Michael Drayton

The complete works. Now first collected.

With introductions and notes by Richard Hooper - Vol. 2

Michael Drayton

The complete works. Now first collected.
With introductions and notes by Richard Hooper - Vol. 2

ISBN/EAN: 9783337732370

Printed in Europe, USA, Canada, Australia, Japan

Cover: Foto ©ninafisch / pixelio.de

More available books at **www.hansebooks.com**

THE COMPLETE WORKS OF

MICHAEL DRAYTON,

NOW FIRST COLLECTED.

WITH INTRODUCTIONS AND NOTES BY

THE REV. RICHARD HOOPER, M.A.

VICAR OF UPTON AND ASTON UPTHORPE, BERKS,

AND EDITOR OF CHAPMAN'S HOMER, SANDYS' POETICAL WORKS, ETC.

VOLUME II.—POLYOLBION.

LONDON:
JOHN RUSSELL SMITH,
SOHO SQUARE.
1876.

POLY-OLBION.

THE NINTH SONG.

THE ARGUMENT.

The Muse here Merioneth vaunts,
And her proud Mountains highly chaunts.
The Hills and Brooks, to bravery bent,
Stand for precedence from descent:
The Rivers for them shewing there   5
The wonders of their Pimblemere.
Proud Snowdon gloriously proceeds
With Cambria's native Princes' deeds.
The Muse then through Carnarvan makes,
And Mon (now Anglesey) awakes   10
To tell her ancient Druids' guise,
And manner of their sacrifice.
Her Rillets she together calls ;
Then back for Flint and Denbigh falls.

OF all the *Cambrian* Shires their heads that bear so
    high,
And farth'st survey their soils with an ambitious eye,
Mervinia[1] for her Hills, as for their matchless crowds,
The nearest that are said to kiss the wand'ring clouds,
Especial audience craves, offended with the throng,   5
That she of all the rest neglected was so long :

[1] *Merionethshire.*

Alleging for herself, When, through the *Saxons'* pride,
The God-like race of *Brute* to *Severne's* setting side
Were cruelly inforc'd, her Mountains did relieve
Those, whom devouring war else ev'rywhere did grieve. 10
And when all *Wales* beside (by fortune or by might)
Unto her ancient foe resign'd her ancient right,
A constant Maiden still she only did remain,
§ The last her genuine laws which stoutly did retain.
And as each one is prais'd for her peculiar things; 15
So only she is rich, in Mountains, Meres, and Springs,
And holds herself as great in her superfluous waste,
As others by their Towns, and fruitful tillage, grac'd.
And therefore, to recount her Rivers from their lins,*
Abridging all delays, *Merrinia* thus begins: 20
¹Though *Dovy*, which doth far her neighboring Floods sur-
  mount
(Whose course, for hers alone *Mountgomery* doth account)
Hath *Angell* for her own, and *Keriog* she doth clear,
With *Towin*, *Gwedall* then, and *Dulas*, all as dear,
Those tributary streams she is maintain'd withall; 25
Yet, boldly may I say, her rising and her fall
My Country calleth hers, with many another brook,
That with their crystal eyes on the *Vergivian* look.
To *Dory* next, of which *Desunny* sea-ward drives,
Lingorrill goes alone: but plenteous *Aron* strives 30
The first to be at sea; and faster her to hie,
Clear *Kessilgum* comes in, with *Hergum* by-and-by.
So *Derry*, *Moothy* draws, and *Moothy* calleth *Caine*,
Which in one channel meet, in going to the Main,
As to their utmost pow'r to lend her all their aids: 35
So *Itro* by the arm *Lanbeder* kindly leads.

* Meres or Pools, from whence Rivers spring.
¹ The Rivers as in order they fall into the *Irish* Sea.

And *Velenrid* the like, observing th' other's law,
Calls *Cunnell;* she again fair *Drurid* forth doth draw,
That from their mother Earth, the rough *Merrinia*, pay
Their mixéd plenteous Springs, unto the lesser Bay   40
§ Of those two noble arms into the land that bear,
Which through *Gwinethia*[1] be so famous everywhere,
On my *Carnarvan* side by nature made my Mound,
As *Dovy* doth divide the *Cardiganian* ground.
The pearly *Conwaye's* head, as that of holy *Dee*,   45
Renownéd Rivers both, their rising have in me :
So, *Luvern* and the *Lue*, themselves that head-long throw
§ Into the spacious Lake, where *Dee* unmix'd doth flow.
Trowerrin takes his stream here from a native lin ;
Which, out of *Pimblemere* when *Dee* himself doth win,   50
Along with him his Lord full courteously doth glide :
So *Rudock* riseth here, and *Cletor* that do guide
Him in his rugged path, and make his greatness way,
Their *Dee* into the bounds of *Denbigh* to convey.
    The lofty Hills, this while attentively that stood,   55
As to survey the course of every several Flood,
Sent forth such echoing shouts (which every way so shrill,
With the reverberate sound the spacious air did fill)
That they were eas'ly heard through the *Vergivian* Main
To *Neptune's* inward Court ; and beating there, constrain   60
That mighty God of sea t' awake : who full of dread,
Thrice threw his three-fork'd Mace about his grisly head,
And thrice above the rocks his forehead rais'd to see
Amongst the high-topp'd Hills what tumult it should be.
So that with very sweat *Cadoridric* did drop,   65
And mighty *Raran* shook his proud sky-kissing top,
Amongst the furious rout whom madness did enrage ;
Until the Mountain-Nymphs, the tumult to assuage,

---

[1] *North-Wales.*

Upon a modest sign of silence to the throng,
Consorting thus, in praise of their *Mervinia*, song : 70
   Thrice famous *Saxon* King, on whom Time ne'er shall prey,
O *Edgar!* who compell'dst our *Ludwall* hence to pay
Three hundred wolves a year for tribute unto thee:
And for that tribute paid, as famous may'st thou be,
O conquer'd *British* King, by whom was first destroy'd 75
§ The multitude of wolves, that long this land annoy'd ;
Regardless of their rape, that now our harmless flocks
Securely here may sit upon the aged rocks ;
Or wand'ring from their walks, and straggling here and there
Amongst the scatt'red cleeves, the lamb needs never fear; 80
But from the threat'ning storm to save itself may creep
Into that darksome cave where once his foe did keep :
That now the clamb'ring goat all day which having fed,
And climbing up to see the sun go down to bed,
Is not at all in doubt her little kid to lose, 85
Which grazing in the vale, secure and safe she knows.
   Where, from these lofty hills[1] which spacious heaven do
Yet of as equal height, as thick by nature set,   [threat,
We talk how we are stor'd, or what we greatly need,
Or how our flocks do fare, and how our herds do feed, 90
When else the hanging rocks, and valleys dark and deep,
The summer's longest day would us from meeting keep.
   Ye *Cambrian* Shepherds then, whom these our Mountains
And ye our fellow Nymphs, ye light *Oreades*,*   [please,
Saint *Helen's* wondrous way, and *Herbert's*, let us go, 95
And our divided Rocks with admiration show.
   Not meaning there to end, but speaking as they were,
A sudden fearful noise surprised every ear.
The Water-Nymphs (not far) *Lin-Teged* that frequent,
With brows besmear'd with ooze, their locks with dew besprent,

---

[1] The wondrous Mountains in *Merionethshire*.
* Nymphs of the Mountains.

Inhabiting the Lake, in sedgy bow'rs below, 101
Their inward grounded grief that only sought to show
Against the Mountain-kind, which much on them did take
Above their wat'ry brood, thus proudly them bespake:
   Tell us, ye haughty Hills, why vainly thus you threat, 105
Esteeming us so mean, compar'd to you so great.
To make you know yourselves, you this must understand,
That our great Maker laid the surface of the Land,
§ As level as the Lake until the general Flood,
When over all so long the troubled waters stood: 110
Which, hurried with the blasts from angry heaven that blew,
Upon huge massy heaps the loosened gravel threw:
From hence we would ye know, your first beginning came.
Which, since, in tract of time, yourselves did Mountains name.
So that the earth, by you (to check her mirthful cheer) 115
May always see (from heaven) those plagues that pouréd were
Upon the former world; as 't were by scars to show
That still she must remain disfigur'd with the blow:
And by th' infectious slime that doomful Deluge left,
Nature herself hath since of purity been reft; 120
And by the seeds corrupt, the life of mortal man
Was short'ned. With these plagues ye Mountains first began.
   But, ceasing you to shame, What Mountain is there found
In all your monstrous kind (seek ye the Island round)
That truly of himself such wonders can report 125
As can this spacious *Lin*, the place of our resort?
That when *Dee* in his course fain in her lap would lie,
Commixtion with her store his stream she doth deny,
By his complexion prov'd, as he through her doth glide.[1]
Her wealth again from his, she likewise doth divide: 130
Those White-fish that in her do wondrously abound,
Are never seen in him; nor are his Salmons found
At any time in her: but as she him disdains,

[1] The wonders of *Lin-teyed*, or *Pemble-mere*.

So he again, from her as wilfully abstains.   [that fall,
Down from the neighbouring Hills, those plenteous Springs
Nor Land-floods after rain, her never move at all.   136
And as in summer's heat, so always is she one,
Resembling that great Lake which seems to care for none :
§ And with stern *Æolus'* blasts, like *Thetis* waxing rank,
She only over-swells the surface of her bank.   140
   But, whilst the Nymphs report these wonders of their
     Lake,
Their further cause of speech the mighty *Snowdon*[1] brake ;
Least, if their wat'ry kind should suff'red be too long,
The licence that they took might do the Mountains wrong.
For quickly he had found that strait'ned Point of Land,   145
Into the *Irish* Sea which puts his pow'rful hand,
Puff'd with their wat'ry praise, grew insolently proud,
And needs would have his Rills for Rivers be allow'd :
Short *Darent*, near'st unto the utmost point of all
That th' Isle of *Gelin* greets, and *Bardsey* in her fall ;   150
And next to her, the *Sawe*, the *Gir*, the *Er*, the *May*,
Must Rivers be at least, should all the world gainsay :
And those, whereas the land lies Eastward, amply wide,
That goodly *Conway* grace upon the other side,
Born near upon her banks, each from her proper *Lin*,   155
Soon from their Mothers out, soon with their Mistress in.
As *Ledder*, her ally, and neighbour *Legwy;* then
Goes *Purloyd, Castell* next, with *Giffin*, that again
Observe fair *Conway's* course: and though their race be short,
Yet they their Sovereign Flood inrich with their resort.   160
And *Snowdon*, more than this, his proper mere did note
(§ Still *Delos*-like, wherein a wand'ring isle doth float)
Was peremptory grown upon his higher ground ;
That Pool, in which (besides) the one-eyed fish are found,
As of her wonder proud, did with the Floods partake.[2]   165

[1] The most famous Mountain of all *Wales*, in *Carnarvanshire*.
[2] The wonders upon the *Snowdon*.

THE NINTH SONG.

So, when great *Snowdon* saw, a faction they would make
Against his general kind ; both parties to appease,
He purposeth to sing their native Princes' praise.
For *Snowdony*, a Hill, imperial in his seat,
Is from his mighty foot unto his head so great,　　　170
That were his *Wales* distrest, or of his help had need,
He all her flocks and herds for many months could feed.[1]
Therefore to do some thing were worthy of his name,
Both tending to his strength, and to the *Britans'* fame,
His Country to content, a signal having made,　　　175
By this oration thinks both parties to persuade:

　Whilst here this general Isle, the ancient *Britans* ow'd,
Their valiant deeds before by *Severne* have been show'd :
But, since our furious foe, these pow'rful *Saxon* swarms
(As merciless in spoil, as well approv'd in arms)　　　180
Here calléd to our aid, *Loëgria* us bereft,
Those poor and scatt'red few of *Brute's* high linage left,
For succour hither came ; where that unmixéd race
Remains unto this day, yet owners of this place :
Of whom no Flood nor Hill peculiarly hath song.　　　185
These, then, shall be my theme: lest Time too much should
　　wrong
Such Princes as were ours, since sever'd we have been ;
And as themselves, their fame be limited between
The *Severne* and our Sea, long pent within this place,
§ Till with the term of *Welsh*, the *English* now embase　　　190
The nobler *Britans'* name, that well-near was destroy'd
With pestilence and war, which this great Isle annoy'd ;
Cadwallader that drave to the *Armoric* shore :
To which, dread *Conan*, Lord of *Denbigh*, long before,
His countrymen from hence auspiciously convey'd :　　　195
Whose noble feats in war, and never-failing aid,

---

[1] The glory of *Snowdon-hill*.

Got *Maximus* (at length) the victory in *Gaul*,
Upon the *Roman* Powers. Where, after *Gratian's* fall,
Armorica to them the valiant Victor gave :
Where *Conan*, their great Lord, as full of courage, drave   200
The *Celts* out of their seats, and did their room supply
With people still from hence; which of our Colony
§ Was Little *Britain* call'd. Where that distressèd King,
Cadwallader, himself awhile recomforting
With hope of *Alan's* aid (which there did him detain)   205
§ Forewarnèd was in dreams, that of the *Britans'* reign
A sempiternal end the angry Powers decreed,
A recluse life in *Rome* injoining him to lead.
The King resigning all, his son young *Edwall* left
With *Alan:* who, much griev'd the Prince should be bereft
Of *Britain's* ancient right, rigg'd his unconquer'd fleet;   211
And as the Generals then, for such an army meet,
His Nephew *Ivor* chose, and *Hiner* for his pheere;
Two most undaunted spirits. These valiant *Britans* were
The first who *West-sex*[1] won. But by the ling'ring war,   215
When they those *Saxons* found t' have succour still from far,
They took them to their friends on *Severne's* setting shore :
Where finding *Edwall* dead, they purpos'd to restore
His son young *Rodorick*, whom the *Saxon* Powers pursu'd :
But he, who at his home here scorn'd to be subdu'd,   220
With *Aldred* (that on *Wales* his strong invasion brought)
Garthmalack, and *Pencoyd* (those famous battles) fought,
That *North* and *South-Wales* sing, on the *West-Sexians* won.
  Scarce this victorious task his bloodied sword had done,
But at *Mount Carno*[2] met the *Mercians*, and with wounds   225
Made *Ethelbald* to feel his trespass on our bounds;
Prevail'd against the *Pict*, before our force that flew;
And in a valiant fight their King *Dalargan* slew.

    [1] The *West-Saxons'* country, comprehending *Devonshire, Somerset, Wiltshire,* and their adjacents.
    [2] A hill near *Aber-gavenny* in *Monmouth*.

THE NINTH SONG.

Nor *Conan's* courage less, nor less prevail'd in ought
Renownéd *Rodorick's* heir, who with the *English* fought   230
The *Herefordian* Field ; as *Ruthlands* red with gore :
Who, to transfer the war from this his native shore,
March'd through the *Mercian* Towns with his revengeful blade;
And on the *English* there such mighty havock made,
That *Offa* (when he saw his Countries go to wrack)   235
From bick'ring with his folk, to keep us *Britans* back,
Cast up that mighty Mound of eighty miles in length,[1]
Athwart from sea to sea. Which of the *Mercians'* strength
A witness though it stand, and *Offa's* name do bear,
Our courage was the cause why first he cut it there :   240
As that most dreadful day at *Gavelford* can tell,
Where under either's sword so many thousands fell
With intermixéd blood, that neither knew their own ;
Nor which went victor thence, unto this day is known.

Nor *Kettle's* conflict then, less martial courage show'd,   245
Where valiant *Mervin* met the *Mercians*, and bestow'd
His nobler *British* blood on *Burthred's* recreant flight.
As *Rodorick* his great son, his father following right,
Bare not the *Saxons'* scorns, his *Britans* to out-brave ;
At *Gwythen*, but again to *Burthred* battle gave ;   250
Twice driving out the *Dane* when he invasion brought.
Whose no less valiant son, again at *Conway* fought
With *Danes* and *Mercians* mix'd, and on their hateful head
Down-show'r'd their dire revenge whom they had murtheréd.

And, were 't not that of us the *English* would report   255
(Abusing of our Tongue in most malicious sort
As often-times they do) that more than any, we
(The *Welsh*, as they us term) love glorified to be,
Here could I else recount the slaught'red *Saxons'* gore
Our swords at *Crosford* spilt on *Severne's* wand'ring shore ;   260

[1] *Offa's* Ditch.

And *Griffith* here produce. *Lewellin's* valiant son
(May we believe our *Bards*) who five pitch'd battles won;
And to revenge the wrongs the envious *English* wrought,
His well-train'd martial troops into the Marches brought
As far as *Wor'ster* walls: nor thence did he retire, 265
Till *Powse* lay well-near spent in our revengeful fire;
As *Hereford* laid waste: and from their plenteous soils,
Brought back with him to *Wales* his prisoners and his spoils.

    Thus as we valiant were, when valour might us steed,
With those so much that dar'd, we had them that decreed.
For, what *Malmutian* laws, or *Martian*, ever were 271
§ More excellent than those which our good *Howell* here
Ordain'd to govern *Wales?* which still with us remain.

    And when all-powerful Fate had brought to pass again,
That as the *Saxons* erst did from the *Britans* win; 275
Upon them so (at last) the *Normans* coming in,
Took from those Tyrants here, what treach'rously they got,
(To the perfidious *French*, which th' angry heavens allot)
Ne'er could that Conqueror's sword (which roughly did decide
His right in *England* here, and prostrated her pride) 280
§ Us to subjection stoop, or make us *Britans* bear
Th' unwieldy *Norman* yoke: nor basely could we fear
His Conquest, ent'ring *Wales;* but (with stout courage) ours
Defied him to his face, with all his *English* Pow'rs.

    And when in his revenge, proud *Rufus* hither came 285
(With vows) us to subvert; with slaughter and with shame,
O'er *Severne* him we sent, to gather stronger aid.

    So, when to *England's* power, *Albania* hers had laid,
By *Henry Beauclarke* brought (for all his devilish wit,
By which he raught the Wreath) he not prevail'd a whit: 290
And through our rugged straits when he so rudely prest,
Had not his provéd mail sate surely to his breast,
A skilful *British* hand his life had him bereft,
As his stern brother's heart by *Tirrill's* hand was cleft.

THE NINTH SONG.

And let the *English* thus which vilify our name, 295
If it their greatness please, report unto our shame
The foil our *Gwyneth* gave, at *Flint's* so deadly fight,
To *Maud* the Empress' son, that there he put to flight;
§ And from the *English* pow'r th' imperial ensign took:
About his pluméd head which valiant *Owen* shook. 300

As when that King again, his fortune to advance
Above his former foil, procur'd fresh powers from *France*,
A surely-levell'd shaft if *Sent-cleare* had not seen,
And in the very loose not thrust himself between
His Sovereign and the shaft, he our revenge had tried: 305
Thus, to preserve the King, the noble subject died.

As *Madock* his brave son, may come the rest among;
Who, like the God-like race from which his grandsires
    sprong,
Whilst here his brothers tir'd in sad domestic strife,
On their unnatural breasts bent either's murtherous knife;
This brave adventurous youth, in hot pursuit of fame, 311
With such as his great spirit did with high deeds inflame,
Put forth his well-rigg'd fleet to seek him foreign ground,
And sailéd West so long, until that world he found
To Christians then unknown (save this adventurous crew)
Long ere *Columbus* liv'd, or it *Vesputius* knew; 316
And put the now-nam'd *Welsh* on *India's* parchéd face,
Unto the endless praise of *Brute's* renownéd race,
Ere the *Iberian* Powers had touch'd her long-sought Bay,
§ Or any ear had heard the sound of *Florida*. 320

§ And with that *Croggen's* name let th' *English* us disgrace;
When there are to be seen, yet, in that ancient place
From whence that name they fetch, their conquer'd grand-
    sires' graves:
For which each ignorant sot unjustly us depraves.
And when that Tyrant *John* had our subversion vow'd, 325
§ To his unbridled will our necks we never bow'd:

Nor to his mighty son ; whose host we did inforce
(His succours cutting off) to eat their warlike horse.
   Until all-ruling Heaven would have us to resign :
When that brave Prince, the last of all the *British* Line,   330
Lewellin, *Griffith's* son, unluckily was slain,
§ As Fate had spar'd our fall till *Edward Longshanks*' reign.
Yet to the stock of *Brute* so true we ever were,
We would permit no Prince, unless a native here.
Which, that most prudent King perceiving, wisely thought
To satisfy our wills, and to *Carnarvan* brought   336
His Queen being great with child, ev'n ready down to lie ;
Then to his purpos'd end doth all his powers apply.
   Through ev'ry part of *Wales* he to the Nobles sent,
That they unto his Court should come incontinent,   340
Of things that much concern'd the Country to debate :
But now behold the power of unavoided Fate.
   When thus unto his will he fitly them had won,
At her expected hour the Queen brought forth a son.
And to this great design, all happ'ning as he would,   345
He (his intended course that clerkly manage could)
Thus quaintly trains us on : Since he perceiv'd us prone
Here only to be rul'd by Princes of our own,
Our naturalness therein he greatly did approve ;[1]
And publicly protests, that for the ancient love   350
He ever bare to *Wales*, they all should plainly see,
That he had found out one, their sovereign Lord to be ;
Com'n of the race of Kings, and (in their Country born)
Could not one *English* word : of which he durst be sworn.
Besides, his upright heart, and innocence was such,   355
As that (he was assur'd) black Envy could not touch
His spotless life in ought. Poor we (that not espy
His subtlety herein) in plain simplicity

[1] A King both valiant and politic.

THE NINTH SONG.

Soon bound ourselves by oath, his choice not to refuse:
When as that crafty King his little child doth choose, 360
Young *Edward*, born in *Wales*, and of *Carnarvan* call'd.
Thus by the *English* craft, we *Britans* were enthrall'd:
    Yet in thine own behalf, dear Country dare to say,
Thou long as powerful wert as *England* every way.
And if she overmuch should seek thee to imbase, 365
Tell her thou art the Nurse of all the *British* race;
And he that was by heaven appointed to unite
(After that tedious war) the Red Rose and the White,
A *Tudor* was of thine, and native of thy *Mon*,
From whom descends that King now sitting on her Throne.

    This speech, by *Snowdon* made, so lucky was to please 371
Both parties, and them both with such content t' appease,
That as before they strove for sovereignty and place,
They only now contend, which most should other grace.

    Into the *Irish* Sea, then all those Rills that ron, 375
In *Snowdon's* praise to speak, immediately begon;
Lewenny, *Lynan* next, then *Gwelly* gave it out,
And *Kerriog* her compeer soon told it all about:
So did their sister-Nymphs, that into *Mena* strain;
The Flood that doth divide *Mon* from the *Cambrian* Main. 380
It *Gorway* greatly prais'd, and *Seint* it loudly song.
So, mighty *Snowdon's* speech was through *Carnarvan* rong;
That scarcely such a noise to *Mon* from *Mena* came,
When with his puissant troops for conquest of the same,
On bridges made of boats, the *Roman* Powers her sought, 385
Or *Edward* to her sack his *English* armies brought:
That *Mona* strangely stirr'd great *Snowdon's* praise to hear,
Although the stock of *Troy* to her was ever dear;
Yet (from her proper worth) as she before all other
§ Was call'd (in former times) her Country *Cambria's* mother,
Persuaded was thereby her praises to pursue, 391
Or by neglect, to lose what to herself was due,

A sign to *Neptune* sent, his boist'rous rage to slake;
Which suddenly becalm'd, thus of herself she spake:
 What one of all the Isles to *Cambria* doth belong   395
(To *Britain*, I might say, and yet not do her wrong)
Doth equal me in soil, so good for grass and grain?
As should my *Wales* (where still *Brute's* offspring doth remain)
That mighty store of men, yet more of beasts doth breed,
By famine or by war constrained be to need,   400
And *England's* neighbouring Shires their succour would deny;
My only self her wants could plenteously supply.
 What Island is there found upon the *Irish* coast,
In which that Kingdom seems to be delighted most
(And seek you all along the rough *Vergivian* shore,   405
Where the incount'ring tides outrageously do roar)
That bows not at my beck, as they to me did owe
The duty subjects should unto their Sovereign show?
§ So that th' *Eubonian Man*, a kingdom long time known,
Which wisely hath been rul'd by Princes of her own,   410
In my alliance joys, as in th' *Albanian* Seas
The *Arrans*,[1] and by them the scatt'red *Eubides*,[1]
Rejoice even at my name; and put on mirthful cheer,
When of my good estate, they by the Sea-Nymphs hear.
 Sometimes within my shades, in many an ancient wood,
Whose often-twined tops great *Phœbus'* fires withstood,   415
§ The fearless *British* Priests, under an aged oak,
Taking a milk-white bull, unstrained with the yoke,
And with an axe of gold from that *Jove*-sacred tree
The Mistletoe cut down; then with a bended knee   420
On th' unhew'd altar laid, put to the hallow'd fires:
And whilst in the sharp flame the trembling flesh expires,
As their strong fury mov'd (when all the rest adore)
Pronouncing their desires the sacrifice before,

     [1] Isles upon the West of *Scotland*.

Up to th' eternal heav'n their bloodied hands did rear: 425
And, whilst the murmuring woods ev'n shudd'red as with
    fear,
Preach'd to the beardless youth, the soul's immortal state,
To other bodies still how it should transmigrate,
That to contempt of death them strongly might excite.
    To dwell in my black shades the Wood-gods did delight,
Untrodden with resort that long so gloomy were, 431
As when the *Roman* came, it strook him sad with fear
To look upon my face, which then was call'd the *Dark;*
Until in after time, the *English* for a mark
Gave me this hateful name, which I must ever bear, 435
And *Anglesey* from them am called everywhere.
    My Brooks (to whose sweet brims the *Sylvans* did resort,
In gliding through my shades, to mighty *Neptune's* Court,
Of their huge oaks bereft) to heaven so open lie,
That now there's not a root discern'd by any eye: 440
My *Brent*, a pretty beck, attending *Mena's* mouth,
With those her sister rills, that bear upon the South,
Gwint, forth along with her *Lewenny* that doth draw;
And next to them again, the fat and moory *Frawe*,
§ Which with my Prince's Court I sometime pleas'd to
    grace, 445
As those that to the West directly run their race.
Smooth *Allo* in her fall, that *Lyawn* in doth take;
Math.mon, that amain doth tow'rds *Moylroniad* make,
The sea-calfs to behold that bleach them on her shore,
Which *Gweyer* to her gets, as to increase her store. 450
Then *Dulas* to the North that straineth, as to see
The Isle that breedeth mice: whose store so loathsome be,
That she in *Neptune's* brack her bluish head doth hide.
    When now the wearied Muse her burthen having ply'd,
Herself awhile betakes to bathe her in the *Sound;* 455
And quitting in her course the goodly *Moniau* ground,

Assays the *Penmenmaur*, and her clear eyes doth throw
On *Conway*, tow'rds the East, to *England* back to go:
Where finding *Denbigh* fair, and *Flint* not out of sight,
Cries yet afresh for *Wales*, and for *Brute's* ancient right. 460

ILLUSTRATIONS.

ORE Western are you carried into *Merioneth, Carnarvan, Anglesey*, and those maritime coasts of *North-Wales*.

14. *The* last *her* genuine laws *which stoutly did retain.*

Under *William Rufus*, the *Norman-English* (animated by the good success which *Robert Fitz-hamon* had first against *Rees ap Tiddour*, Prince of *South-Wales*, and afterward against *Jestin*, Lord of *Glamorgan*) being very desirous of these *Welsh* territories; *Hugh*, surnamed *Wolfe*,[1] Earl of *Chester*, did homage to the King for *Tegengl* and *Ryvonioe*, with all the land by the sea unto *Conwey*. And thus pretending title, got also possession of *Merioneth*, from *Gruffith ap Conan*, Prince of *North-Wales:* but he soon recovered it, and thence left it continued in his posterity, until *Lhewelyin ap Gruffith*, under *Edward* I., lost it, himself, and all his dominion. Whereas other parts (of *South* and *West-Wales* especially) had before subjected themselves to the *English* Crown; this, through frequency of craggy mountains, accessible with too much difficulty, being the last strong refuge until that period of fatal conquest.

[1] Powel. ad Caradoc. Lhancarv.; et Camden.

41. *Of those two noble* arms *into the land that bear.*

In the confines of *Merioneth* and *Cardigan*, where these Rivers jointly pour themselves into the *Irish* Ocean, are these two arms or creeks of the sea, famous, as he saith, through *Gwinethia* (that is one of the old titles of this *North-Wales*) by their names of 𝕮𝖗𝖆𝖊𝖙𝖍 𝕸𝖆𝖎𝖔𝖗 and 𝕮𝖗𝖆𝖊𝖙𝖍 𝕭𝖆𝖈𝖍𝖆𝖓, *i.e.*, as it were, the Great Haven, and the Little Haven; 𝕮𝖗𝖆𝖊𝖙𝖍,[1] in *British*, signifying a tract of sand whereon the sea flows, and the ebb discovers.

48. *Into that spacious* Lake *where* Dee *unmix'd doth flow.*

That is *Lhin-tegid* (otherwise called by the *English, Pemelsmere*) through which, *Dee* rising in this part runs whole and unmixed, neither Lake nor River communicating to each other water or fish; as the Author anon tells you. In the ancients,[2] is remembered specially the like of *Rhosne* running unmixed, and (as it were) over the Lake of *Geneva;* as, for a greater wonder, the most learned *Casaubon*[3] hath delivered also of *Arva*, running whole through *Rhosne;* and divers other such like are in *Pliny's* collection of Nature's most strange effects in waters.

76. *The multitude of* Wolves *that long this land annoy'd.*

Our excellent *Edgar* (having first enlarged his name with diligent and religious performance of charitable magnificence among his *English*, and confirmed the far-spread opinion of his greatness, by receipt of homage at *Chester* from eight Kings; as you shall see in and to the next Song) for increase of his benefits towards the Isle, joined with preservation of his Crown-duties, converted the tribute of the *Welsh*

---

[1] Girald. Itinerar. 2. cap. 6.
[2] Ammian. Marcel. Hist. 15.; Pomp. Mel. lib. 2.; Plin. Hist. Nat. 2. cap. 103.
[3] Ad Strabon. lib. δ.

THE NINTH SONG.

into three hundred Wolves a year, as the Author shews. The King that paid it;

Thre per he hult is terme rent at the berthe was behinde
Vor he sende the Ring word that he ne mighte ne mo binde,

As, according to the story my old Rhymer delivers it. Whom you are to account for this *Ludwall* King of *Wales* in the *Welsh* history, except *Howel* ap *Jeraf*, that made war against his uncle *Iago*, delivered his father, and took on himself the whole Principality towards the later years of *Edgar*, I know not. But this was not an utter destruction of them; for, since that time,[1] the Manor of *Piddlesey* in *Leicestershire* was held by one *Henry* of *Angage, per serjeantium capiendi lupos*, as the inquisition delivers it.

95. *S.* Helen's *wondrous way* ———

By *Festeneog* in the confines of *Caernarvan* and *Merioneth* is this highway of note; so called by the *British*, and supposed made by that *Helen*, mother to *Constantine* (among her other good deeds) of whom to the last Song before.

109. *As* level *as the lake until the* general Flood.

So is the opinion of some Divines,[2] that, until after the Flood, were no mountains, but that by congestion of sand, earth, and such stuff as we now see hills strangely fraughted with, in the waters they were first cast up. But in that true Secretary of Divinity and Nature, *Selomoh*,[3] speaking as in the person of *Wisdom*, you read; *Before the mountains were founded, and before the hills I was formed*, that is, before the world's beginning; and in Holy Writ elsewhere,[4] *the mountains ascend, and the valleys descend to the place where Thou didst*

---
[1] Itin. *Leicest.* 27. Hen. 3. in Archiv. Turr. *Londin.*
[2] His post alios refragatur B. *Pererius* ad Genes. 1. quæst. 101.
[3] Proverb. 8.   [4] Psalm. 104.

found them; good authorities to justify mountains before the Flood. The same question hath been of Isles, but I will peremptorily determine neither.

130. *And with stern Æolus' blasts, like* Thetis *waxing rank.*

The South-West wind constrained between two hills on both sides of the Lake, sometimes so violently fills the River out of the Lake's store, that both have been affirmed (but somewhat against truth) never to be disturbed, or overflow, but upon tempestuous blasts, whereas indeed (as *Powel* delivers) they are overfilled with rain and land-floods, as well as other waters; but most of all moved by that impetuous wind.

162. *Still* Delos-like *wherein a wand'ring Isle doth float.*

Of this Isle in the water on top of *Snowdon,* and of oneeyed Eels, Trouts, and Perches, in another Lake there, *Girald* is witness. Let him perform his word; I will not be his surety for it. The Author alludes to that state of *Delos,* which is feigned[1] before it was with pillars fastened in the sea for *Latona's* child-birth.

190. *That with the term of* Welsh *the* English *now imbase.*

For this name of *Welsh* is unknown to the *British* themselves, and imposed on them, as an ancient and common opinion is, by the *Saxons,* calling them *Walsh, i.e., strangers.* Others fabulously have talk of *Wallo* and *Wandolena,* whence it should be derived. But you shall come nearer truth, if upon the community of name, customs, and original, twixt the *Gauls* and *Britons,* you conjecture them called *Walsh,* as it were, *Gualsh* (the *W* often-times being instead of the *Gu*), which expresses them to be *Gauls* rather than strangers;

---

[1] Pindar. ap. Strabon. lib. 10.

although in the Saxon (which is observed¹) it was used for the name of *Gauls*, *Strangers*, and *Barbarous*, perhaps in such kind as in this Kingdom the name of *Frenchman*,² hath by inclusion comprehended all kind of Aliens.

203. *Was* Little Britain *call'd*————

See a touch of this in the passage of the Virgins to the Eighth Song. Others affirm, that under *Constantine*,³ of our *Britons'* Colonies were there placed; and from some of these the name of that now Dukedom to have had its beginning. There be⁴ also that will justify the *British* name to have been in that tract long before, and for proof cite *Dionysius*⁵ *Afer*, and *Pliny*;⁶ but for the first, it is not likely that he ever meant that Continent, but this of ours, as the learned tell you; and for *Pliny*, seeing he reckons his *Britons* of *Gaul* in the confines of the now *France*, and Lower *Germany*, it is as unlikely that twixt them and Little *Bretaigne* should be any such habitude. You want not authority, affirming that our *Britons* from them,⁷ before they from ours, had deduction of this national title; but my belief admits it not. The surer opinion is to refer the name unto those *Britons*, which (being expelled the Island at the entry of the *Saxons*) got them new habitation in this maritime part, as beside other authority an express assertion is in an old fragment of a *French* history,⁸ which you may join with most worthy *Camden's* treatise on this matter; whither (for a learned declaration of it) I send you.

¹ Buchanan. Scotic. Hist. 2.
² Bract. lib. 3. tract. 2. cap. 15. Leg. G. Conquest. et D. Coke in Cas. Calvin.
³ Malmesb. de Gest. Reg. 1.
⁴ Paul Merul. Cosmog. part. 2. lib. 3. cap. 31.
⁵ V. Eustath. ad eundem.
⁶ Hist. Nat. lib. 4. cap. 17. quem super Ligerim Britanos hos situs dixisse, miror P. Merulam tam constanter affirmasse.
⁷ Bed. lib. 1. cap. 3. quem secutus P. Merula.
⁸ Ex Ms. Cænob. Floriac. edit. per P. Pithæum.

206. *Forewarnéd was* in dreams *that of the* Britons' *reign.*

Cadwallader driven to forsake this land, especially by reason of plague and famine, tyrannizing among his subjects, joined with continual irruptions of the *English*, retired himself into Little *Bretaigne*, to his cousin *Alan* there King: where, in a dream, he was admonished by an angel (I justify it but by the story) that a period of the *British* Empire was now come, and until time of *Merlin's* prophecy, given to King *Arthur*, his country or posterity should have no restitution; and further, that he should take his journey to *Rome*, where for a transitory he might receive an eternal Kingdom. *Alan*, upon report of this vision, compares it with the *Eagle's* prophecies, the *Sibyll's* verses, and *Merlin;* nor found he but all were concording in prediction of this ceasing of the *British* Monarchy.[1] Through his advice therefore, and a prepared affection, *Cadwallader* takes voyage to *Rome*, received of *PP. Sergius*, with holy tincture, the name of *Peter*, and within very short time there died; his body very lately under Pope *Gregory* the XIII. was found[2] buried by S. *Peter's* Tomb, where it yet remains; and *White* of *Basingstoke* says, he had a piece of his raiment of a chesnut colour, taken up (with the corpse) uncorrupted; which he accounts, as a *Romish* pupil, no slight miracle. It was added among *British* traditions, that, when *Cadwallader's* bones[3] were brought into this Isle, then should the posterity of their Princes have restitution: concerning that, you have enough to the Second Song. Observing concurrence of time and difference of relation in the story of this Prince, I know not well how to give myself or the reader satisfaction. In *Monmouth*, *Robert* of *Glocester*, *Florilegus*, and their followers,

[1] See to the Second Song.
[2] Anton. Major. ap. Basingstoch. lil. 9. not. 32.
[3] Ranulph. Higden. lib. 5. cap. 20.

Cadwallader is made the son of *Cadwallo* King of the *Britons* before him; but so, that he descended also from *English-Saxon* blood; his mother being daughter to *Penda* King of *Mercland*. Our Monks call him King of *West-Saxons*, successor to *Kentwine*, and son to *Kenbrith*. And where *Caradoc Lhancarvan* tells you of wars twixt *Ine* or *Ivor* (successor to *Cadwallader*) and *Kentwine*, it appears in our chronographers that *Kentwine* must be dead above three years before. But howsoever these things might be reconcileable, I think clearly that *Cadwallader* in the *British*, and *Cedwalla*[1] King of *West-Saxons* in *Bede*, *Malmesbury*, *Florence*, *Huntingdon*, and other stories of the *English*, are not the same, as *Geffrey*, and, out of *Girald*, *Randall* of *Chester*, and others since erroneously have affirmed. But strongly you may hold, that *Cadwallo* or *Caswallo*, living about 840, slain by *Oswald* King of *Northumberland*, was the same with *Bede's* first *Cedwalla*, whom he calls King of *Britons*, and that by misconceit of his two *Cedwals* (the other being, almost fifty years after, King of *West-Saxons*) and by communicating of each other's attributes upon indistinct names, without observation of their several times, these discordant relations of them, which in story are too palpable, had their first being. But to satisfy you in present, I keep myself to the course of our ordinary stories, by reason of difficulty in finding an exact truth in all. Touching his going to *Rome;* thus: Some will, that he was Christian before, and received of *Sergius* only Confirmation; others, that he had there his first Baptism, and lived not above a month after; which time (to make all dissonant) is extended to eight years in *Lhancarvan*. That, one King *Cedwall* went to *Rome*, is plain by all, with his new-imposed name and burial there: For his baptism before, I have no

---

[1] Cedwalla Rex *Britonum* Bed. Hist. Eccles. 3. cap. 1. cæterum v. Nennium ap. Camd. in Ottadinis pag. 664. et 665. et Bed. lib. 5. cap. 7.

direct authority but in *Polychronicon;* many arguments proving him indeed a well-willer to Christianity, but as one that had not yet received its holy testimony. The very phrase in most of our Historians is plain that he was baptized; and so also his epitaph then made at *Rome,* in part here inserted.

> [1] *Percipiénsque alacer redivivæ præmia vitæ,*
> *Barbaricam rabiem, nomen et inde suum*
> *Conversus convertit orans: Petrumque vocari,*
> *Sergius antistes jussit, ut ipse pater*
> *Fonte renascentis, quem Christi gratia purgans*
> *Protinus ablatum rexit in arce poli.*

This shows also his short life afterward, and agrees fully with the *English* story. His honorable affection to Religion, before his cleansing mark of regeneration, is seen in that kind respect given by him to *Wilfrid* first Bishop of *Selesey* in *Sussex;* where the Episcopal See of *Chichester* (hither was it translated from *Selesey,* under *William* the Conqueror) acknowledges in public monuments rather him founder than *Edilwalch* the first Christian King of that Province, from whom *Cedwalla* violently took both life and kingdom: nor doth it less appear, in that his paying Tenths of such spoils, as by war's fortune, accrued to his greatness; which notwithstanding, although done by one then not received into the Church of either Testament, is not without many examples among the ancient *Gentiles,* who therein imitating the *Hebrews,* tithed much of their possessions, and acquired substance to such Deities as unhallowed religion taught them to adore; which, whether they did upon mystery in

---

[1] Bed. Eccles. Hist. lib. 5. cap. 7. *Englished* in substance, if you say, *He was baptized, and soon died.* A. CHR. 688. Judicious conjecture cannot but attribute all this to the *West-Saxon Cedwall,* and not the *British.* See to the Eleventh Song.

THE NINTH SONG.   25

the number, or, therein as paying first fruits (for the word בכרות which was for *Abel's* offerings, and מעשר for *Melchisedech's* tithes, according to that less* calculation in *Cabalistic* concordance of identities in different words, are of equal number, and by consequence of like interpretation) I leave to my reader. Speaking of this, I cannot but wonder at that very wonder of learning *Joseph Scaliger*,[1] affirming, tithes among those ancients only payable to *Hercules*: whereas by express witness of an old inscription[2] at *Delphos*, and the common report of *Camillus*, it is justified, that both *Greeks* and *Romans* did the like to *Apollo*, and no less among them and others together, was to *Mars*,[3] *Jupiter*,[4] *Juno*,[5] and the number of Gods in general, to whom the *Athenians* dedicated the Tenth part of *Lesbos*.[6] He which the Author, after the *British*, calls here *Ivor*, is affirmed the same with *Ine* King of *Westsex* in our Monkish Chronicles, although there be scarce any congruity twixt them in his descent. What follows is but historical and continued succession of their Princes.

272. *More excellent than those which our good* Howel *here*.

For, *Howel Dha* first Prince of *Southwales* and *Powis*, after upon death of his cousin *Edwal Voel*, of *Northwales* also, by mature advice in a full Council of Barons and Bishops, made divers universal constitutions. By these *Wales* (until *Edward* I.) was ruled. So some say; but the truth is, that before *Ed*. I. conquered *Wales*, and, as it seems, from twenty-eighth but especially thirty-fifth of

---

* Ratio Cabalistica Minor, secundum quam è Centenario quolibet et Denario unitatem accipiunt, reliquos numeros in utroque vocabulo retinentes uti Archangel. Bergonovens in Dog. Cabalisticis.
[1] Ad Festum. verb. Decuna.
[2] Clemens Alexand. Strom. *a* et Steph. περὶ πολ. in ᾿Αβορίγιν. tantundem: præter alios quam plurimos.
[3] Lucian. περὶ ᾿Ορχήσεως, et Varro ap. Macrob. 3. cap. 11.
[4] Herodot. *a*. [5] Samii apud Herodot. *c*. [6] Thucydid. Hist. γ.

Hen. III. his Empire enlarged among them, the *English* King's Writ did run there. For when *Ed.* I. sent Commission[1] to *Reginald* of *Grey, Thomas* Bishop of S. *Dewies,* and *Walter* of *Hopton,* to enquire of their customs, and by what laws they were ruled, divers Cases were upon oath returned, which by, and according to, the King's law, if it were between Lords or the Princes themselves, had been determined; if between Tenants, then by the Lord's seising it into his hands, until discovery of the title in his Court; but also that none were decided by the laws of *Howel Dha.* Of them, in *Lhuyd's* annotations to the *Welsh Chronicle,* you have some particulars, and in the Roll which hath aided me. Touching those other of *Molmutius* and *Martia,* somewhat to the Ninth Song.

281. *Us to subjection stoop, or makes us* Britons *bear*
    Th' unwieldy Norman *yoke*————

Snowdon properly speaks all for the glory of his country, and follows suppositions of the *British* story, discording herein with ours. For in *Matthew Paris,* and *Florilegus,* under the year 1078 I read that the *Conqueror* subdued *Wales,* and took homage and hostages of the Princes; so of *Hen.* I. 1113, *Hen.* II. in 1157 and other times; Of this *Hen.* II. hath been understood that prophecy of *Merlin, When the freckle-faced Prince* (so was the King) *passes over* **Rhyd Pencarn,**[*] *then should the* Welsh *forces be weakened.* For he in this expedition against *Rees* **ap** *Gryffith* into *South-Wales,* coming mounted near that ford in *Glamorgan,* his steed madded with sudden sound of trumpets, on the bank violently, out of the purposed way, carries him through the ford: which compared with that of *Merlin* gave to the *British* army no small discomfiture; as a

---
[1] Rot. Claus. de ann. 9. *Ed.* I. in Archiv. *Turr. Londin.*
[*] The Ford at the Rock's head.

Cambro-Briton,[1] then living, hath delivered. But, that their stories and ours are so different in these things, it can be no marvel to any that knows how often it is used among Historians,[2] to flatter their own nation, and wrong the honour of their enemies. See the first note here for *Rufus* his time.

299. *And from the* English *Power the imperial* Standard took.

Henry of *Essex*, at this time Standard-bearer to *Hen*. II. in a strait at *Counsylth* near *Flint*, cast down the Standard, thereby animating the *Welsh*, and discomfiting the *English*, adding much danger to the dishonour. He was afterward accused by *Robert* of *Montfort*, of a traitorous design in the action. To clear himself, he challenges the combat: they both, with the royal assent and judicial course by law of arms, enter the lists; where *Montfort* had the victory, and *Essex* pardoned for his life; but forfeiting[3] all his substance, entered Religion, and professed in the Abbey of *Reading*, where the combat was performed. I remember a great Clerk[4] of those times says, that *Montfort* spent a whole night of devotions to S. *Denis* (so I understand him, although his copy seem corrupted) which could make Champions invincible; whereto he refers the success. That it was usual for combatants to pray over-night to several Saints, is plain by our Law-annals.[5]

320. *Or any ear had heard the sound of* Florida.

About the year 1157 *Madoc*, brother to *David* ap *Owen*, Prince of *Wales*, made this sea-voyage; and, by proba-

[1] Girald. Itinerar. 1. cap. 6.
[2] De quo si placet, videas compendiosè apud Alberic. Gentil. de Arm. Rom. 1. cap. 1.
[3] Gul. de Novo Burgo lib. 2. cap. 5.
[4] Joann. Sarisburiens. Ep. 159.
[5] 30. *Ed*. III. fol. 20.

bility, those names of *Capo de Breton* in *Norumbeg*, and *Pengwin* in part of the Northern *America*, for a *White Rock* and a *White-headed Bird*, according to the *British*, were relics of this discovery. So that the *Welsh* may challenge priority, of finding that New World, before the *Spaniard, Genoway*, and all other mentioned in *Lopez, Marineus, Cortez*, and the rest of that kind.

321. *And with that* Croggin's *name let th'* English *us disgrace.*

The first cause of this name, take thus: In one of *Henry* the II. his expeditions into *Wales*, divers of his Camp sent to assay a passage over *Offa's-Dike*, at *Croyen* Castle were entertained with prevention by *British* forces, most of them there slain, and, to present view. yet lying buried. Afterward, this word *Crogen*,[1] the *English* used to the *Welsh*, but as remembring cause of revenge for such a slaughter, although time hath made it usual in ignorant mouths for a disgraceful attribute.

326. *To his unbridled will our necks* we never bow'd.

Sufficiently justifiable is this of King *John*, although our Monks therein not much discording from *British* relation, deliver, that he subdued all *Wales;* especially this Northern* part unto *Snowdon*, and received twenty hostages for surety of future obedience. For, at first, *Lhewelin* ap *Jorwerth*, Prince of *North-Wales*, had by force joined with stratagem the better hand, and compelled the *English* Camp to victual themselves with horse-flesh; but afterward indeed upon a second rode made into *Wales*, King *John* had the conquest. This compared with those changes ensuing

[1] Gutyn Owen in *Lhewelin* ap *Jorwerth*.
* Note that *North-wales* was the chief Principality, and to it *South-wales* and *Powis* paid a tribute, as out of the laws of *Howel Dha* is noted by *Doctor Powel*.

upon the Pope's wrongful uncrowning him, his Barons' rebellion, and advantages in the mean time taken by the *Welsh*, proves only that, his winnings here were little better than imaginary, as on a Tragic Stage. The stories may, but it fits not me to inform you of large particulars.

332. *As Fate had spar'd our fall till* Edward Longshankes' *reign.*

But withal observe the truth of Story in the mean time. Of all our Kings until *John*, somewhat you have already. After him, *Hen.* III. had wars with *Lhewelin* ap *Jorwerth ;* who (a most worthy Prince) desiring to bless his feebler days with such composed quiet, as inclining age affects, at last put himself into the King's protection. Within short space dying, left all to his sons, *David* and *Gruffyth ;* but *David* only being legitimate. had title of government. He by charter[1] submits himself and his Principality to the *English* Crown, acknowledges that he would stand to the judgment of the King's Court, in controversies 'twixt his brother and himself, and that what portions soever were so allotted to either of them, they would hold of the Crown in chief ; and briefly makes himself and his Barons (they joining in doing homage) Tenants, and subjects of *England*. All this was confirmed by oath, but the oath, through favour, purchased at *Rome*, and delegate authority in that kind to the Abbots of *Conwy* and *Kemer*, was (according to persuasion of those times, the more easily induced, because gain of Regal liberty was the consequent) soon released, and in lieu of obedience, they all drew their rebellious swords ; whereto they were the sooner urged, for that the King had transferred the Principality of *Wales*[2] (by name of

[1] Charta Davidis 25. Hen. 3. *Senen*, wife of *Gruffith* then imprisoned, was with others a pledge for her husband's part.
[2] In Archiv. Scaccar. et Polydor. Hist. Angl. 16.

unà cum Conquestu nostro Walliæ) to Prince *Edward Long-shankes* (afterward *Edward* I.) since when our Sovereign's eldest sons have borne that hopeful title. But when this *Edward*, after his father, succeeded in the *English* Crown,[1] soon came that fatal conversion, here spoken of by the Author, even executed in as great and worthy a Prince, as ever that third part of the Isle was ruled by; that is *Lhewelin* ap *Gruffyth*, who (after uncertain fortune of war, on both sides, and revolting of *Southwales*) was constrained to enter a truce (or rather subjection) resigning his Principality to be annexed wholly to the Crown, after his death, and reserving, for his life only, the Isle of *Anglesey* and five Baronies in *Snowdon*, for which the King's Exchequer should receive a yearly rent of one thousand marks, granting also that all the Baronies in *Wales* should be held of the King, excepting those five reserved, with divers other particulars in *Walsingham*, *Matthew* of *Westminster*, *Nicholas Trivet*, and *Humfrey Lhuyd*, at large reported. The Articles of this instrument were not long observed, but at length the death of *Lhewelin*, spending his last breath for maintenance of his ancestors' rights against his own covenant, freely cast upon King *Edward* all that, whereof he was, as it were, instituted there. What ensued, and how *Wales* was governed afterward, and subject to *England*, Stories and the Statute of *Ruthlan*[2] will largely show you; and see what I have to the Seventh Song. In all that follows concerning *Edward* of *Carnarvan*, the Author is plain enough. And concluding, observe this proper personating of *Snowdon* Hill, whose limits and adjacent territories are best witnesses, both of the *English* assaults, and pacifying covenants between both Princes.

[1] 1277.   [2] 12. Ed. 1.

THE NINTH SONG. 31

390. *Was call'd in former times her country* Cambria's mother.

In the *Welsh* Proverb **Mon*** mam **Cymbry**;[1] in such sense as *Sicile* was styled *Italy's* Store-house,[2] by reason of fertile ground, and plenteous liberality of corn thence yearly supplied. And *Girald* tells me, that this little Isle was wont to be able to furnish all *Wales* with such provision, as *Snowdon* Hills were for pasture. Of its antiquities and particulars, with plain confutation of that idle opinion in *Polydore, Hector Boethius,* and others, taking the (now-called) Isle of *Man* for this *Mon* (now *Anglesey*) learned *Lhuyd* in his Epistle to *Ortelius* hath sufficient. Although it be divided as an Isle (but rather by a shallow ford, than a sea: and in the *Roman* times, we see by *Tacitus*, that *Paulinus* and *Agricola's* soldiers swam over it) yet is it, and of ancient time hath been, a County by itself, as *Caernarvan*, *Denbigh*, and the rest neighbouring.

409. *So that the* Eubonian Man, *a Kingdom long time known*.

It is an Isle lying twixt *Cumberland*, and the *Irish Doun* County, almost in the mid-sea, as long since *Julius Caesar* could affirm, calling it *Mona*,[3] which being equivalent, as well for this, as for *Anglesey*, hath with imposture blinded some knowing men. *Nennius* (the eldest Historian amongst us extant) gives it the name of *Eubonia-manay*, like that here used by the Author. It was of ancient time governed by Kings of its own, as you may see in the Chronicle of *Ruffin*, deduced from time of *S. Edward*, into the reign of *Edward* the Second. After this, the government of the *English* and *Scots* were now and then interchanged in it, being at last recovered, and with continuance, ruled by such as the favour of our Sovereigns (to whose Crown it belonged[4]) honoured with that title *King of Man.* It is at

---

* *Mon* the mother of *Wales.*   [1] Girald. Itinerar. 2. cap. 7. et 9.
[2] Strabo. lib. 7.   [3] Commentar. 5.   [4] Walsingh. in *Ed.* II.

this day, and since time of *Henry* IV. hath been, in that noble family of the *Stanleys* Earls of *Derby*[1]; as also is the patronage of the Bishopric of *Sodor*, whereto is all judicial government of the Isle referred. There was long since a controversy, whether it belonged to *Ireland* or *England* (for you may see in the Civil law,[2] with which, in that kind, ours somewhat agrees, that all lesser Isles are reckoned part of some adjoining continent, if both under the same Empire) and this by reason of the equal distance from both. To decide it, they tried if it would endure venomous beasts, which is certainly denied of *Ireland;* and, finding that it did,[3] adjudged it to our *Britain*. The other Isles here spoken of lie further North by *Scotland*, and are to it subject.

417. *The fearless* British Priests *under an aged* oak.

He means the *Druids;* because they are indeed, as he calls them, *British* Priests, and that this Island was of old their Mother: whence, as from a Seminary, *Gaul* was furnished with their learning. Permit me some space more largely to satisfy you in their *NAME, PROFESSION, SACRIFICE, PLACES* of *Assembling*, and lastly, *SUBVERSION*. The name of *Druids* hath been drawn from Δρῦς, *i.e., an Oak*, because of their continual[4] using that tree as superstitiously hallowed; according as they are called also Σαρονίδαι or Σαρωνίδες,[5] which likewise, in *Greek*, is *Old Oak*. To this compare the *British* word 𝔇𝔢𝔯𝔴 of the same signification, and, the original here sought for, will seem surely found. But one,[6] that derives all from *Dutch*, and

---

[1] Camden. in Insulis.
[2] Ulpian ff. de Judiciis l. 9. et verb. fig. l. 99.
[3] Topograph. Hibern. dist. 2. cap. 15.
[4] Plin. Hist. Nat. 16. cap. 44.
[5] Diodor. Sicul. de Antiquorum gestis fab. σ.
[6] Goropius Gallic. 5.

THE NINTH SONG. 33

prodigiously supposes that the first tongue spoken, makes them so styled from **Trow wis,** *i.e.*, *truly wise*, so expressing their nature in their name. Nor is this without good reason of conjecture (if the ground were true) seeing that their like in proportion among the *Jews* and *Gentiles* were called (until *Pythagoras* his time) *Wise-men,** and afterward by him turned into the name of Philosophers, *i.e.*, *Lovers of wisdom;* and perhaps the old *Dutch* was, as some learned think, communicated to *Gaul,* and from thence hither; the conjecture being somewhat aided in that attribute which they have in *Pomponius*,[1] calling them *Masters of wisdom.* A late great Scholar[2] draws it from **Trutin,** in an old *Dutch* copy of the Gospel, signifying, as he says, *God;* which might be given them by *hyperbole* of superstitious reverence; nay, we see that it is justifiable by Holy Writ, so to call great Magistrates and Judges; as they were among the people. But that word *Trutin* or *Truchtin* in the old Angelical salutation, *Zachary's* Song, and *Simeon's,* published by *Vulcan,* is always *Lord;* as this **Giwihit si truchtin got Israelo,** *i.e.*, *Blessed be the Lord God of Israel,* and so in the *Saxon* Ten Commandments,[3] Ic eom Dpihten ðin God, *i.e.*, *I am the Lord thy God.* These are the etymologies which savour of any judgment. To speak of King *Druis* or *Sarron,* which that *Dominican* Friar[4] hath cozened vulgar credulity withal, and thence fetch their name, according to Doctor *White* of *Basingstoke,* were with him to suffer, and, at once, offer imposture. Of them all, I incline to the first, seeing it meets in both tongues *Greek* and *British;* and somewhat the rather too,

---

* אמרו הכמים. i.e. *dixerunt sapientes*, Capnio de Art. Cabalistic. l. 3. quod Hebræis in usu ut αὐτὸς ἔφη Pythagoræis, nec Druidum discipulis refragari sententiis Magistrorum fas erat.

[1] Geograph. 3. cap. 2.
[2] Paul. Merula Cosmog. part. 2. lib. 3. cap. 11.
[3] Præfat. ad Leg. Aluredi Saxonic.
[4] Berosus (ille Annianus subdititius) Chaldaic. Antiquitat. 5.

because Antiquity did crown their infernal Deities (and from *Dis*, if you trust *Cæsar*, the *Gauls*, and by consequence our *Britons*, upon tradition of these Priests, drew their descent) with Oak; as *Sophocles*[1] hath it of *Hecate*, and *Catullus*[*] of the Three Destinies. Neither will I desire you to spend conceit upon examination of that supposition which makes the name[2] corrupted from 𝔇𝔲𝔯𝔠𝔢𝔯𝔤𝔩𝔦𝔦𝔰, which in *Scottish* were such as had a holy charge committed to them; whereupon, perhaps, *Bale* says S. *Columban* was the Chief of the *Druids:* I reckon that among the infinite fables and gross absurdities, which its author hath, without judgment, stuffed himself withal. For their *PROFESSION*, it was both of learning Profane and Holy (I speak in all, applying my words to their times): they sat as Judges, and determined all causes emergent, civil and criminal, subjecting the disobedient, and such as made default to interdicts, and censures, prohibiting them from sacred assemblies, taking away their capacities in honourable offices, and so disabling them, that (as our now out-laws, excommunicates, and attainted persons) they might not commence suit against any man. In a multitude of verses they delivered what they taught, not suffering it to be committed to writing, so imitating both *Cabalists*, *Pythagoreans*, and ancient Christians;[3] but used in other private and public business *Greek* letters, as *Cæsar's* copies have; but hereof see more to the Tenth Song. Their more private and sacred learning consisted in Divinity, and Philosophy (see somewhat of that to the First Song), which was such, that although I think you may truly

---

[1] In 'Ριζοτόμ. apud Scholiast. Apollonii uti primùm didici à Josepho Scaligero in Conjectaneis.
[*] De nuptiis Pelei et Thetidos. 308. *His Corpus tremulum*, &c., ubi vulgatis deest ista, quæ, antiquorum codicum fide, est vera lectio, uti Scalig.
[2] Hector Boeth. Scot. Hist. 2.
[3] Cæl. Rhodigin. Antiq. lect. 10. cap. 1.

say with *Origen*,[1] that, before our Saviour's time, *Britain* acknowledged not one true God, yet it came as near to what they should have done, or rather nearer, than most of other, either *Greek* or *Roman*, as by their positions in *Cæsar*, *Strabo*, *Lucan*, and the like discoursing of them, you may be satisfied. For although *Apollo*, *Mars*, and *Mercury* were worshipped among the vulgar *Gauls*, yet it appears that the *Druids'* invocation was to one *All-healing*[2] or *All-saving* power. In Morality, their instructions were so persuasive, and themselves of such reverence, that the most fiery rage of *Mars* kindled among the people, was by their grave counsels often quenched.[3] Out of *Pliny* receive their form of ritual *SACRIFICE* (here described by the Author) thus: In such gloomy shadows, as they most usually for contemplation retired their ascending thoughts into, after exact search, finding an Oak, whereon a Mistletoe grew, on the sixth day of the Moon (above all other times) in which was beginning of their year, they religiously and with invocation brought with them to it a ceremonial banquet, materials for sacrifice, with two white Bulls, filleted on the horns, all which they placed under the Oak. One of them, honoured with that function, clothed all in white, climbs the tree, and with a golden knife or scythe cuts the Mistletoe, which they solemnly wrapped in one of their white garments. Then did they sacrifice the Bulls, earnestly calling on the *All-healing** Deity to make it prosperous and happy on whomsoever they shall bestow it, and accounted it both preservative against all poisons, and a remedy against barrenness. If I should imagine by this *All-healing* Deity to be meant *Apollo*, whom they worshipped under name of *Belin* (as I tell you to the Eighth Song) my conjecture were

---

[1] Ad Jehezkel. 4. [2] Plin. Hist. Nat. 16. cap. 44.
[3] Strab. Geograph. iv.   * Omnia sanantem.

every way receivable; seeing that *Apollo*[1] had both among *Greeks* and *Latins* the Divine titles of 'Αλεξίκακος,* Λοίμιος, *Medicus*, and to him the invocation was 'Ιὴ Παιάν,† all concurring in the same proof; but also if they had (as probability is enough to conjecture it) an Altar inscribed for this devotion, and used *Greek* letters (which to the next Song shall be somewhat examined) I could well think the dedication thus conceived.

ΒΕΛΙΝΩι.‡
ΤΩι.
ΠΑΝΑΚΕΙ.
OR,
ΒΕΛΙΝΩι. ΘΕΩι.§

Which, very probably, was meant by some, making in *Latin* termination, and nearer *Apollo's* name

DEO
ABELLIONI.‖

As, an Inscription, in *Gaul*, to abiding memory committed by that most noble *Joseph Scaliger*[2] is read; and perhaps some relics or allusion to this name is in that

DEO
SANCTO BELA-
TUCADRO......

yet remaining in *Cumberland*.[3] Nor is it strange that *Apollo's* name should be thus far of ancient time, before communication of religion twixt these Northern parts and

---

[1] Macrob. Saturnal. cap. 17.
* All three words as much as *Physician*. † Heal *Apollo*.
‡ To All-healing *Apollo*: et *Salutaris Apollo* in Numm. Apud Goltzium. in Thes. § To God *Belin*. ‖ To God *Abellio*.
[2] Ausoniarum. Lect. 1. cap. 9. [3] Camd. ibid.

the learned *Gentiles*, seeing that *Cæsar* affirms him for one of their Deities; and, long before that, *Abaris* (about the beginning of the *Olympiads*[1]) an *Hyperborean* is recorded for *Apollo's*[2] Priest among the utmost *Scythians*, being further from *Hellenism* than our *British*. But I return to the Mistle: Hereto hath some referred[3] that which the *Sibyl* counselled *Æneas* to carry with him to *Proserpine;*

——————— *latet arbore opacâ*
Aureus et foliis et lento vimine ramus
Junoni infernæ dictus sacer: hunc tegit omnis
Lucus, et obscuris claudunt convallibus umbræ. *

Which may as well be so applied, as to Chymistry;[4] seeing it agrees also with what I spake before of *Dis*, and that, *Virgil* expressly compares it to the Mistle,

——————— *quod non sua seminat arbos,*†

for it springs out of some particular nature of the oaken stem, whereupon it is called by an old poet Δρυὸς Ιδρῶς:‡ and although it be not ordinarily found upon oaks, yet, that ofttimes it is, any apothecary can tell, which preserveth it for medicine, as the Ancients used to make lime of it to catch birds: of which *Argentarius*[5] hath an admonitory epigram to a black-bird, that she should not sing upon the oak, because that

——————— ἐπ' ὀρνίθεσσι φέρει τὸν ἀνάρσιον Ἰξόν,§

but on the vine, dedicated to *Bacchus*, a great favourite of

[1] Hippostrat. ap. Suid in *Abar*.   [2] Malchus Vit. Pythagoræ.
[3] Virgil Æneid. 6. Petr. Crinit. Hist. Poet. 6. cap. 10.
* She directs him to seek a golden branch in the dark woods, consecrate to *Proserpine*.
[4] Bracesch. in Ligno vitæ.   † *Which grows not of itself.*
‡ *Sweat of the Oak.* Ion apud Athenænm Deipnosoph. 10.
[5] Antholog. a. cap. ξ.   § *Bred lime to catch her.*

singers. Upon this *Druidian* custom,[1] some have grounded that unto this day used in *France*, where the younger country-fellows, about New-Year's tide, in every village give the wish of good fortune at the inhabitants' doors, with this acclamation, *Au guy l'an neuf ;** which, as I remember, in *Rablais* is read all one word, for the same purpose. Whether this had any community with the institution of that Temple[2] 'Ἰξευτηρίας τύχης† in *Antium*, or that *Ovid* alluded to it in that verse, commonly cited out of him,

At (some read *ad*) *Viscum Druidæ, Viscum clamare solebant;*‡

I cannot assure you, yet it is enough likely. But I see a custom in some parts among us, in our language (nor is the digression too faulty) the same in effect; I mean the yearly 𝔴𝔞𝔰-𝔥𝔞𝔦𝔩𝔢 in the country on the vigil of the New-Year, which had its beginning, as some say,[3] from that of *Ronix* (daughter to *Hengist*) her drinking to *Vortigern*, by these words, 𝔏𝔬𝔲𝔢𝔯𝔡 𝔨𝔦𝔫𝔤 𝔴𝔞𝔰-𝔥𝔢𝔦𝔩,§ he answering her by direction of an interpreter, 𝔇𝔯𝔦𝔫𝔠-𝔥𝔢𝔦𝔩𝔢,∥ and then,[4]

𝔎𝔲𝔰𝔱𝔢 𝔥𝔦𝔯𝔢 𝔞𝔫𝔡 𝔰𝔦𝔱𝔱𝔢 𝔥𝔦𝔯𝔢 𝔞𝔡𝔬𝔲𝔫𝔢 𝔞𝔫𝔡 𝔤𝔩𝔞𝔡 𝔡𝔯𝔬𝔫𝔨𝔢 𝔥𝔦𝔯𝔢 𝔥𝔢𝔦𝔩
𝔄𝔫𝔡 𝔱𝔥𝔞𝔱 𝔴𝔞𝔰 𝔱𝔥𝔬 𝔦𝔫 𝔱𝔥𝔦𝔰 𝔩𝔞𝔫𝔡 𝔱𝔥𝔢 𝔟𝔢𝔯𝔰𝔱 𝔴𝔞𝔰-𝔥𝔞𝔦𝔩
𝔄𝔰 𝔦𝔫 𝔩𝔞𝔫𝔤𝔞𝔤𝔢 𝔬𝔣 𝔖𝔞𝔵𝔬𝔶𝔫𝔢 𝔱𝔥𝔞𝔱 𝔪𝔢 𝔪𝔦𝔤𝔥𝔱 𝔢𝔲𝔢𝔯𝔢 𝔦𝔴𝔦𝔱𝔢
𝔄𝔫𝔡 𝔰𝔬 𝔴𝔢𝔩 𝔥𝔢 𝔭𝔞𝔦𝔱𝔥 𝔱𝔥𝔢 𝔣𝔬𝔩𝔠 𝔞𔟐𔠀𔠁𔠂, 𝔱𝔥𝔞𝔱 𝔥𝔢 𝔦𝔰 𝔫𝔬𝔱 𝔭𝔲𝔱 𝔥𝔬𝔯𝔶𝔲𝔱𝔢.

Afterward it appears that 𝔚𝔞𝔰-𝔥𝔞𝔦𝔩𝔢 and 𝔇𝔯𝔦𝔫𝔠-𝔥𝔢𝔦𝔩 were the usual phrases of quaffing among the *English*, as we see

---

[1] Io. Goropius Gallic. 5. et alii.   * *To the Mistle, this New Year.*
[2] Plutarch. Problem. Rom. οδ. Cœlius Rhodigin. Antiq. lect. 18. cap. 14.
† As if you should say of *Misthed Fortune.*
‡ *To the Mistle, the Druids used to cry.*
[3] Galfred. Monumeth. 1. 3. cap. 1.   § *Lord King, a health.*
∥ *Drink the health.*   [4] Rob. Glocestrens.

in *Thomas de la Moore*,[1] and before him the old *Havillan*,[2] thus:

> *Ecce vagante cifo distento gutture* wass=heil
> *Ingeminant* wass=heil————

But I rather conjecture it a usual ceremony among the *Saxons* before *Hengist*, as a note of health-wishing (and so perhaps you might make it wish=heil), which was expressed among other nations in that form of drinking to the health of their mistresses and friends,

> *Benè* vos, benè nos, benè te, benè me, benè nostram etiam Stephanium,*

in *Plautus*,[3] and infinite other testimonies of that nature (in him *Martial, Ovid, Horace,* and such more) agreeing nearly with the fashion now used; we calling it a *Health,* as they did also in direct terms;† which, with an Idol called *Heil,* anciently worshipped at *Cerne* in *Dorsetshire*,[4] by the *English-Saxons,* in name expresses both the ceremony of Drinking, and the New-Year's acclamation (whereto in some parts of this kingdom is joined also solemnity of drinking out of a cup,‡ ritually composed, decked, and filled with country liquor) just as much and as the same which that *All-healing Deity,* or *All-helping* medicine did among the *Druids.* You may to all this add, that, as an earnest of good luck to follow the New Year beginning, it was usual[5] among the *Romans,* as with us, and I think, in all *Europe,* at this day is, to greet each other with auspicious gifts. But hereof you say I unfitly expatiate: I omit, therefore, their sacrificing of

---

[1] Vita *Edwardi* II.
* Sub intellige ζῆσθαι aut quid simile.
† *Propino tibi salutem plenis faucibus.*
[4] Camdenus.
[5] Ovid. Fastor. 1. Fest. in Strena.

[2] In Architren. lib. 2.
[3] In Sticho.
Plautus eâdem comœdiâ.
‡ The *Wasshail-boll.*

human bodies, and such like, and come to the *PLACES* of
their assembly. This was about *Chartres* in *Gaul*, as *Cæsar*
tells us; *Paul Merula* (for affinity of name) imagines it to
be *Dreux*, some eight miles on this side *Chartres*. And per-
adventure the *Galatians'* public Council called *Drymenetum*[1]
had hence original. The *British Druids* took this Isle of
Anglesey (then well-stored with thick woods and religious
groves, insomuch that it was called 𝔍𝔫𝔦𝔰=𝔇𝔬𝔴𝔦𝔩*) for their
chief residence; as, in the *Roman*[2] story of *Paulinus* and
Agricola's adventuring on it, is delivered. For their *SUB-
VERSION;* under *Augustus* and *Tiberius* they were prohibited *Rome;*[3] and *Claudius* endeavoured it in *Gaul*[4]; yet in
the succeeding Emperors' times there were of them left, as
appears in *Lampridius* and *Vopiscus*, mentioning them in their
lives; and, long since that, *Procopius*,[5] writing under *Jus-
tinian* above five hundred years after *Christ*, affirms that
then the *Gauls* used sacrifices of human flesh, which was a
part of *Druidian* doctrine. If I should upon testimony of,[6]
I know not what, *Veremund, Campbell*, and the *Irish Cornill*,
tell you that some hundred and sixty years before *Christ*,
Finnan King of *Scotland* first gave them the Isle, or that
King *Crathlint* in *Diocletian's* persecution, turned their religion into Christianism, and made *Amphibalus* first Bishop of
Sodor, I should fabulously abuse time, as they have ignorantly mistook that Isle of *Man* for this. Or to speak of
the supposed their 𝔇𝔯𝔲𝔱𝔱𝔢𝔫𝔣𝔲𝔰𝔰, *i.e.*, a pentagonal figure,
ingraven with 'ΥΓΙΕΙΑ or 'Υγεία (it is the same, in fashion,

[1] Strab. Geograph. xii.
* *The Dark Isle*, Brit.
[2] Tacit. Annal. 14. et Vit. Agricolæ.
[3] Sueton. lib. 5. cap. 24. et Plin. Hist. Nat. 30. cap. 1.
[4] Senec. in Apocoloc. et Sueton. ubi suprà.
[5] De Bell. Gothic. β.
[6] Hector. Boet. Scotor. Hist. 2. et 6.

THE NINTH SONG. 41

with the victorious seal of *Antiochus Soter*,[1] being admonished by *Alexander* in a dream, to take it) which in *Germany* they reckon for a preservative against hobgoblins, were but to be indulgent to old wives' traditions. Only thus much for a corollary, I will note to you; *Conrad Celtes*[2] observes, to be in an Abbey at the foot of *Vichtelberg* Hill, near *Voitland*, six statues, of stone, set in the church-wall, some seven foot every one tall, bare head and foot, cloaked and hooded, with a bag, a book, a staff, a beard hanging to his middle, and spreading a mustachio, an austere look and eyes fixed on the earth; which he conjectures to be images of them. Upon mistaking of *Strabo*, and applying what he saith in general, and bracelets and gold chains of the *Gauls*, to the *Druids*, I once thought that *Conrad* had been deceived. But I can now upon better advice incline to his judgment.

445. *Which with my* Princes' Court *I sometimes pleas'd to grace.*

For, as in *South-Wales*, *Caermardhin*, and afterward *Dinevowr;* in *Powis*, *Shrewsbury*, and then *Mathraval*, so in *North-Wales* was *Aber-fraw*, in *Anglesey*, chief place of the Princes' residence.[3]

Lest (by reason of the composition in print) some pages should have been idle, and because also here is so much of the *Welsh* Story, I inserted this Chronology of the Kings and Princes of *Wales*, from *Arthur*, until the end of the *British* blood in them.

[1] Lucian. ὑπὲρ τοῦ ἐν τῇ προσαγορεύσει πταίσματος; Alii et habetur apud Agrippam. in 3. de Occultâ Philosoph. cap. 31. atque ex Antiochi nummis apud I. Reuchlinum. in 3. de arte Cabalisticâ.
[2] Tract. de Hercyniâ Sylvâ.
[3] Pris. in Descript. Wall.

Of Christ.

516   Arthur succeeded his father *Uther Pendragon:* of his death, see to the Third Song.[1]

542   *Constantine,* son to *Cador* Duke of *Cornwall* (understand *Governor* or *Lord Lieutenant;* for, neither in those times nor long after, was any such title particularly honorary): he lies buried at *Stonehenge.*

545   *Aurelius Conan.*

578   *Vortipor.*

581   *Malgo.*

586   *Catheric.* In his time the *Britons* had much adverse fortune in war with the *Saxons,* and then, most of all, made that secession into *Wales* and *Cornwall,* yet in name retaining hereof remembrance.

About 600   *Cadwan.*

About 630   *Cadwalin* or *Cadwallo:* the *Britons* as in token of his powerful resistance and dominion against the *Saxons,* put him,* being dead, into a brazen Horse, and set it on the top of the West gate of *London:* it seems he means *Ludgate.*

676   *Cadwallader,* son to *Cadwallo.* Of him and his name, see before. Nor think I the *British* and *English* Chronicles, concerning him, reconcileable. In him the chief monarchy and glory of the *British* failed.

688   *Ivor,* song to *Alan,* King of *Armoric Britain.* This *Ivor* they make (but I examine it not now)

---

[1] I will not justify the times of this *Arthur,* nor the rest, before *Cadwallader;* so discording are our Chronologers: nor had I time to examine, nor think that any man hath sufficient means to rectify them.

* This report is, as the *British* story tells, hardly justifiable, if examined.

THE NINTH SONG. 43

Of Christ.
            Ine King of *West-Saxons* in our Monks; that is,
            he which began the *Peter-pence* to *Rome*.
720   *Roderic Molwinoc*, son of *Edwal* **Dwrch**.*
755   *Conan Tindaethwy*, son of *Roderic*.
Near 820   *Merrin Urich*, in right of his wife *Esyllt*,
            daughter and heir to *Roderic*.
843   *Roderic Mawr*, son to *Merrin* and *Esyllt*.
            Among his sons was the tripartite division of
            Wales (as to the Seventh Song) into *Powise*,
            North, and *South-Wales*.
877   *Anarawd*, son to *Roderic*.
913   *Edward Voel*, son of *Anarawd*.
940   *Howel Dha*, cousin-german to *Edwal*, having,
            before, the Principality of *South-Wales* and *Powis*.
            This is he whose Laws are so famous and in-
            quired of in *Rot. Claus. Wall. 9. Ed. 1.* in the
            Tower.
948   *Ieraf* and *Iago*, sons of *Edwal Voel*.
982   *Howel* **ap** *Ieraf*.
984   *Cadwalhon* **ap** *Ieraf*.
986   *Meredith* **ap** *Owen*.
992   *Edwal* **ap** *Meiric*.
1003   *Ædan* **ap** *Blegored*.
1015   *Lhewelin* **ap** *Sitsyllht*.
1021   *Iago* **ap** *Edwal* **ap** *Meyric*.
1037   *Gruffyth* **ap** *Lhewelin*.
1061   *Blethin* and *Rhywallon* **ap** *Conrin*.
1073   *Trahaern* **ap** *Caradoc*.
1078   *Gruffyth* **ap** *Conan*. He reformed the *Welsh*
            Poets and Minstrels, and brought over others
            out of *Ireland* to instruct the *Welsh*; as to the
            Fourth Song.

                            * The *Roo*.

Of Christ.

1137   *Owen Gwineth* **ap** *Gruffyth* **ap** *Conan.*
1169   *David* **ap** *Owen Gwineth.* In his time, *Mador* his brother discovered part of the West *Indies.*
1194   *Lhewelin* **ap** *Iorwerth* **ap** *Owen Gwineth.*
1240   *David* **ap** *Lhewelin* **ap** *Iorwerth.*
1246   *Lhewelin* **ap** *Gruffyth* **ap** *Lhewelin* **ap** *Iorwerth;* the last Prince of *Wales* of the *British* blood.
1282   *Edward* I. conquered *Wales,* and got the Principality, *Lhewelin* then slain; and since that (*Henry* III. before gave it also to his son Prince *Edward*) it hath been in the eldest sons, and heirs-apparent of the *English* Crown.

But note, that after the division among *Roderic Mawr's* sons, the Principality was chiefly in *North-Wales,* and the rest as tributary to the Prince of that part: and for him as supreme King of *Wales,* are all these deductions of time and persons, until this last *Lhewelin.*

THE TENTH SONG.

THE ARGUMENT.

The serious Muse herself applies
To Merlin's ancient prophecies,
At Dinas Emris; where he show'd
How Fate the Britans' rule bestow'd.
To Conway next she turns her tale, 5
And sings her Cluyd's renownéd Vale;
Then of Saint Winifrid doth tell,
And all the wonders of her Well;
Makes Dee, Bruit's history pursue:
At which, she bids her Wales Adieu. 10

WHILE thus taking breath, our way yet fair in view,
    The Muse her former course doth seriously pursue.
From *Penmen's*[1] craggy height to try her saily wings,
    Herself long having bath'd in the delicious springs
(That trembling from his top through long-worn crannies
    creep, 5
To spend their liquid store on the insatiate deep)
She meets with *Conway* first, which lieth next at hand:
Whose precious orient pearl,[2] that breedeth in her sand,
Above the other Floods of *Britain* doth her grace:
Into the *Irish* Sea which making out her race, 10

---

[1] *Penmenmaure.*   [2] Pearl in the River *Conway.*

Supply'd by many a mere (through many several rills
Into her bosom pour'd) her plenteously she fills.
O goodly River! near unto thy sacred spring
§ Prophetic *Merlin* sate, when to the *British* King
The changes long to come, auspiciously he told.   15
Most happy were thy Nymphs, that wond'ring did behold
His graver wrinkled brow, amazed and did hear
The dreadful words he spake, that so ambiguous were.
Thrice happy Brooks, I say, that (every way about)
Thy tributaries be: as is that Town, where-out   20
Into the sea thou fall'st, which *Conway* of thy name
Perpetually is call'd, to register thy fame.
For thou, clear *Conway*, heard'st wise *Merlin* first relate
The Destinies' decree, of *Britain's* future fate;
Which truly he foretold proud *Vortiger* should lose: 25
As, when him from his seat the *Saxons* should depose:
The forces that should here from *Armoric*[1] arrive,
Yet far too weak from hence the enemy to drive:
And to that mighty King, which rashly undertook
A strong-wall'd tower to rear, those earthly spirits that shook
The great foundation still, in Dragons' horrid shape,   31
That dreaming Wizard told; making the mountain gape
With his most powerful charms, to view those caverns deep;
And from the top of *Brith*,* so high and wondrous steep,
Where *Dinas Emris* stood, show'd where the Serpents fought,
The White that tore the Red; from whence the Prophet
          wrought   36
The *Britans*' sad decay then shortly to ensue.

O! happy ye that heard the man who all things knew
Until the general Doom, through all the world admir'd:
By whose prophetic saws ye all became inspir'd;   40
As well the forked *Aeage*, that near'st her fountain springs,

---

[1] *Little Britain* in *France*.   * Part of the *Snowdon*.

With her belovéd maid, *Melandidar*, that brings
Her flow, where *Conway* forth into the sea doth slide
(That to their Mistress make to the *Denbighian* side)
As those that from the hills of proud *Carnarvan* fall.
This scarce the Muse had said, but *Cluyd* doth quickly call
Her great recourse, to come and guard her while she glide
Along the goodly Vale (which with her wealthy pride
Much beautifies her banks; so naturally her own,
That *Dyffren Cluyd* by her both far and near is known)
[1]With high embattled hills that each way is enclos'd
But only on the North: and to the North dispos'd,
Fierce *Boreas* finds access to court the dainty Vale:
Who, whisp'ring in her ear with many a wanton tale,
Allures her to his love (his leman her to make)
As one that in himself much suff"reth for her sake.

The *Orcades*,[2] and all those *Eubides*[2] imbrac'd
In *Neptune's* aged arms, to *Neptune* seeming chaste,
Yet prostitute themselves to *Boreas;* who neglects
The *Calidonian* Downs, nor ought at all respects
The other inland Dales, abroad that scatt'red lie,
Some on the *English* earth, and some in *Albany;*
But, courting *Dyffren Cluyd*, her beauty doth prefer.
Such dalliance as alone the North-wind hath with her,
Orithya[3] not enjoy'd, from *Thrace* when he her took,
And in his saily plumes the trembling Virgin shook:
But through the extreme love he to this Vale doth bear,
Grows jealous at the length, and mightily doth fear
Great *Neptune*, whom he sees to smug his horrid face:
And, fearing lest the God should so obtain her grace,
From the Septentrion cold, in the breem freezing air,
Where the bleak North-wind keeps, still domineering there,

---
[1] The situation of *Dyffren Cluyd*.
[2] Isles upon the North-east and West of *Scotland*.
[3] In the sixth book of Ovid's Metamorph.

From *Shetland* straddling wide, his foot on *Thuly* sets :
Whence storming, all the vast *Deucalidon* he threats,
And bears his boist'rous waves into the narrower mouth   75
Of the *Vergivian* Sea : where meeting, from the South,
Great *Neptune's* surlier tides, with their robustious shocks,
Each other shoulder up against the griesly rocks ;[1]
As strong men when they meet, contending for the path :
But, coming near the coast where *Cluyd* her dwelling hath,   80
The North-wind (calm become) forgets his ire to wreak,
§ And the delicious Vale thus mildly doth bespeak :

   Dear *Cluyd*, th' aboundant sweets, that from thy bosom flow,
When with my active wings into the air I throw,
Those hills, whose hoary heads seem in the clouds to dwell,
Of agéd become young, enamour'd with the smell   85
Of th' odoriferous flowers in thy most precious lap :
Within whose velvet leaves, when I myself enwrap,
They suffocate with scents ; that (from my native kind)
I seem some slow perfume, and not the swiftest wind.   90
With joy, my *Dyffren Cluyd*, I see thee bravely spread,
Surveying every part, from foot up to thy head ;
Thy full and youthful breasts, which in their meadowy pride,
Are branch'd with rivery veins, meander-like that glide.
I further note in thee, more excellent than these   95
(Were there a thing that more the amorous eye might please)
Thy plump and swelling womb, whose mellowy glebe doth bear
The yellow ripened sheaf, that bendeth with the ear.

   Whilst in this sort his suit he amorously preferr'd,
Moylvennill near at hand, the North-wind overheard :   100
And, vexéd at the heart, that he a Mountain great,
Which long time in his breast had felt love's kindly heat,
As one whom crystal *Cluyd* had with her beauty caught,
Is for that River's sake near of his wits distraught,

---

[1] The Tides out of the North and South Seas, meeting in S. George's Channel.

THE TENTH SONG.   49

With inly rage to hear that Valley so extoll'd;   105
And yet that Brook whose course so batfull makes her mould,
And one that lends that Vale her most renownéd name,
Should of her meaner far be over-gone in fame.
Wherefore, *Moylevennill* will'd his *Cluyd* herself to show:
Who, from her native fount as proudly she doth flow,   110
Her handmaids *Manian*[1] hath, and *Hespin*,[1] her to bring
To *Ruthin*. Whose fair seat first kindly visiting,
To lead her thence in state, *Lewenny* lends her source:
That when *Moylevennill* sees his River's great recourse,
From his intrenchéd top is pleas'd with her supplies.   115
Claweddock cometh in, and *Istrad* likewise hies
Unto the Queen-like *Cluyd*, as she to *Denbigh* draws:
And on the other side, from whence the Morning daws,
Down from the *Flintian* Hills, comes *Wheler*, her to bear
To sacred *Asaph's* See, his hallow'd Temple; where   120
Fair *Elwy* having won her sister *Aled's* power,
They entertain their *Cluyd* near mighty *Neptune's* bower:
Who likewise is sustain'd by *Senion*, last that falls,
And from the Virgin's Well doth wash old *Ruthland's* walls.

Moylevennill with her sight that never is suffic'd,   125
Now with excessive joy so strongly is surpris'd,
That thus he proudly spake: On the *Gwynethian* ground
(And look from East to West) what Country is there crown'd
As thou *Tegenia*[2] art? that, with a Vale so rich
(Cut thorough with the *Cluyd*, whose graces me bewitch)   130
The fruitfull'st of all *Wales*, so long hast honour'd been:
As also by thy Spring, such wonder who dost win,
§ That naturally remote, six *British* miles from sea,
And rising on the firm, yet in the natural day
Twice falling, twice doth fill, in most admiréd wise.   135
When *Cynthia* from the East unto the South doth rise,

[1] Riverets running into *Cluyd* out of *Denbigh* and *Flintshire*.
[2] Part of the Vale called *Tey-Engle*, i.e., Fair England.

VOL. II.   4

That mighty *Neptune* flows, then strangely ebbs thy Well ;
And when again he sinks, as strangely she doth swell ;¹
§ Yet to the sacred Fount of *Winifrid* gives place ;
Of all the *Cambrian* Springs of such especial grace,　　140
That oft the *Devian* Nymphs,* as also those that keep
Amongst the coral-groves in the *Vergivian* Deep,
Have left their wat'ry bowers, their secret safe retire,
To see her whom report so greatly should admire
(Whose waters to this day as perfect are and clear,　　145
As her delightful eyes in their full beauties were,
A virgin while she liv'd) chaste *Winifrid :* who chose
Before her maiden-gem she forcibly would lose,
To have her harmless life by the lewd rapter spilt :
For which, still more and more to aggravate his guilt,　　150
The liveless tears she shed, into a Fountain turn.
And, that for her alone the water should not mourn,
The pure vermilion blood, that issu'd from her veins,
Unto this very day the pearly gravel stains ;
As erst the white and red were mixéd in her cheek.　　155
And, that one part of her might be the other like,
Her hair was turn'd to moss; whose sweetness doth declare,
In liveliness of youth, the natural sweets she bare :
And of her holy life the innocence to show,
Whatever living thing into this Well you throw,　　160
She strongly bears it up, not suff'ring it to sink.
Besides, the wholesome use in bathing, or in drink,
Doth the diseaséd cure, as thereto she did leave
Her virtue with her name, that Time should not bereave.

　　Scarce of this tedious tale *Moylerennill* made an end,　　165
But that the higher *Yale*,² whose being doth ascend
Into the pleasant East, his loftier head advanc'd.
This Region, as a man that long had been intranc'd

---

¹ A Fountain ebbing and flowing, contrary to the course of the sea.
* Of *Dee*.　　² A place mountainous, and somewhat inaccessible.

THE TENTH SONG.

(Whilst thus himself to please, the mighty Mountain tells
Such farlies* of his *Cluyd*, and of his wondrous Wells)   170
Stood thinking what to do : lest fair *Tegenia*, plac'd
So admirably well, might hold herself disgrac'd
By his so barren site, being mountainous and cold,
To nothing more unlike than *Dyffren's* batfull mould ;
And in respect of her, to be accounted rude.   175
 Yale, for he would not be confounded quite by *Cluyd*
(And for his common want, to coin some poor excuse)
Unto his proper praise, discreetly doth produce
A Valley, for a Vale, of her peculiar kind ;
In goodness, breadth, and length, though *Dyffren* far behind :
On this yet dare he stand, that for the natural frame,   181
§ That figure of the Cross, of which it takes the name,
Is equal with the best, which else excell it far :
And by the power of that most sacred Character,
Respect beyond the rest unto herself doth win.   185
 When now the sterner *Dee* doth instantly begin
His ampler self to show, that (down the verdant dale)
Strains, in his nobler course along the rougher *Yale*,
T' invite his favouring Brooks : where from that spacious lin
Through which he comes unmix'd, ¹first *Alwin* falleth in :   190
And going on along, still gathering up his force,
Gets *Gerrow* to his aid, to hasten on his course.
With *Christioneth* next, comes *Keriog* in apace.
Out of the leaden Mines, then with her sullied face
Clawedock casts about where *Gwenrow* she may greet,   195
Till like two loving friends they under *Wrexam* meet.
Then *Alen* makes approach (to *Dee* most inly dear)
Taking *Tegiddog* in ; who, earnest to be there,
For haste, twice under earth her crystal head doth run :
When instantly again, *Dee's* holiness begun,   200

  * Strange things.
  ¹ The Rivers in the East of *Denbigh*, falling into *Dee*.

By his contracted front and sterner waves, to show
That he had things to speak, might profit them to know;
A Brook, that was suppos'd much business to have seen,
Which had an ancient bound[1] twixt *Wales* and *England* been,
And noted was by both to be an ominous Flood,   205
That changing of his fords, the future ill, or good,
Of either Country told; of either's war, or peace,
The sickness, or the health, the dearth, or the increase:
And that of all the Floods of *Britain*, he might boast
His stream in former times to have been honor'd most,   210
When as at *Chester* once King *Edgar* held his Court,
§ To whom eight lesser Kings with homage did resort:
That mighty *Mercian* Lord, him in his barge bestow'd,
And was by all those Kings about the river row'd.
For which, the hallow'd *Dee* so much upon him took.   215
And now the time was come, that this imperious Brook
The long-traducéd *Brute* determin'd to awake,
And in the *Britans'* right thus boldly to them spake:

   O ye the ancient race of famous *Brute* that be,
§ And thou the Queen of Isles, Great *Britain;* why do ye   220
Your grandsire's God-like name (with a neglectful ear)
In so reproachful terms and ignominy hear,
By every one of late contemptuously disgrac'd;
That he whom Time so long, and strongly, hath imbrac'd,
Should be rejected quite? The reason urgéd why,   225
Is by the general foe thus answer'd by-and-by:
That *Brutus*, as you say, by sea who hither came,
From whom you would suppose this Isle first took the name,
Merely fictitious is; nor could the *Romans* hear
(Most studious of the truth, and near'st those times that
     were)   230
Of any such as he: nay, they who most do strive,
From that great stock of *Troy* their linage to derive,

[1] See to the Eighth Song.

In all the large descent of *Iülus*, never found
That *Brute*, on whom we might our first beginning ground.
   To this assertion, thus I faithfully reply ;
And as a friend to truth, do constantly deny
Antiquity to them, as nearer to those times,
Their writings to precede our ancient *British* rhymes :
But that our noble *Bards* which so divinely sung
That remnant of old *Troy*, of which the *Britans* sprung,   240
Before those *Romans* were, as proof we can produce ;
§ And learning, long with us, ere 't was with them in use.
And they but idly talk, upbraiding us with lies.
§ That *Geffray Monmouth*, first, our *Brutus* did devise,
Not heard of till his time our Adversary says :
When pregnantly we prove, ere that Historian's days,
A thousand ling'ring years, our Prophets clearly song
The Britain-founding *Brute*, most frequent them among.
From *Taliessen* wise (approvéd so with us,
That what he spake was held to be oraculous,   250
So true his writings were) and such immortal men
As this now-waning world shall hardly hear again
In our own genuine tongue, that natives were of *Wales*,
Our *Geffray* had his *Brute*.   Nor were these idle tales,
(As he may find, the truth of our descents that seeks)
Nor fabulous, like those deviséd by the *Greeks :*
But from the first of Time, by Judges still were heard,
Discreetly every year[1] correcting where they err'd.
   And that whereon our foe his greatest hold doth take,
Against the handled cause and most doth seem to make,   260
Is, that we show no book our *Brutus* to approve ;
But that our idle *Bards*, as their fond rage did move,
Sang what their fancies pleas'd.   Thus do I answer these :
That th' ancient *British* Priests, the fearless *Druidés*,
That minist'red the laws, and were so truly wise,

[1] At the *Stethva:* see to the Fourth Song.

That they determin'd states, attending sacrifice,
§ To letters never would their mysteries commit,[1]
For which the breasts of men they deem'd to be more fit.
Which questionless should seem from judgment to proceed.
For, when of Ages past we look in books to read,   270
We retchlessly discharge our memory of those.
So when injurious Time, such monuments doth lose
(As what so great a work, by Time that is not wrack'd?)
We utterly forego that memorable act:
But when we lay it up within the minds of men,   275
They leave it their next Age; that, leaves it hers again:
So strongly which (methinks) doth for Tradition make,
As if you from the world it altogether take,
You utterly subvert Antiquity thereby.
For though Time well may prove that often she doth lie,   280
Posterity by her yet many things hath known,
That ere men learn'd to write, could no way have been shown:
For, if the Spirit of God did not our faith assure
The Scriptures be from heav'n, like heav'n divinely pure,
Of *Moses'* mighty works, I reverently may say   285
(I speak with godly fear) Tradition put away,
In pow'r of human wit it eas'ly doth not lie
To prove before the Flood the Genealogy.
Nor anything there is that kindlier doth agree
With our descent from *Troy* (if things compar'd may be)   290
Than peopling of this place, near to those Ages, when
Exiled by the *Greeks*, those poor world-wand'ring men
(Of all hope to return into their Country reft)
Sought shores whereon to set that little them was left:
From some such god-like race we questionless did spring,   295
Who soon became so great here once inhabiting.
So barbarous nor were we as many have us made,
And *Cæsar's* envious pen would all the world persuade,

[1] The *Druids* would not commit their mysteries to writing.

His own ambitious ends in seeking to advance,
When with his *Roman* power arriving here from *France*, 300
If he the *Britans* found experienc'd so in war,
That they with such great skill could wield their arméd car;
And, as he still came on, his skilful march to let,
Cut down their aged oaks, and in the rivers set
The sharp steel-pointed stakes, as he the fords should pass;
I fain would understand how this that Nation was 305
So ignorant he would make, and yet so knowing war.

But, in things past so long (for all the world) we are
Like to a man embark'd, and travelling the deep:
Who sailing by some hill, or promontory steep 310
Which juts into the sea, with an amazéd eye
Beholds the cleeves thrust up into the lofty sky.
And th' more that he doth look, the more it draws his sight;
Now at the craggy front, then at the wondrous weight:
But, from the passéd shore still as the swelling sail 315
(Thrust forward by the wind) the floating barque doth hail,
The mighty giant-heap, so less and lesser still
Appeareth to the eye, until the monstrous hill
At length shows like a cloud; and further being cast,
Is out of kenning quite: So, of the Ages past; 320
Those things that in their Age much to be wond'red were,
Still as wing-footed Time them farther off doth bear,
Do lessen every hour. When now the mighty prease,
Impatient of his speech, intreat the Flood to cease,
And cry with one consent, the *Saxon* state to show, 325
As angry with the Muse such labour to bestow
On *Wales*, but *England* still neglected thus to be.

And having pass'd the time, the honorable *Dee*
At *Chester* was arriv'd, and bade them all adieu:
When our intended course, with *England* we pursue. 330

ILLUSTRATIONS.

RETURNING into the land, the Muse leads you about *Denbigh* and *Flint*, most Northern and maritime shires of *Wales;* which conclude these seven last books dedicated to the glory of that third part of Great *Britain.*

14. *Prophetic* Merlin *sate, when to the* British *King.*

In the first declining state of the *British* Empire (to explain the Author in this of *Merlin*) *Vortigern,* by advice of his Magicians, after divers unfortunate successes in war, resolved to erect a strong Fort in *Snowdon* Hills (not far from *Conwey's* head in the edge of *Merioneth*) which might be as his last and surest refuge, against the increasing power of the *English.* Masons were appointed, and the work begun; but what they built in the day, was always swallowed up in the earth, next night. The King asks counsel of his Magicians, touching this prodigy; they advise that he must find out a child which had no father, and with his blood sprinkle the stones and mortar, and that then the Castle would stand as on a firm foundation. Search was made, and in *Caer-Merdhin* (as you have it to the Fifth Song) was *Merlin Ambrose* found: he, being hither brought to the King, slighted that pretended skill of those Magicians as palliated ignorance; and with confidence of a more knowing spirit, undertakes to show the true cause of that amazing ruin of the stone-work; tells them that in the earth was a great water, which could endure continuance of no heavy superstruction. The workmen digged to discover the truth, and found it so. He then beseeches the King to cause them make further inquisition, and affirms, that in the bottom of it were two sleeping Dragons: which proved so likewise, the one *white*, the other *red;* the *white* he interpreted for the *Saxons*, the *red* for the *Britons:* and upon this event here in *Dinas Emrys*,[1] as they call it, began he those prophecies to *Vortigern*, which are common in the *British* story. Hence questionless was that fiction of the Muses' best pupil, the noble *Spenser*,[2] in supposing *Merlin* usually to visit his old *Timon*, whose dwelling he places

—————— *low in a valley greene*
Under the foot of Rauran *mossie hore*
From whence the River Dee *as silver cleene*
His tumbling billows rols with gentle rore.

For this *Rauran-Vaur* Hill is there by in *Merioneth:* but observe withal, the difference of the *Merlins*, *Ambrose*, and *Sylvester*, which is before to the Fourth Song; and permit it only as poetical, that he makes King *Arthur* and this *Merlin* of one time. These prophecies[3] were by *Geffrey* ap *Arthur* at request of *Alexander* Bishop of *Lincoln* under *Hen*. I. turned into *Latin*, and some three hundred years since had interpretation bestowed on them by a *German* Doctor, one *Alanus de Insulis*, who never before, but twice since that happy inauguration and mighty increase of do-

[1] *Ambrose's Bury*. Itinerar. 2. cap. 8.
[2] *Faery Q*. Lib. 1. Cant. 9. Stanz. 4.
[3] *Merlin's* Prophecies.

minion in our present Sovereign hath been imprinted. It is certain that ofttimes they may be directly and without constraint applied to some event of succeeding time; as that which we have before to the Fifth Song of *Cuerleon*, and this, *the Isle shall again be named after Brute ;*[1] which is now seen by a public edict, and in some of his Majesty's present coins, and with more such: yet seeing learned men[2] account him but a professor of unjustifiable Magic, and that all prophecies either fall true, or else are among the affecters of such vanity perpetually expected, and that of later time the Council of *Trent* have by their Expurgatories prohibited it, I should abuse you, if I endeavoured to persuade your belief to conceit of a true foreknowledge in him.

82. *And the delicious* Vale *thus mildly doth bespeak.*

If your conceit yet see not the purpose of this Fiction, then thus take it. This Vale of Cluid (for so is the *English* of 𝔇𝔶𝔭𝔥𝔯𝔶𝔫 𝔆𝔩𝔴𝔶𝔡,) extended from the middle of *Denbighshire* to the sea, about eighteen miles long, and some five in breadth, having those three excellences, a fertile soil, healthful air, and pleasant seat for habitation, washed through the middle with this River, and encompassed on the East, West, and South with high mountains, freely receives the wholesome blasts of the North wind (much accounted of among builders and geoponics for immission of pure air) coming in from that part which lies open to the sea: whereupon the Muse very properly makes the Vale here *Boreas* his beloved; and in respect of his violence against the waters, supposeth him jealous of *Neptune ;* whose ravishing waves in that troubled *Irish* Sea and the depressed state of the Valley warrants it. And for that of

---

[1] Great *Britain.* [2] Wier. de præstigiis Demon. 2. cap. 16. alii.

THE TENTH SONG. 59

Molvennil's love to the River, wantonly running by him, I know your conceit cannot but apprehend it.

133. *That naturally remote six British miles from sea.*

It is in the Parish of *Kilken* in *Flintshire*, where it ebbeth and floweth[1] in direct opposite times to the sea, as the Author describes; they call it 𝔉𝔦𝔫𝔬𝔫 𝔏𝔯𝔦𝔫𝔟𝔬:[2] Such a one is there about a furlong from the *Severne* Sea, by *Newton* in *Glamorganshire*,[3] and another ebbing and flowing (but with the common course of the Moon, ascending or setting) by *Dinevor*[4] in *Caermerdhinshire*. Nor think I any reasons more difficult to be given, than those which are most specially hidden, and most frequently strange in particular qualities of Floods, Wells, and Springs; in which (before all other) Nature seems as if she had, for man's wonder, affected a not intelligible variety, so different, so remote from conceit of most piercing wits; and such unlooked-for operations both of their first and second qualities (to use the School phrase of them) are in every Chronographer, Naturalist, and Historian.

139. *Yet to the sacred* fount *of* Winifrid *gives place.*

At *Haliwell*, a maritime village near *Basingwerke* in *Flint*, is this *Winifrid's* Well, whose sweetness in the moss, wholesomeness for bath, and other such useful qualities have been referred to her martyrdom in this place. But *D. Powel* upon *Girald*, in effect thus: *Hen.* II. in his first *Welsh* expedition fortified the Castle of *Basingwerke*, and near by made a Cell for *Templars*, which continued there until their dissolution under *Edward* II.* and was after converted to a

[1] Hum. Lhuid. descript.
[2] Powel ad Girald. Itinerar. l. cap. 10.
[3] Stradling. ap. Camd.
[4] Girald. Itinerar. l. cap. 10.
* 5. Ed. II.

nest of lubberly Monks, whose superstitious honouring her more than truth, caused this dedication of the Fountain; so much to their profit (in a kind of merchandise then too shamefully in request) that they had large guerdons (it belonging to the Cell) of those which had there any medicine, beside increasing rents which accrued to them yearly out of Pardons to such as came thither in solemn Pilgrimage. This title of exaction they purchased of *PP. Martin* V. under *Henry* the Fifth and added more such gaining pretences to themselves in time of *Hen.* VII. by like authority; nor, until the more clear light of the Gospel, yet continuing its comfortable beams among us, dissipated those foggy mists of error and smoke-selling imposture, ended these collected revenues. The Author follows the Legend; but observe times compared, and you shall find no mention of this Well, and the healthful operations of it, until long after the supposed time of S. *Winifred's* martyrdom.

182. *That figure of the* Cross *of which it takes the name.*

Depressed among mountains this Valley expresses the form of a *Cross,* and so is called the *Cross Vale,* and in *British* **Lhan Gwest.**

212. *To whom* eight *lesser* Kings *with* homage *did resort.*

Upon comparing our Stories, I find them to be *Kenneth* of *Scotland, Malcome* of *Cumberland, Malcuze* King of the Isles (whom *Malmesbury* gives only the name of *Archpirate*) *Donald, Siffreth, Howel, Iago,* and *Inchithill* Kings of *Wales.* All these, he (thus touched with imperious affection of glory) sitting at the stern, compelled to row him over *Dee;* his greatness as well in fame as truth, daily at this time increasing, caused multitudes of aliens to admire and visit his Court, as a place honoured above all other by this so mighty and worthy a Prince: and, through that abundant confluence, such vicious courses followed by example, that, even now was the age, when first the more simple and frugal natures of the *English* grew infected with what (in some part) yet we languish. For, before his time, the *Angles* hither traduced, being *homines integri*,* and using, *naturali simplicitate sua defensare, aliena non mirari*, did now learn from the *stranger-Saxons* an uncivil kind of fierceness, of the *Flemings* effeminacy, of the *Danes* drunkenness, and such other; which so increased, that, for amendment of the last, the King was driven to constitute quantities in quaffing-bowls by little pins of metal set at certain distances, beyond which none durst swallow in that provocation of good fellowship.

220. *As thou, the* Queen of Isles, *Great Britain*———

Both for excellence in soil and air, as also for large continent she hath this title. And although in ancient time of the *Greeks* (that hath any story or chorography) *Sardinia* was accounted the greatest Isle,[1] and by some *Sicily*, as the old verses of the *Seven*[2] tells us, and that by *Ptolemy*[3] the East *Indian Taprobran*, now called *Sumatra*, had pre-eminence of quantity before this of ours; yet certainly, by comparison of that with this, either according to the measure took of it by *Onesicrit*[4] upon *Alexander's* commandment, or what later time teaches us, we cannot but affirm with the Author here in substance, that

———————οὐδέ τις ἄλλη
Νήσοις ἐν πάσῃσι Βρετανίσιν ἰσοφαρίζει,†

* Honest men, by simplicity of nature, looking only to their own, neglecting others. *Malmesbur.*
[1] Scylax. Caryand. in περιπλ. edit. per D. Hoeschelium.
[2] Eustath. ad Dionys. Afrum.
[3] Geograph. lib. ζ. cap. ε.   [4] Solin. Polyhist. cap. 66.
† No other Isle is equal to *Britain.*

as, long since, *Dionysius Afer* of our *Britain*, which hath given cause to call it *Another world*, as the attributes of it in *Virgil, Horace, Claudian*, and others justify.

242. *And* learning *long* with us *ere 'twas with them in use*.

For the *Druids*, being in profession very proportionate in many things to *Cabalistic* and *Pythagorean* doctrine, may well be supposed much ancienter than any that had note of learning among the *Romans*,[1] who before *Livius Salinator*, and *Nævius, Ennius, Pacuvius, Accius*, and others, not much preceding *Cæsar*, can scarce show steps of poesy, nor before *Fabius Pictor, Valerius Antias*, and some such now left only in their names (although by pretence of *Annius* there be a piece of *Pictor* published) can produce the title of a story; whereas we have some[2] that make that supposed eldest Historian (of the *Gentiles*) extant, *Dares Phrygius*, translated by *Cornelius Nepos*, and dedicated to *Sallust*, to have lived here, but indeed upon no such warrant, as I dare trust.

244. *Our* Geffrey Monmouth *first our* Brutus *to devise*.

It was so laid to *Geffrey's* charge (he was Bishop of S. *Asaph's*, under King *Stephen*) by *John* of *Whethamsted*, Abbot of S. *Alban's, William Petit*, called *William* of *Newborough*, and some other: but plainly (let the rest of his story, and the particulars of *Brute* be as they can) the name of *Brute* was long before him in *Welsh* (out of which his story was partly translated) and *Latin* testimonies of the *Britains*, as I have, for the Author, more largely spoken, to the First Song. And (a little to continue my first justification, for this time) why may not we as well think that many stories and relations, anciently written here, have been by the *Picts, Scots, Romans, Danes, Saxons*, and *Normans*, devoured up from posterity, which perhaps, had they been left to us,

[1] V. Liv. Decad. 1. lib. 6.   [2] Bal. centur. 1.

would have ended this controversy? Shall we doubt of what *Livy, Polybius, Halicarnasseus, Plutarch, Strabo,* and many others have had out of *Fabius, Antias, Chereas, Solylus, Ephorus, Theopompus, Cato, Quadrigarius,* with infinite other, now lost, writers, because we see not the self authors? No, Time hath ransacked more precious things, and even those super-excellent books wherein that incomparable *Solomon* wrote from the cedar to the hyssop, were (upon fear of the facile multitudes too much respecting natural causes in them divinely handled) by King *Ezechias* suppressed from succeeding ages, if my authority[1] deceive not. So that the loss in this, and all kinds, to the commonwealth of letters, hath been so grievous and irreparable, that we may well imagine, how error of conceit in some, envy in others, and hostile invasion hath bereft us of many monuments most precious in all sorts of literature, if we now enjoyed their instructing use: and to conclude, the antiquities of these original ages are like those of *Rome,* between it built and burnt by the *Gauls; Cum vetustate nimiâ obscurœ, velut quœ* (as *Livy* says[2]) *magno ex intervallo loci vix cernuntur* : tum quod perrarœ per eadem tempora Literœ fuêre, una custodia fidelis memoriœ rerum gestarum ; et quod, etiamsi quœ in commentariis Pontificum aliisque publicis privatisque erant monumentis, incensâ urbe, pleraque interiere.* But all this in effect the Muse tells you in the Sixth Canto.

267. *To letters never would their mysteries commit.*

What they taught their Scholars for matter of law, Heathenish religion, and such learning as they here were presidents of, was delivered only by word of mouth[3] ; and,

[1] In Zerror Hammor. apud Munst. ad Exod. 13.   [2] Dec. 1. lib. 6.
* Worn away by devouring Time, and the enemy's ransacking the city, &c. Of the *Druids* see fully to the Ninth Song.
[3] Cæsar. de Bell. Gallic. lib. 6.

lest memory unused might so fail, they permitted not commission of their lectures and instructions to the custody of writing, but delivered all in a multitude of verses and *Pythagorean* precepts, exactly imitating the *Cabalists;* which, until of late time, wrote not, but taught and learned by mouth and diligent hearing of their *Rabbins*. In other matters, private and public (so is *Cæsar's* assertion), they used Greek letters,* which hath made some think that they wrote *Greek*. But be not easily thereto persuaded. Perhaps they might use *Greek* characters,[1] seeing that those which the *Greeks* then had, and now use, were at first received from strangers,[2] and as likely from the *Druids* as from any other; for it is sufficiently justifiable out of old coins, inscriptions, and express assertion,[3] that the ancient character among the *Greeks* was almost the same with that which is now the *Latins*. But thence to collect that therefore they wrote or spake *Greek*, is as if you should affirm the *Syriac* Testament to be *Hebrew*, because published in *Hebrew* letters; or some *Latin* Treatises *Saxon*, because in that character; or that the *Saxons* wrote *Irish*, because they used the *Irish* form of writing[4]; or that those books which are published in *Dutch* by some *Jews* in a special kind of *Hebrew* letter, should also be of the same tongue. Observe but this passage in *Cæsar:* He sends by a *Gaul* (allured to this use against his country by large rewards) a letter to *Q. Cicero*, being then besieged about where now is *Tourney*,† *et Græcis conscripsit literis, ne, intercepta epistolâ, nostra* (saith he himself) *ab hostibus con-*

* Græcis literis utuntur.
[1] What language and letters the *Druids* used.
[2] Varro de Ling. Lat. 7.
[3] Plin. Hist. Nat. 7. cap. 58. et, si placet, videas Annianos illos, Archilochum de Temporibus, et Xenophontem in Æquivocis.
[4] Camd. in Hibernia. etc., Per Græcas literas in arâ Ulyssis in confinio Rhetiæ et Germaniæ, apud Tacitum, Lipsius characteres solummodò intelligit.
† Neruii. de Bello Gallic. 5.

silia cognoscantur.* To what purpose did he thus, if the *Gauls*, or their Statesmen the *Druids*, understood *Greek*? I know what he[1] writes of those tables of account found in the now *Switzerland*, but shall not soon believe that they had much more *Greek* in them than the character. If you object *Strabo* his affirmance,[2] that the *Gauls* (for as long as I speak of them in general in this kind, I well include our *Druids*, as sufficient reason is elsewhere given) were grown such lovers of that tongue, ὥστε καὶ τὰ συμβόλαια Ἑλληνιστί γράφειν,† it is soon answered, that he speaks only of those about *Marsilles*, which was, and is well known to all men to have been, a Colony of *Phocians*, out of the now *Natolia* (which were *Greeks*) by appointment of Fate arriving at the mouth of *Rhosne*, about time of *Tarquin* the *Proud;* where *Protis*, one of their chief leaders, entertained by *Nannus* King of that coast, was chosen (according to their custom) in a banquet by *Gyptis* the King's daughter for her husband. Hereto success grew so fortunate, that honourable respect on both sides joined with imitation of *Greek* civility (after this city built near their arrive) it seemed, as my author says,[3] as if *Gaul* had been turned into *Greece*, rather than *Greece* to have travelled into *Gaul*. Wonder not then why, about *Marsilles*, *Greek* was so respected, nor why in the *Romaunt-French* now such Hellenisms are: here you see apparant Original of it; yet conclude, upon the former reasons, that the *Druids* and *Gauls* used a peculiar tongue, and very likely the same with the now *Welsh*, as most-learned *Camden* hath even demonstrated; although I know some great scholars there are, which still suspend their judgment, and make it a doubt, as ever things of such

---

* Wrote it in *Greek*, lest the enemy might, by intercepting the letters, discover his design.
[1] De Bell. Gallic. 1.   [2] Geograph. δ.
† That they wrote their instruments of contract in *Greek*.
[3] Trog. Pomp. Hist. 43.

antiquity will be. But (if you will) add hereto that of the famous and great lawyer *Hotoman*,[1] who presumes that the word *Græcis** in *Cæsar's* text is crept in by ignorance of transcribers, as he well might, seeing those Commentaries, titled with name of *J. Cæsar*, commonly published, and in divers MSS. with *J. Celsus*, are very imperfect, now and then abrupt, different in style, and so variable in their own form, that it hath been much feared by that great critic *Lipsius*,[2] lest some more impolite hand hath sewed many patches of base cloth into that more rich web, as his own metaphor expresses it. And if those characters which are in the pillars at *Y-Voellas* in *Denbighshire* are of the *Druids*, as some imagine (yet seeming very strange and uncouth) then might you more confidently concur in opinion with *Hotoman*. In sum, I know that *Græcis literis* may be taken as well for the language (as in *Justin*[3] I remember, and elsewhere) as for the character: but here I can never think it to be understood in any but the last sense, although you admit *Cæsar's* copy to be therein not interpolated. It is very justifiable which the Author here implies, by slighting *Cæsar's* authority in *British* originals, in respect that he never came further into the Isle than a little beyond *Thames* towards *Barkeshire*[4]; although some of ours idly talk of his making the *Bath*, and being at *Chester*, as the *Scottish* Historians most senselessly of their 𝕵𝖚𝖑𝖎𝖘 𝕳𝖔𝖋𝖋 built by him which others refer to *Vespasian*,[5] some affirm it a Temple of God *Terminus*[6]; whereas it seems expressly to be built by *Carausius*, in time of *Diocletian*, if *Nennius* deceive us not. But, this out of my way.

[1] Franco-Gall. cap. 2. quem v. etiam ad Cæsar. Com. *Greek.
[2] Elect. 2. cap. 7. Epistolic. quæst. 2. cap. 2.
[3] Hist. Lib. 20. in extremâ.
[4] Cæsarem si legas, tibi ipsi satisfacias, verùm et ita Leland ad Cyg. Cant. in Baln.
[5] Veremund. ap. Hect. Boet. Hist. 3.
[6] Buchanan. Hist. 4. in Donaldo.

THE ELEVENTH SONG.

THE ARGUMENT.

The Muse, her native earth to see,
Returns to England over Dee;
Visits stout Cheshire, *and there shows*
To her and hers, what England *owes;*
And of the Nymphets sporting there
In Wyrrall, *and in* Delamere.
Weever, *the great devotion sings*
Of the religious Saxon *Kings;*
Those Riverets doth together call,
That into him, and Mersey *fall;*
Thence bearing to the side of Peak,
This zealous Canto off doth break.

WITH as unwearied wings, and in as high a gait
As when we first set forth, observing every state,
The Muse from *Cambria* comes, with pinions
    summ'd and sound:
And having put herself upon the *English* ground,
First seizeth in her course the noblest *Cestrian* shore;
Of our great *English* bloods as careful here of yore,
As *Cambria* of her *Brute's* now is, or could be then;
For which, our proverb calls her, *Cheshire, chief of men.*

§ And of our Counties, place of Palatine doth hold,
And thereto hath her high Regalities enroll'd ; 10
Besides, in many Fields since Conquering *William* came,
Her people she hath prov'd, to her eternal fame.
All, children of her own, the leader and the led,
The mightiest men of bone, in her full bosom bred :
And neither of them such as cold penurious need 15
Spurs to each rash attempt ; but such as soundly feed,
Clad in warm *English* cloth; and maim'd should they return
(Whom this false ruthless world else from their doors would
   spurn)
Have livelihood of their own, their ages to sustain.
Nor did the Tenants' pay the Landlord's charge maintain : 20
But as abroad in war, he spent of his estate ;
Returning to his home, his hospitable gate
The richer and the poor stood open to receive.
They, of all *England*, most to ancient customs cleave,
Their Yeomanry and still endeavour'd to uphold. 25
For rightly whilst herself brave *England* was of old,
And our courageous Kings us forth to conquests led,
Our Armies in those times (ne'er through the world so dread)
Of our tall Yeomen were, and footmen for the most ;
Who (with their bills and bows) may confidently boast, 30
§ Our *Leopards* they so long and bravely did advance
Above the *Flower-delice*, ev'n in the heart of *France*.
  O ! thou thrice happy Shire, confined so to be
Twixt two so famous Floods, as *Mersey* is, and *Dee*.[1]
Thy *Dee* upon the West from *Wales* doth thee divide ; 35
Thy *Mersey* on the North, from the *Lancastrian* side,
Thy natural sister Shire ; and link'd unto thee so,
That *Lancashire* along with *Cheshire* still doth go.
As tow'rds the *Derbian Peak*, and *Moreland* (which do draw
More mountainous and wild) the high-crown'd *Shutlingslawe*

[1] The general bounds of *Cheshire*.

And *Molcop* be thy mounds, with those proud hills whence
    rove   41
The lovely sister Brooks, the silvery *Dane* and *Dore;*
Clear *Dove*, that makes to *Trent;* the other to the West.
But, in that famous Town, most happy of the rest
(From which thou tak'st thy name) fair *Chester*, call'd of old
§ *Carelegion;* whilst proud *Rome* her conquests here did hold,
Of those her legions known the faithful station then,   47
So stoutly held to tack by those near *North-Wales'* men;
Yet by her own right name had rather called be,
§ As her the *Britan* term'd, *The Fortress upon Dee*,   50
Then vainly she would seem a Miracle to stand,
Th' imaginary work of some huge Giant's hand:
Which if such ever were, Tradition tells not who.
    But, back awhile my Muse: to *Weever* let us go,
Which (with himself compar'd) each *British* Flood doth
    scorn;   55
His fountain and his fall, both *Chesters* rightly born;
The country in his course that clean through doth divide,
Cut in two equal shares upon his either side:
And, what the famous Flood far more than that enriches,
The bracky Fountains are, those two renowned *Wyches*,   60
The *Nant-wyche*, and the *North;* whose either briny Well,
For store and sorts of salts, make *Weever* to excell.
Besides their general use, not had by him in vain,
§ But in himself thereby doth holiness retain
Above his fellow Floods: whose healthful virtues taught,   65
Hath of the Sea-gods oft caus'd *Weever* to be sought
For physic in their need: and *Thetis* oft hath seen,
When by their wanton sports her *Nereides* have been
So sick, that *Glaucus'* self hath failed in their cure:
Yet *Weever*, by his salts, recovery durst assure.   70
And *Amphitrité* oft this Wizard River led
Into her secret walks (the depths profound and dread)

Of him (suppos'd so wise) the hid events to know
Of things that were to come, as things done long ago.
In which he had been prov'd most exquisite to be ; 75
And bare his fame so far, that oft twixt him and *Dee*,
Much strife there hath arose in their prophetic skill.
    But to conclude his praise, our *Weever* here doth will
The Muse, his source to sing ; as how his course he steers :
Who from his natural spring, as from his neighbouring
    meres 80
Sufficiently supply'd, shoots forth his silver breast,
As though he meant to take directly toward the East ;
Until at length it proves he loit'reth, but to play
Till *Ashbrooke* and the *Lee* o'ertake him on the way,
Which to his journey's end him earnestly do haste : 85
Till having got to *Wyche*, he taking there a taste
Of her most savoury salt, is by the sacred touch
Forc'd faster in his course, his motion quick'ned much
To *North-wyche* : and at last, as he approacheth near,
Dane, Whelock draws, then *Crock*, from that black ominous
    mere, 90
Accounted one of those that *England's* wonders make ;
Of neighbours, *Black-mere* nam'd, of strangers, *Brereton's-
    Lake ;*
Whose property seems far from Reason's way to stand :
For, near before his death that's owner of the land,
She sends up stocks of trees, that on the top do float ; 95
By which the world her first did for a wonder note.
    His handmaid *Howty* next, to *Weever* holds her race :
When *Peerer* with the help of *Pickmere*, make apace
To put-in with those streams his sacred steps that tread,
Into the mighty waste of *Mersey* him to lead. 100
Where, when the Rivers meet, with all their stately train,
Proud *Mersey* is so great in ent'ring of the Main,
As he would make a show for empery to stand,

And wrest the three-fork'd mace from out grim *Neptune's* hand;
To *Cheshire* highly bound for that his wat'ry store,   105
As to the grosser loughs* on the *Lancastrian* shore.
From hence he getteth *Goyt* down from her *Peakish* spring,
And *Bollen*, that along doth nimbler *Birkin* bring
From *Maxfield's* mighty wilds, of whose shagg'd *Sylvans* she
Hath in the rocks been woo'd, their paramour to be :   110
Who in the darksome holes and caverns kept her long,
And that proud Forest made a party to her wrong.
Yet could not all intreat the pretty Brook to stay;
Which to her sister stream, sweet *Bollen*, creeps away.
To whom, upon their road she pleasantly reports   115
The many mirthful jests, and wanton woodish sports
In *Maxfield* they have had; as of that Forest's fate :
Until they come at length, where *Mersey* for more state
Assuming broader banks, himself so proudly bears,
That at his stern approach, extended *Wyrrall*[1] fears,   120
That (what betwixt his Floods of *Mersey* and the *Dee*)
In very little time devouréd he might be :
Out of the foaming surge till *Hilbre* lifts his head,
To let the fore-land see how richly he had sped.
Which *Mersey* cheers so much, that with a smiling brow   125
He fawns on both those Floods; their amorous arms that throw
About his goodly neck, and bar'd their swelling breasts :
On which whilst lull'd with ease, his pleaséd cheek he rests,
The *Naiades*, sitting near upon the aged rocks,
Are busied with their combs, to braid his verdant locks,   130
Whilst in their crystal eyes he doth for *Cupids* look :
But *Delamere* from them his fancy quickly took,
Who shews herself all drest in most delicious flowers;

* Meres, or standing Lakes.
[1] A poetical description of *Wyrrall*.

And sitting like a Queen, sees from her shady bowers
The wanton Wood-Nymphs mix'd with her light-footed Fauns.
To lead the rural routs about the goodly lawns,   130
As over holt[1] and heath, as thorough frith[2] and fell[3];
And oft at Barley-break, and Prison-base, to tell
(In carols as they course) each other all the joys,
The passages, deceits, the sleights, the amorous toys   140
The subtile Sea-Nymphs had, their *Wyrrall's* love to win.
  But *Weever* now again to warn them doth begin
To leave these trivial toys, which inly he did hate,
That neither them beseem'd, nor stood with his estate
(Being one that gave himself industriously to know   145
What monuments our Kings erected long ago:
To which, the Flood himself so wholly did apply,
As though upon his skill the rest should all rely)
And bent himself to shew, that yet the *Britans* bold,
Whom the laborious Muse so highly had extoll'd,   150
Those later *Saxon* Kings excell'd not in their deeds,
And therefore with their praise thus zealously proceeds:
  Whilst the Celestial Powers th' arrivéd time attend,
When o'er this general Isle the *Britans'* reign should end,
And for the spoiling *Pict* here prosp'rously had wrought, 155
Into th' afflicted land which strong invasion brought,
And to that proud attempt, what yet his power might want,
The ill-disposéd heavens, *Brute's* offspring to supplant,
Their angry plagues down-pour'd, insatiate in their waste
(Needs must they fall, whom Heaven doth to destruction
  haste).   160
And that which lastly came to consummate the rest,
Those prouder *Saxon* powers (which liberally they prest
Against th' invading *Pict*, of purpose hiréd in)
From those which paid them wage, the Island soon did win;

[1] A wood growing on a hill or knoll.
[2] High wood.   [3] Low coppice.

And sooner overspread, being masters of the field;   165
Those, first for whom they fought, too impotent to wield,
A land within itself that had so great a foe;
And therefore thought it fit them wisely to bestow:
Which over *Severne* here they in the mountains shut,
And some upon that point of *Cornwall* forth they put.   170
Yet forcéd were they there their stations to defend.
 Nor could our men permit the *Britans* to descend
From *Jove* or *Mars* alone; but brought their blood as high,
§ From *Woden*, by which name they styléd *Mercury.*
Nor were the race of *Brute*, which ruléd here before,   175
More zealous to the Gods they brought unto this shore
Than *Hengist's* noble heirs; their idols that to raise,
§ Here put their *German* names upon our weekly days.
 These noble *Saxons* were a nation hard and strong,
On sundry lands and seas in warfare nuzzled long;   180
Affliction throughly knew; and in proud Fortúne's spite,
Even in the jaws of Death had dar'd her utmost might:
Who under *Hengist* first, and *Horsa*, their brave Chiefs,
From *Germany* arriv'd,[1] and with the strong reliefs
Of th' *Angles* and the *Jutes*, them ready to supply,   185
Which anciently had been of their affinity,
By *Scythia* first sent out, which could not give them meat,
Were forc'd to seek a soil wherein themselves to seat.
Them at the last on *Dansk* their ling'ring fortune drave,
Where *Holst* unto their troops sufficient harbour gave.   190
These with the *Saxons* went, and fortunately wan:
Whose Captain, *Hengist*, first a kingdom here began
In *Kent;* where his great heirs, ere other Princes rose
Of *Saxony's* descent, their fulness to oppose,
With swelling *Humber's* side their empire did confine.   195
And of the rest, not least renownéd of their line,

[1] See, concerning their coming, to the First, Fourth, and Eighth Songs.

§ Good *Ethelbert* of *Kent*, th' first Christ'ned *English* King,
To preach the Faith of Christ, was first did hither bring
Wise *Augustine* the Monk, from holy *Gregory* sent.
This most religious King, with most devout intent,   200
That mighty Fane to *Paul*, in *London* did erect,
And privileges gave, this Temple to protect.
  His equal then in zeal, came *Ercombert* again,
From that first Christ'ned King, the second in that reign.
The gluttony then us'd severely to suppress,   205
And make men fit to prayer (much hind'red by excess)
§ That abstinence from flesh for forty days began,
Which by the name of *Lent* is known to every man.
  As mighty *Hengist* here, by force of arms had done,
§ So *Ella* coming in, soon from the *Britans* won   210
The Countries neighbouring *Kent:* which lying from the Main,
Directly to the South did properly obtain
The Southern *Saxons'* name; and not the last thereby
Amongst the other reigns which made the Heptarchy :
So in the high descent of that South-*Saxon* King,   215
We in the bead-roll here of our religious bring
Wise *Ethelwald :* alone who Christian not became,
But willing that his folk should all receive the name,
§ Saint *Wilfrid* (sent from *York*) into his realm receiv'd,
(Whom the *Northumbrian* folk had of his See bereav'd)   220
And on the South of *Thames* a seat did him afford,
By whom that people first receiv'd the saving Word.
  As likewise from the loins of *Erchinwin* (who rais'd
Th' East-*Saxons'* kingdom first) brave *Sebert* may be prais'd :
Which, as that King of *Kent*, had with such cost and state   225
Built *Paul's ;* his greatness so (this King to imitate)
Began the goodly Church of *Westminster* to rear :
The primer *English* Kings so truly zealous were.

Then *Sebba** of his seed, that did them all surpass,
Who fitter for a shrine than for a sceptre was,   230
(Above the power of flesh, his appetite to sterve,
That his desiréd Christ he strictly might observe)
Even in his height of life, in health, in body strong,
Persuaded with his Queen, a lady fair and young,
To separate themselves, and in a sole estate,   235
After religious sort themselves to dedicate.
   Whose nephew *Uffa* next, inflam'd with his high praise,
(Enriching that proud Fane his grandsire first did raise)
Abandonéd the world he found so full of strife,
And after liv'd in *Rome* a strict religious life.   240
   Nor these our Princes here, of that pure *Saxon* strain,
Which took unto themselves each one their several reign,
For their so godly deeds deservéd greater fame,
Than th' *Angles* their Allies, that hither with them came ;
Who sharing-out themselves a kingdom in the East,   245
With th' Eastern *Angles*' name their circuit did invest,
By *Uffa* in that part so happily begun :
Whose successors the crown for martyrdom have won
From all before or since that ever suff'red here ;
Redwald's religious sons : who for their Saviour dear,   250
By cruel heathenish hands unmercifully slain,
Amongst us evermore rememb'red shall remain,
And in the roll of Saints must have a special room,
Where *Derwald* to all times with *Erpenwald* shall come.
   When in that way they went, next *Sebert* them succeeds,
Scarce seconded again for sanctimonious deeds :   256
Who for a private life when he his rule resign'd,
And to his cloister long had strictly him confin'd,
A corslet for his cowl was glad again to take
His country to defend (for his religion's sake)   260
Against proud *Penda*, com'n with all his Pagan power,

   * *Sebba*, a Monk in Paul's.

Those Christ'ned *Angles* then of purpose to devour :
And suff'ring with his folk, by *Penda's* heathenish pride,
As he a Saint had liv'd, a constant Martyr died.
 When, after it fell out, that *Offa* had not long   265
Held that by cruel force, which *Penda* got by wrong,
§ Adopting for his heir young *Edmond*, brought him in,
Even at what time the *Danes* this Island sought to win :
Who Christ'ned soon became, and as religious grown
As those most heathenish were who set him on his throne,
Did expiate in that place his predecessor's guilt,   271
Which so much Christian blood so cruelly had spilt.
For, taken by the *Danes*, who did all tortures try,
His Saviour Jesus Christ to force him to deny ;
First beating him with bats, but no advantage got,   275
His body full of shafts then cruelly they shot ;
The constant martyr'd King, a Saint thus justly crown'd.
To whom even in that place, that Monument renown'd
Those after-Ages built to his eternal fame.
What *English* hath not heard Saint *Edmond Bury's** name ?
 As of those *Angles* here, so from their loins again,   281
Whose hands hew'd out their way to the *West-Sexian* reign
(From *Kenrick*, or that claim from *Cerdick* to descend)
A partnership in fame great *Ina* might pretend
With any King since first the *Saxons* came to shore.   285
Of all those Christ'ned here, who highlier did adore
The God-head than that man ? or more that did apply
His power t' advance the Church in true sincerity ?
Great *Glastenbury* then so wondrously decay'd,
Whose old foundation first the ancient *Britons* lay'd,   290
He gloriously rebuilt, enriching it with plate,
And many a sumptuous cope, to uses consecrate :
Ordaining godly laws for governing this Land,
Of all the *Saxon* Kings the *Solon* he shall stand.

     * In *Suffolk*.

From *Otta*[1] (born with him who did this Isle invade)   295
And had a conquest first of the *Northumbrians* made,
And tributary long of mightier *Hengist* held,
Till *Ida* (after born) the *Kentish* power expell'd,
And absolutely sat on the *Dierian* seat,
But afterward resign'd to *Ethelfrid* the Great :   300
An army into *Wales* who for invasion led,
At *Chester* and in fig't their forces vanquished :
Into their utter spoil, then public way to make,
The long-Religious House of goodly *Bangor* brake,
§ And slew a thousand Monks, as they devoutly pray'd.   305
For which his cruel spoil upon the Christians made
(Though with the just consent of Christian *Saxons* slain)
His blood the heathenish hands of *Redwald* did distain.
That murth'rer's issue next this Kingdom were exil'd :
And *Edwyn* took the rule ; a Prince as just and mild   310
As th' other faithless were : nor could time ever bring
In all the Seven-fold Rule an absoluter King ;
And more t' advance the Faith, his utmost power that lent :
§ Who re-ordained *York* a Bishop's government ;
And so much lov'd the poor, that in the ways of trade,   315
Where fountains fitly were, he iron dishes made,
And fast'ned them with chains the wayfarer to ease,
And the poor Pilgrims' thirst, there resting, to appease.

As *Mercia*, 'mongst the rest, sought not the least to raise
The saving Christian Faith, nor merits humbler praise.   320
§ Nor those that from the stem of *Saxon Cred.i* came
(The *Britans* who expuls'd) were any whit in fame,
For piety and zeal, behind the others best ;
Though heathenish *Penda* long and proudly did infest
The Christ'ned neighbouring Kings, and forc'd them all to bow ;   325
Till *Oswy* made to God a most religious vow,

[1] *Otta*, brother to *Hengist*.

Of His aboundant grace would He be pleas'd to grant,
That he this Panim Prince in battle might supplant.
A recluse he would give his daughter and delight,
Sweet *Alfled* then in youth, and as the morning bright: 330
And having his request, he gave as he obtain'd;
Though his unnatural hands succeeding *Wulpher* stain'd
In his own children's blood, whom their dear mother had
§ Confirm'd in Christ's belief, by that most reverend *Chad:*
Yet to embrace the Faith when after he began 335
(For the unnatural'st deed that e'er was done by man)
If possible it were to expiate his guilt,
Here many a goodly House to holy uses built:
And she (to purge his crime on her dear children done)
A crownéd Queen, for him, became a veiléd Nun. 340
 What Age a godlier Prince than *Etheldred* could bring?
Or than our *Kinred* here, a more religious King?
Both taking them the cowl, th' one here his flesh did tame,
The other went to *Rome*, and there a monk became.
 So, *Ethelbald* may well be set the rest among: 345
Who, though most vainly given when he was hot and young,
Yet, by the wise reproof of godly Bishops brought
From those unstay'd delights by which his youth was caught,
He all the former Kings of *Mercia* did exceed,
§ And (through his rule) the Church from taxes strongly
 freed. 350
Then to the Eastern sea, in that deep wat'ry Fen
(Which seem'd a thing so much impossible to men)
He that great Abbey built of *Crowland;* as though he
Would have no others' work like his foundation be.
 As, *Offa* greater far than any him before: 355
Whose conquests scarcely were suffic'd with all the shore,
But over into *Wales* adventurously he shot
His *Mercia's* spacious mere,[1] and *Powsland* to it got.

[1] *Offa's* Ditch.

This King, even in that place, where with rude heaps of
  stones
§ The *Britans* had interr'd their Proto-martyr's bones,   360
That goodly Abbey built to *Alban* ; as to show
How much the sons of *Brute* should to the *Saxons* owe.
  But when by powerful Heaven it was decreed at last,
That all those Seven-fold Rules should into one be cast
(Which quickly to a head by *Britrik's*[1] death was brought)   365
Then *Egbert*, who in *France* had carefully been taught,
Returning home, was King of the *West-Sexians* made.
Whose people, then most rich and potent, him persuade
(As once it was of old) to Monarchize the land.
Who following their advice, first with a warlike hand   370
The *Cornish* overcame ; and thence, with prosperous sails,
O'er *Severne* set his powers into the heart of *Wales* ;
And with the *Mercians* there a bloody battle wag'd :
Wherein he wan their rule; and with his wounds enrag'd,
Went on against the rest. Which, sadly when they saw   375
How those had sped before, with most subjective awe
Submit them to his sword : who prosperously alone
Reduc'd the Seven-fold Rule to his peculiar Throne,
§ (Extirping other styles) and gave it *England's* name
Of th' *Angles*, from whose race his nobler fathers came.   380
  When scarcely *Egbert* here an entire Rule began,
But instantly the *Dane*[2] the Island over-ran ;
A people, that their own those *Saxons* paid again.
For, as the *Britans* first they treacherously had slain,
This third upon their necks a heavier burthen lay'd   385
Than they had upon those whom falsely they betray'd.
And for each other's states, though oft they here did toil,
§ A people from their first bent naturally to spoil,
That cruelty with them from their beginning brought.

[1] *Egbert's* predecessor.   [2] See to the First Song.

Yet when the Christian Faith in them had throughly
    wrought,
Of any in the world no story shall us tell,
Which did the *Saxon* race in pious deeds excell:
That in these drowsy times should I in public bring
Each great peculiar act of every godly King,
The world might stand amaz'd in this our Age to see
Those goodly Fanes of theirs, which irreligious we
Let every day decay; and yet we only live
By the great freedoms then those Kings to these did give.
    Wise *Seybert* (worthy praise) preparing us the seat
§ Of famous *Cambridge* first, then with endowments great
The Muses to maintain, those Sisters thither brought.
    By whose example, next, religious *Alfred* taught,
Renowned *Oxford* built t' *Apollo's* learned brood;
And on the hallowed bank of *Isis'* goodly Flood,
Worthy the glorious Arts, did gorgeous Bowers provide.
§ He into several Shires the Kingdom did divide.
    So, valiant *Edgar*, first, most happily destroy'd
The multitudes of wolves, that long the land annoy'd.
And our good *Edward* here, the Confessor and King,
(Unto whose sumptuous Shrine our Monarchs off'rings
    bring)
That cank'red Evil cur'd, bred twixt the throat and jaws.
When Physic could not find the remedy nor cause,
And much it did afflict his sickly people here,
He of Almighty God obtain'd by earnest pray'r,
This Tumour by a King might curéd be alone:
§ Which he an heir-loom left unto the *English* Throne.
So, our Saint *Edward* here, for *England's* general use,
§ Our Country's Common Laws did faithfully produce,
Both from th' old *British* writ, and from the *Saxon* tongue.
    Of Forests, Hills, and Floods, when now a mighty throng
For audience cry'd aloud; because they late had heard,

THE ELEVENTH SONG.

That some high *Cambrian* Hills the *Wrekin* proudly dar'd
With words that very much had stirr'd his rancorous spleen.
Where, though clear *Severne* set her princely self between
The *English* and the *Welsh*, yet could not make them cease.
Here, *Weever*, as a Flood affecting godly peace,   426
His place of speech resigns; and to the Muse refers
The hearing of the cause, to stickle all these stirs.

ILLUSTRATIONS.

NOW are you newly out of *Wales*, returned into *England*: and, for conveniency of situation, imitating therein the ordinary course of Chorography, the first Shire Eastward (from *Denbigh* and *Flint*, last sung by the Muse) *Cheshire* is here surveyed.

6. *Of our great* English *bloods as careful* ———

For, as generally in these Northern parts of *England*, the Gentry is from ancient time left preserved in continuance of Name, Blood, and Place; so most particularly in this *Cheshire*, and the adjoining *Lancashire:* which, out of their numerous families, of the same name, with their chief Houses and Lordships, hath been observed.[1]

9. *And, of our* Counties, *place of* Palatine *doth hold*.

We have in *England* three more of that title, *Lancaster, Durham*, and *Ely*: and, until later time,[2] *Hexamshire* in the Western part of *Northumberland* was so reputed. *William* the *Conqueror* first created one *Hugh Wolfe*, a *Norman*, Count *Palatine* of *Chester*, and gave the Earldom to hold, *as freely*

---

[1] Camden. in Cornav. et Brigant.
[2] Stat. 14. *Eliz.* cap. 13.

e King held his Crown. By this supremacy of liberty he
e to himself *Barons*, which might assist him in Council,
had their Courts and Cognizance of Pleas in such sort
rding the Earldom, as other Barons the Crown. *Ego*
*s Hugo et mei Barones confirmavimus ista omnia,** is sub-
ed to a Charter, whereby he founded the Monastery of
'erburg there. For the name of *Palatine*, know, that in
nt time under the Emperors of declining *Rome*, the
of *Count Palatine* was; but so, that it extended first
to him which had care of the Household and Imperial
ue¹; which is now (so saith *Wesembech*² : I affirm it
as the *Marshal* in other Courts; but was also commu-
ed by that honorary attribute of *Comitiva Dignitas* to
others, which had anything proportionate, place or
t, as the Code teacheth us. In later times both in
any (as you see in the *Palgrave* of *Rhine*) in *France*
h the Earldom of *Champagne* shows long time since in
rown; yet keeping a distinct Palatine Government, as
*Pithou*³ hath at large published) and in this Kingdom
were hereditarily honored with it, as being near the
e in the Court (which they, as we, called *the Palace*)
by their state-carriage, gained full opinion of their
, and ability in government, by delegate power of ter-
es to them committed, and hereafter titled *Countes de*
s, as our Law Annals call them. If you desire more
culars of the power and great state of this Palatine
om, I had rather (for a special reason) send you to the
age of *Hen.* III. and Queen *Elianor* in *Matthew Paris;*
John Scot, then Earl of *Chester*, bare before the King
lward's Sword, called **Curtein,** which the Prince at

Earl *Hugh* and my *Barons* have confirmed all this.
  de Offic. Com. Sac. Palat. v. Euseb. de vit. Constantin. δ. et
ib. 12.   ² In Paratit. C. 1. tit. 34.
vre i. des Comtes de Champagne et Brie. De Palatinorum
rum nomine Sarisbur. Policrat. 6. cap. 16. et Epist. 263.

Coronation of *Henry* IV. is recorded to have done as]
of *Lancaster*[1]; and wish you to examine the passages t
with what *Bracton*[2] hath of Earls, and our Year-book
the *High Constable* of *England*, than here offer it m
To add the royalties of the Earldom, as Courts, Off
Franchises, forms of Proceeding, even as at *Westminst*
the diminution of its large liberties by the Statute o
sumption,[4] were to trouble you with a harsh digressio1

31. *Our* Leopards *they so long and bravely did advanc*
He well calls the Coat of *England*, *Leopards*. Neithe
you justly object the common blazon of it by nar
Lions, or that assertion of *Polydore's* ignorance,[5] telli1
that the Conqueror bare three *Fleurs-de-lis*, and *three*
as quartered for one Coat, which hath been, and is, ;
men know, at this present borne in our Sovereign's arr
France and *England*; and so, that the quartering o
Fleurs was not at all until *Ed*. III. to publish his title
gain the *Flemish* forces (as you have it in *Froissart*) ba
French arms,[6] being then *Azure semy with Fleurs-de-li*;
were afterward contracted to three in time of *Hen*
Charles VI. because he would bear different from the *E*
King, who notwithstanding presently seconded the ch
to this hour continuing. Nor could that *Italian* have
into any error more palpable, and in a professed anti
so ridiculous. But to prove them anciently Leopards,
ergo (saith *Matthew Paris*[7]) *Imperator* (that is *Frederi*
Regi Anglorum tres Leopardos in signum Regalis Cly
*quo tres Leopardi transeuntes figurantur.** In a M

---

[1] Archiv. in Tur. Lond. iam verò et typis commiss. apud C
Jurisdict. Cur.   [2] De acq. rer. dom. cap. 1€
[3] 6. *Hen.* 8. Kelaway. et v. Brook. tit. Prerogat. 31.
[4] 27. *Hen.* 8. cap. 24.   [5] A gross error of *Polydore*
[6] V. Stat. 14. *Ed.* III.   [7] 19. *Hen.* 3.
* The Emperor sent to *Hen.* III. three *Leopards*, as allud
the arms of *England*.

cer's Confessio Amantis, which the printed books have

*Ad laudem Christi, quem tu Virgo peperisti,
Sit laus* RICHARDI, *quem sceptra colunt* Leopardi.

ıd *Edward* IV.[1] granted to *Lewes* of *Bruges* Earl of *Win-*
r, that he should bear *d'Azure, a dix Muscles enarme
Canton de Nostre Propre armes d'Engleterre, Cestassavoir
oules ung Leopard passant d'Or, arme d'Azur*, as the
ıt speaks: and likewise *Hen.* VI.[2] to King's College in
ridge, gave a Coat Armour, three Roses, and *Summo
partitum principale de Azoreo cum Francorum flore deque
ɔ cum peditante Leopardo*, and calls them *Porcellæ Armo-
quæ nobis in regnis Angliæ et Franciæ jure debentur regio.*
ow it is otherwise now received, but withal, that
:es, being supreme Judges of Honor and Nobility, may
rarily change their Arms in name and nature; as was
³ upon return out of the Holy War in *Godfrey* of
ne's time; and it seems it hath been taken indifferently,
her you call them the one or other, both for similitude
lineaments and composture (as in the bearing of *Nor-
y*, the County of *Zutphen*, and such more) being bla-
l in *Hierom de Bara*, and other *French* heralds, *Lion-
rds:* and for that even under this *Hen.* VI. a great
nt in heraldry,[4] and a writer of that kind, makes the
sion of the *Lion* of *Guienne* to the Coat of *Normandy*
h was by *Hen.* II. his marriage with Queen *Elianor*,
ced from *Lewes* of *France*) to be the first three *Lions*
by the *English* Kings.

aerlegion *whilst proud* Rome *her conquests here did hold.*
u have largely in that our most learned Antiquary, the

ıt. 12. *Ed.* 4. part. 1. memb. 12.
ıt. 27. *Hen.* 6. num. 46.   ³ Pont. Heuter. de Vet. Belgio. 2.
ichol. Upton. de Re Militari. lib. 3.

cause of this name from the tents of
about *Vespasian's* time. I will only n
long since found fault with *Willian*
affirming it so called, *quòd ibi Emeriti
resedére**; whereas it is plain, that *Jul*
near this territory. Perhaps, by *Julii*
(then Lieutenant here) so named, and
tion laid on that best of the Monks, u
reading *Militarium* for *Julianarum*, as
tends, I find not sufficiently warrantal
MS. very ancient, as near *Malmesbur*
may be, and heretofore belonging to tl
tine's in *Canterbury*, evidently persuade

50. ——— *the Fortress* ;

At this day in *British* she is called (
𝔇𝔟𝔶,[4] *i.e.*, *the City of Legions upon the r*
antiquaries have referred the name
builder of it: I, nor they, know not w
But indeed ridiculously they took 𝔏
Leon the Great; to whom the Author

64. *But in himself thereby doth* h

He compares it with *Dee's* title pre
reason given before to the Seventh So
of the salt-pits at *Northwich*, *Nantwic*
on his banks) hath this attribute, and
suit to him, and kind entertainment fo
and prophecy; justifiable in general,
Tryphon their surgeon, which our e:
done; and in particular cause, upon tl

[1] In *Deva* ad Cyg. Cant.   [2]
* Because the old soldiers of *Julius* his leg
[3] Conjectura in Malmesburiensem.
[4] Humf. Lhuid. in Breviario.   †

THE ELEVENTH SONG. 87

divinely honored name of Salt; of which, if you observe it used in all sacrifices by express commandment[1] of the true God, the מלח ברית* in Holy Writ, the religion of the Salt, set first, and last taken away as a symbol[2] of perpetual friendship, that in *Homer*[3] Πάσσε δ' ἁλὸς θείοιο,† the title of 'Ἁγνίτης‡ given it by *Lycophron*,[4] and passages of the Ocean's medicinable epithets[5] because of his saltness, you shall see apparant and apt testimony.

174. *From Woden, by which name they styléd Mercury.*

Of the *Britons'* descent from *Jove*, if you remember but *Æneas* son to *Anchises* and *Venus*, with her derivation of blood from *Jupiter's* parents, sufficient declaration will offer itself. For this of *Woden*, see somewhat to the Third Song. To what you read there, I here more fitly add this: *Woden*, in *Saxon* genealogies, is ascended to as the chief ancestor of their most royal progenies; so you may see in *Nennius, Bede, Ethelwerd, Florence of Worcester*, an *Anonymus de Regali Prosupiâ, Huntingdon*, and *Hoveden*, yet in such sort that in some of them they go beyond him, through *Frithwald, Frealaf, Frithulf, Fin, Godulph, Geta*, and others, to *Seth;* but with so much uncertainty, that I imagine many of their descents were just as true as the *Theogony* in *Hesiod, Apollodorus*, or that of *Prester John's* sometimes deriving himself[6] very near from the loins of *Salomon*. Of this *Woden*, beside my authors named, special mention is found in *Paul Warnfred*,[7] who makes *Frea* his wife (others call her *Fricco*, and by her understand *Venus*) and *Adam* of *Breme*,[8] which describe him as *Mars*, but in *Geffrey* of *Mon*-

[1] Levit. 2. comm. 13. et Num. 18.   * Salt of the Covenant.
[2] Cæl. Rhodigin. Antiq. Lect. 12. cap. 1. vid. Plutarch. Sympos. t. cap. 10.   [3] Iliad. ι. vid. Lips. Saturnal. 1. cap. 2.
† He sprinkled it with divine Salt.   ‡ A Cleanser.
[4] In Cassandrâ.   [5] Cæl. Ant. Lect. 11. cap. 22.
[6] Damian a *Goes* de Morib. Æthiopum.
[7] De Longobard. 1. cap. 8.   [8] Hist. Ecclesiast. lib. 4. cap. 91.

mouth, and *Florilegus*, in *Hengist's* own person, he is affirmed the same with *Mercury*, who by *Tacitus'* report was their chief Deity; and that also is warranted in the denomination of our *Wodensday* (according to the *Dutch* 𝔚𝔬𝔡𝔢𝔫𝔰𝔡𝔞𝔤𝔥) for the fourth day of the week, titled by the ancient planetary account with name of *Mercury*. If that allusion in the Illustrations of the Third Song to *Merc.* allow it him not, then take the other first taught me by *Lipsius*[1] fetching *Wodan* from 𝔚𝔬𝔫 or 𝔚𝔦𝔫, which is to *gain*, and so make his name *Wondan* expressing in that sense the self name[2] Ἐρμῆς κερδῶος,* used by the *Greeks*. But without this inquiry you understand the Author.

178. *Here put the* German *names upon the* weekly days.

From their *Sunnan* for the Sun, *Monan* for the Moon, *Tuisco*, or *Tuisto* (of whom see to the Fourth Song) for *Mars*, *Woden* for *Mercury*, *Thor* for *Jupiter*, *Fre*, *Frie*, or *Frigo* for *Venus*, *Saturn* for *Saturn*, they styled their days Sunnan-bæȝ, Monan-bæȝ, ʈuiɼcons-bæȝ, podenɼ-bæȝ, þoɼɼ-bæȝ, ꝼɼiȝ-bæȝ, Sæʈeꝼnɼ-bæȝ: thence came our days now used, *Sunday*, *Munday*, *Tuesday*, *Wodensday*, *Thursday*, *Friday*, *Saturday;* which planetary account was very ancient among the *Egyptians*[3] (having much *Hebrew* discipline), but so superstitious, that, being great astronomers and very observant of mysteries produced out of number and quantity, they began on the *Jewish* Sabbath and imposed the name of *Saturn*, on the next the *Sun*, then the *Moon*, as we now reckon, omitting two planets in every nomination, as you easily conceive it. One might seek, yet miss the reasons of that form; but nothing gives satisfaction equal to that of all-penetrating *Joseph Scaliger*,[4] whose intended reason for it

---

[1] Ad. Tacit. Germ. not. 32.   [2] Lucian. in Timone.
* *Mercury* president of *gain*.   [3] Dion. Hist. Rom. λζ.
[4] De Emendat. Temp. l. Eundem de hâc re Prolegom. et lib. 7. doctorem merito agnoscimus.

is thus. In a circle describe an heptagonal and equilateral figure; from whose every side shall fall equilateral triangles, and their angles respectively on the corners of the inscribed figure, which are noted with the planets after their not interrupted order. At the right side of any of the bases begin your account, from that to the oppositely noted planet, thence to his opposite, and so shall you find a continued course in that order (grounded perhaps among the ancients upon mysteries of number, and interchanged government by those superior bodies over this habitable orb) which some have sweated at, in inquiry of proportions, music distances, and referred it to planetary hours: whereas they (the very name of hour for a twenty-fourth part of a day, being unusual till about the *Peloponnesiac* war) had their original of later time than this hebdomadal account, whence the hourly from the morning of every day had his breeding, and not the other from this, as pretending and vulgar astrologers receive in supposition. At last, by *Constantine* the Great, and Pope *Sylvester*, the name of *Sun-day* was turned into the *Lord's-day*[1]; as it is styled *Dominicus et* Κυριακή; of *Saturday*, into the *Sabbath;* and the rest not long afterward named according to their numeral order, as the *First, Second,* or *Third Feria* (that is *Holiday*, thereby keeping the remembrance of *Easter-week*, the beginning of the Ecclesiastic year, which was kept every day holy) for *Sunday, Munday, Tuesday*. You may note here that *Cæsar*[2] was deceived in telling us,

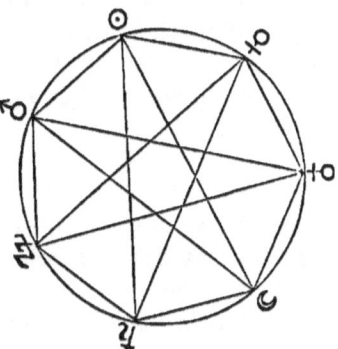

[1] Nicephor. Callist. Eccles.' Hist. ζ. cap. μς. Polyd. Invent. Rer. 6. cap. 5.
[2] Comment. Gallic. 6.

the *Germans* worshipped no other Gods but *quos cernunt, et quorum opibus apertè juvantur,** Solem, Vulcanum, and Lunam, *reliquos ne famâ quidem accepisse;* for you see more than those thus honoured by them, as also they had[1] their Єoþcen Monaþ for *April,* dedicated to some adored Power of that name: but blame him not; for the discovery of the Northern parts was but in weakest infancy, when he delivered it.

197. *Good* Ethelbert *of* Kent *first* Christ'ned English King.

About the year 600 Christianity was received among the *Saxons;* this *Ethelbert* (being first induced to taste that happiness by *Bertu* his Queen, a Christian, and daughter to *Hilperic* (or *Lothar* the II.) King of *France*) was afterward baptized by *Augustine* a Monk sent hither, with other workmen for such a harvest, by Pope *Gregory* the I. zealously being moved to conversion of the *English* nation: so that after the first coming of *Hengist* they had lived here one hundred and fifty years by the common account without tincture of true religion: nor did the *Britons* who had long before (as you see to the Eighth Song) received it, at all impart it by instruction, which *Gildas* imputes to them for merit of divine revenge. *White* of *Basingstoke*[2] (I must cite his name, you would laugh at me if I affirmed it) refers to *Kent's Paganism,* and *British Christianity* before this conversion, the original of our vulgar by-word, *Nor in Christendom, Nor in Kent.*

207. *That* abstinence *from flesh for* forty days *began.*[3]

Began it here. So understand him; for plainly that fasting-time was long before in other Churches, as appears in

---

* Whom they see and have daily use of, as the *Sun, Moon,* and the *Fire,* by name of *Vulcan.*   [1] Bed. Lib. de Temporibus.
[2] Hist. 7. not. 24.   [3] 640.

the Decreeing Epistle[1] of Pope *Telesphorus*, constituting that the Clergy should fast from *Quinquagesima* (that is, *Shrove-sunday*) to *Easter*, whereas the Laity and they both were before bound but to six weeks accounted, as now, from the first *Sunday* in *Lent*; so that, even from the first[2] of Christianity, for remembrance of our Saviour, it seems, it hath been observed, although I know it hath been referred to *Telesphorus*, as first author. He died in 140 of *Christ*. But if you compare this of him with that of Pope *Melchiades*[3] (some hundred and seventy years after) taking away the fast upon *Sunday*, and *Thursday*, you will lose therein forty days, and the common name of *Quadragesime;* but again find it thus. S. *Gregory*[4] (after both these) makes *Lent* to be so kept, that yet no fasting be upon *Sundays;* because (among other reasons) he would have it as the tenth of time consecrated to *God* in prayer and abstinence (and the Canonists,[5] how justly I argue not, put it in their division of Personal Tithes) then, in this form, after the exception, calculates out his number. From the first *Sunday* in *Lent* to *Easter* are six weeks, that is, forty-two days, whence six *Sundays* subtracted, remain thirty-six, which (fractions avoided) is the quotient of three hundred and sixty-five, being the number of the common year divided by ten. But seeing that holy number (as he calls it) of forty, which our Saviour honoured with His fasting, is by this reckoning excluded, he adds, to the first week, the four last days of the *Quinquagesima*, that is, *Ash-Wednesday, Thursday, Friday*, and *Saturday;* so keeping both his conceit of tithing, and also observation of that number, which we remember only (not able to imitate) in our assayed abstinence. For proof of

[1] Dist. 4. c. 4. statuimus et ibid. D. Ambrosius.
[2] Ita etiam Baronius, sed et vide Eusebii Chronic. in sixto. 1.
[3] Dist 4. de Consecrat. c. 14. Iciunium.
[4] In Homil. Dist. 5. de Consecrat. c. 16.
[5] Rebuff Tract. de Decim Quæst. 3. num. 31.

this in *Erconbert*, both *Bede* and *Malmesbury*, beside their
later followers, are witnesses. Their *Saxon* name near ours
was Lenȝcten-fæſten,[1] as the other Four Fasts ẏmbṗen
fæſten.

210. *So* Ella *coming in soon from the* Britons *won.*

Near forty years after the *Saxons'* first arrival, *Ælla* (of
the same nation) with his sons *Plencing*, or *Pleting*, *Cimen*,
and *Cissa* landed at *Cimenshore* in *the* now *Sussex* (it is supposed to be near the *Witterings* by *Chichester*[2]) and having
his forces increased by supply, after much bloodshed twixt
him and the *Britons*, and long siege of the City *Andredceaster*, now *Newenden* in *Kent* (as learned *Camden* conjectures)
got supreme dominion of those Southern parts, with title of
King of *Sussex*, whose son and successor *Cissa's* name, is yet
there left in Cıſſa-ceaſtep[*] for *Chichester* and in a Hill encircled with a deep trench for military defence, called *Cissburie*, by Offington. The Author fitly begins with him after
the *Kentish*; for he was the first that made the number of
the *Saxon* Kings plural, by planting and here reigning over
the *South Saxons*[3]*:* and as one was always in the Heptarchy,
which had title of *First*, or *Chief King of the Angles* and
Saxons, so this *Ælla* not only was honoured with it,[4] but
also the prerogative by priority of time, in first enjoining
it, before all other Princes of his nation : But his dominion
afterward was for the most part still under the *Kentish* and
West Saxon Kings.

219. *Saint* Wilfrid *sent from* York *into his realm receiv'd.*

This *Wilfrid* Archbishop of *York* expelled that See by

[1] Canut. Leg. 16.
[2] Ex antiq. Chartâ Eccles. Selesens. ap. Camden.
[*] So is it called in Florent. Wigorn. page 331.
[3] Kingdom of *Sussex*.
[4] Ethelwerd. Hist. 3. cap. 2. ; Bed. Hist. 2. cap. 5.

THE ELEVENTH SONG. 93

Egfrid King of *Northumberland*, was kindly received by *Edilwalch* (otherwise *Ethelwalch*, being before Christened through religious persuasion of his godfather *Wulpher* King of *Mercland*) and converted the *South Saxons* to the Gospel. He endowed this *Wilfrid* with *Selsey* a cherronese in *Sussex*, and was so founder of a Bishopric, afterward translated, under the *Norman* Conqueror, to *Chichester*, whose Cathedral Church in public Monuments honours the name of *Cedwalla* (of whom see to the Ninth Song) King of *West Sex* for her first creator: but the reason of that was rather because *Cedwalla* after death of *Edilwalch* (whom he slew) so honoured *Wilfrid*,[1] *ut* *Magistrum et Dominum omni Provinciæ eum præfecit, nihil in totâ Provinciâ sine illius assensu faciendum arbitratus;* whereupon it was, as it seems, thought fit (according to course of yielding with the sway of fortune) to forget *Edilwalch*, and acknowledge *Cedwalla* (then a Pagan) for first Patron of that Episcopal dignity. It is reported that three years, before this general receipt there of Christ's profession, continued without rain; insomuch that Famine, and her companion Pestilence, so vexed the Province, that in multitudes of forty or fifty at a time, they used, hand in hand, to end their miseries in the swallowing waves of their neighbouring Ocean: But, that all ceased upon *Wilfrid's* preaching; who taught them also first (if *Henry* of *Huntingdon's* teaching deceive me not) to catch all manner of fish, being before skilled only in taking of eels.[2] I know, some[3] make *Eadbert* Abbot of the Monastery in *Selsey*, under King *Ine*, first Bishop there, adding, that before his time the Province was subject to *Winchester;* but that rightly understood discords not; that is, if you refer

[1] Malmesb. de Gest. Pontific. 3.
* That he committed the supreme government of that Province to him.
[2] *Sussex* men taught to catch fish.
[3] Matth. Westmonasteriensis.

it to instauration of what was discontinued by *Wilfrid's* return to his Archbishopric.

268. *Adopting for his heir young* Edmund ─────

Penda King of *Mercland* had slain *Sigebert* (or *Sebert*) and *Anna* Kings of *East-Angles*, and so in dominion might be said to have possessed that Kingdom; But *Anna* had divers successors of his blood, of whom, *Ethelbirth* was traitorously slain in a plot dissembled by *Offa* King of *Mercland*, and this part of the Heptarchy confounded in the *Mercian* Crown. Then did *Offa* adopt this S. *Edmund* a *Saxon*, into name of successor in that kingdom: which he had not long enjoyed but that through barbarous cruelty, chiefly of one *Hinguar* a *Dane* (*Polydore* will needs have his name *Agner*) he was with miserable torture martyred upon the 19th of November,[1] whither his Canonization directeth us for holy memory of him.

305. *And slew a* thousand Monks *as they devoutly pray'd.*

You may add two hundred to the Author's number. This *Ethelfrid* or *Edilfrid* King of *Northumberland*, aspiring to increase his territories, made war against the bordering *Britons*. But as he was in the field, by *Chester*, near the onset, he saw, with wonder, a multitude of Monks assembled in a place by, somewhat secure; demanded the cause, and was soon informed that they were there ready to assist his enemies' swords with their devout orisons, and had one called *Brocmail*, professing their defence from the *English* forces. The King no sooner heard this, but *Ergo* (saith he, being a heathen) *si adversus nos ad Dominum suum clamant, profecto et ipsi quamvis arma non ferant, contra nos pugnant, qui adversis nos imprecationibus persequuntur**; pre-

[1] 870.
* If they pray to their God against us, then plainly they fight against us.

sently commands their spoil : which so was performed by his soldiers, that twelve hundred were in their devotions put to the sword. A strange slaughter of Religious persons, at one time and place ; but not so strange as their whole number in this one Monastery, which was two thousand one hundred, not such idle lubberly sots as later times pestered the world withal, truly pictured in that description[1] of (their character) Sloth.

———————————With two slimy eyne
I must sit said the Segge, or else I must needs nap,
I may not stond ne stoupe, ne without mi stole kneele,
Were I brought abed (but if my talende it made)
Should ne ringing do me rise, or I were ripe to dine.
He began Benedicite with a belke, and his brest knoked
And raskled, and rored, and rut at the last;
If I should dye by this daie, me lyste not to loke.
I can not perfitly my Pater nost, as the Priest it singeth
But I can rimes of Robin Hod, and Randall of Chester,
But of our Lord or our Lady I lerne nothing at all.
I am occupied eberie day, holy day and other,
With idle tales at the Ale, and other while in Churches.
Gods paine and his passion full selde thinke I thereon
I bisited neber seblemen, ne settred folke in pittes,
I habe leber here an Harlotrie, or a somers game,
Or leasings to laugh at and bilye my neighbours,
Then all that eber Marke made, Math, Iohn and Lucas.
And Vigiles and fasting daies all these let I passe,
And lie in bed in Lent, and mi Lemman in mine armes.
I habe ben Priest and Parson passing thyrtie winter,
Yet can I nether Sol fe ne sing, ne Saints libes read,
But I can find in a feild, or in a furlong an hare
Better then in Beatus Vir, Or in Beati Omnes.

[1] Rob. de Langland, sive Joannes Malverne, Pass. 5.

Not such were those *Bangor* Monks: but they *Omnes de labore manuum suarum vivere solebant.** Observe here the difference twixt the more ancient times and our corrupted neighbour ages, which have been so branded, and not unjustly, with dissembled bestial sensualities of Monastic profession, that in the universal Visitation under *Hen.* VIII. every Monastery afforded shameful discovery of Sodomites and incontinent Friars; in *Canterbury* Priory of *Benedictins* nine Sodomites; in *Battell* Abbey fifteen and, in many other, like proportion; larger reckoning will not satisfy if you account their Wenches, which married and single (for they affected that variety) supplied the wants of their counterfeited solitariness, so that, hereupon, after an account of six hundred Convents of Monks and Friars, with Mendicants, in this kingdom, when time endured them, *Je laisseray,* saith one,[1] *maintenant au Lecteur calculer combien pur le moins devoint estre de fils de putains en Angletere, je di seulement fils de Moines et de Putaines.*† These were they who admired all for *Hebrew* or *Greek* which they understood not, and had at least (as many of our now professing ⲧFormalists) *Latin* enough to make such a speech as *Rablais* hath to Gargantua for *Paris* Bells, and call for their *Vinum Cos;* which, in one of them personated, receive thus from a noble poet :[2]

Fac extrà: nihil hoc: extrà totum sit oportet,
Sobriè enim justè atque piè potare jubet Lex.
Vinum lætificat cor hominis, præcipuè Cos.
Gratia sit Domino, Vinum Cos, inquit, habemus.

How my reader tastes this, I know not; therefore I will-

* All lived of handy labour.
[1] H. Stephen on l'Entroduct. au Traité de la Conformité, etc. 1. chap. 21.
† I leave it to the reader to guess, how many Bastards the Monks and Friars got for the Laity.
[2] Jan. Douz. Satyr. 5.

ingly quit him; and add only, that *William* of *Malmesbury* grossly errs in affirming that this *Bangor*[1] is turned into a Bishopric; but pardon him, for he lived in his Cloister and perhaps was deceived by equivocation of name, there being in *Caernarvan* a Bishopric of the same title to this day, which somebody later hath on the other side ill taken for this.[2]

314. *Who re-ordained* Yorke *a Bishop's government.*

For in the *British* times it had a Metropolitic See (as is noted to the Ninth Song) and now by *Edwine* (converted to Christian discipline both through means of his wife *Ethelburg*, daughter to *Ethelbert* King of *Kent*, and religious persuasion of God's Ministers) was restored to the former dignity, and *Paulinus*, in it, honoured with name of Archbishop, being afterwards banished that Province, and made Bishop of *Rochester*, which some have ignorantly made him before.

321. *Nor those that in the stem of* Saxon Crida *came.*

Most of our Chronologers begin the *Mercian* race-royal with *Penda;* But *Henry* of *Huntingdon* (not without his proofs and followers) makes *Crida* (grandfather to *Penda*) first in that Kingdom.

334. *Confirmed in* Christ's *belief by that most reverend* Chad.

This *Wulpher*, son to *Penda* restored to his father's Kingdom, is reported[3] with his own hands to have slain his two sons, *Wulphald* and *Rufin*, for that they privily withdrew themselves to that famous S. *Chad*, or *Cedda*, Bishop of *Lichfield*, for instruction in the Christian Faith; and all this

---
[1] In Hist. et Lib. 4. de Pontificib. in Dorcecestrensibus.
[2] Ant. lib. Academ. per Europ. edit. 1590.
[3] Robert. de *Swapham* in Hist. Petroburgens. ap. Camd. in Stafford, et Northampton, et J. Stoveum.

is supposed to be done where the now *Stone* in *Staffordshire* is seated. Hereupon the Author relies. But, the credit of it is more than suspicious, not only for that in Classic authority I find his issue only to be *Kenred*, and S. *Werburge* (by *Ermengild* daughter to *Ercombert* of *Kent*) but withal that he was both Christian, and a great Benefactor to the Church. For it appears by consent of all, that *Peada, Weda,* or *Penda* (all these names he hath) eldest son of the first *Penda*, first received in *Middle Engle* (part of *Mercland*) the Faith, and was baptized by *Finnan* Bishop of *Lindisfarne** : after whose violent death, in spite of *Oswy* King of *Northumberland, Immin, Ebba,* and *Edberth,* gentlemen of power in *Mercland,* saluted *Wulpher* (brother to *Peada*) King of all that Province, who was then, as it seems (by *Florence* of *Worcester* and *Bede's* reporting of four Bishops in succession preferred by him) of Christian name : But howsoever he was at that time, it is certain that in the second or third years of his reign, he was godfather to King *Edilwalch* of *Sussex,* and bestowed on him as a gift in token of that spiritual adoption, the *Isle* of *Wight* with another territory in *West Saxony,* and gave also to S. *Cedda* (made, by consent of him and King *Oswy,* Bishop of *Lindisfarne*) fifty Hides of land (a *Hide*,† a *plough-land,* or a *Carue,* I hold clearly equivalent) towards foundation of a Monastery. All this compared, and his life, in our Monks, observed,

---

* It is that now called *Holy Island,* by East the utmost parts of *Northumberland,* whence the Bishopric about 995 was translated to *Durham.*

† Ita enim apud Matth. Paris, Huntingdon. Th. Walsingham. docemur, licet alii 100 Acris, alii aliter definiunt. Cæterùm quod me maximè movet, et absque hæsitatione in hanc sententiam pedibus ire cogit, en tibi ex *Dunstani* Chartâ (An. 963) quâ *Terræ partem concedit septem Aratrorum quæd Anglicè dicitur septem Hidas.* Nec immemorem hic te vellem vocabuli illius apud Jur. Cons. nostros, Ꮳiꝺe et Ꮳaine; quod Arvum restibile interpretari haùt ignorat *Dupendius* quispiam.

hardly endures this note of persecution; which in respect of his foundership of *Peterborough* Abbey, *Robert* of *Swapham* a Monk there reporting it, or those from whom he had it, might better in silence have buried it, or rather not so ungratefully feigned it. I only find one thing notably ill of him; that he, first of the English Kings, by Simony made a Bishop, which was *Wine* of *London*, as *Malmesbury* is author.

350. *And (through his Rule) the* Church *from* Taxes *strongly freed*.

Ethelbald King of *Mercland*, Founder of *Crowland* Abbey in *Lincolnshire*, a great, martial, and religious Prince, in a Synod held (*Cuthbert* then Archbishop of *Canterbury*) enlarged Ecclesiastic liberty in this form, *Donationem meam me vivente concedo, ut omnia Monasteria et Ecclesiæ Regni mei à publicis Vectigalibus, Operibus, et Oneribus absolvantur, nisi Instructionibus Arcium vel Pontium, quæ nunquam ulli possunt relaxari;* i.e., He discharged all Monasteries and Churches of all kind of taxes, works, and imposts, *excepting such as were for building of Forts* and *Bridges*, being (as it seems the law was then) not releasable. For, beside the authority of this Statute of *Ethelbald*, it appears frequent in Charters of the *Saxon* times, that, upon Endowment, and Donations, to Churches with largest words of exemption, and liberty from all secular charges, the conclusion of the *Habendum*, was, *Exceptis istis tribus, Expeditione, Pontis, Arcisve constructione,** which among common Notaries or Scriveners was so well known, that they called it by one general name, *Trinoda Necessitas*,† as out of *Cedwalla's* Charter to *Wilfrid*, first Bishop of *Selsey*,¹ of the Manor of *Pagenham* (now *Pagham*)

---

* Excepting those three, Aid in war, mending of Bridges and Forts. vid. Chartam hujusmodi apud D. Ed. Cok. in Epist. ad lib. 6.
† A three-knotted necessity.   ¹ 680.

in *Sussex*, I have seen transcribed; whereupon in a Deliberative (concerning Papal exactions, and subjection of Church-living) held under *Hen.* the Third,[1] after examination of ancient Kings' Indulgence to the Clergy, it was found, that; *Non adeò libertati dederunt hujusmodi possessiones, quin Tria sibi reservarent semper propter publicam regni utilitatem, videlicet, Expeditionem, Pontis, et Arcis reparationes, vel refectiones, ut per ea resisterent hostium incursionibus**; although by words of a Statute of *Ethelulph* King of *West-Saxons* in the year 855 made by advice both of Laity and Spirituality, the Church was quitted also of those three Common-wealth causes of Subsidy, but enjoyed it not; for, even the Canons[2] themselves subject their possessions to these services and duties, and upon interpretation of a Charter made by *Henry Beauclerc*, Founder of the Priory of S. *Oswald* in *Yorkshire*, containing words of immunity and liberty of tenure, as general and effectual as might be, a great lawyer[3] long since affirmed that yet the House was not freed of repairing *Bridges* and *Causies*. But all lands, as well in hands of Clerks as Lay, were subjected to particular tenures after the Conquest: and so these kind of charges and discharges being made rather *feodal* (as *Bracton*[4] calls them) than *personal*, use of them in Charters consequently ceased. I note here to students of antiquity, that, where the printed *Ingulph* says this was done by *Ethelbald* in the third year of his reign, they must with correction make it the twenty-third,[5] as is, without scruple, apparant in the date of the Synod,[6] which was 745 of our Saviour.

[1] Math. Paris, pag. 838.
* They always reserved those that so they might the better be furnished against the enemies' invasion.
[2] Gregor. Decret. tit. de Imm. Eccles. c. Pervenit. 2.
[3] Knivet 44. Ed. 3. fol. 25. a.
[4] De Acquir. rer. Dom. 2. cap. 16. §. 8.
[5] Ingulphus emendatus.   [6] Malmesb. Lib. de Gest. Pontif. 1.

THE ELEVENTH SONG.

360. *The* Britons *had interred their* Proto-martyr's *bones.*

In that universal persecution under *Diocletian*, and *Herculius*, this Isle gave, in S. *Alban*, testimony of Christian profession; even to his last breath drawn among tormenting enemies of the Cross.[1] His death (being the first Martyr, as the Author here calls him, that this country had) was at *Werlamcester* (*i.e.*, the old *Verulam*) where by the Abbey of S. *Alban's* was afterward erected.[2]

379. (*Extirping other styles*) *and gave it* England's[*] *name.*

Look back to the last note on the First Song. Thus, as you see, hath the Muse compendiously run through the Heptarchy, and united it in name and empire under *Egbert* King of *West-Saxons*: after whom, none but his successors had absolute power in their Kingdoms, as course of story shows you.[3] Likely enough I imagine, that as yet expectation of the reader is not satisfied in these Seven Kingdoms, their beginnings, territory, and first Christianity; therefore as a corollary receive this for the eye's more facile instruction.

		Began in	*First received the* Faith *in*
Comprehended in	I. *Kent* { The now Kent.	I. *Hengist* 456,[4] from whose son *Oisc* the succeeding Kings were called *Oiscings*.	I. *Ethelbert*,597, of *Augustine* from *Gregory* 1.
	II. *South Sex* { Sussex. Surrey.	II. In *Ælla* about 491.	II. *Edilwalch* 661, and the whole Country converted by *Wilfrid* 679.

[1] See the Author in the Sixteenth Song.   [2] 760 aut circiter.
[*] Ann. Circa 800.   [3] See the Sixteenth Song.
[4] I follow here the ordinary Chronology of our Monks.

			Began in	First received the Faith in
Comprehended in	III. West-Sex.	Cornwall. Devonshire. Dorset. Somerset. Wilton. Southampton. Berkshire. Lancaster.	III. Certic, 519, whose grandfather was Gewise, and thence his people and posterity called Gewises.	III. Kinegils 635, baptized by Birin first Bishop of Dorchester in Oxfordshire.
	IV. Northumberland.	Yorke. Durham. Westmerland. Northumberland, and the neighbouring territory to Edinburgh Frith; whither from Tine was the name of Bernicland, and what lay on this side Tine, called Deirland.	IV. Ida 547, taking all Bernicland, as Ælla twelve years after began in Deirland; but both Kingdoms soon were confounded in one.	IV. Edwin 625, Christened by Paulin first Archbishop (in the Saxon times) of Yorke.
	V. Est-Sex.	Essex. Middlesex. Part of Hereford.*	V. Sleda after some (others say in Erchinwin before him) about 580, both uncertain, and their successors.	V. Sebert 604, dipped in holy tincture by Mellitus, first Bishop of London.

* i.e., Hertford.—ED.

THE ELEVENTH SONG.

		Began in	First received the Faith in
Comprehended in	VI. *Est-Angle.*	*Norfolk. Suffolk. Cambridge-shire.* Part of *Ely.*	VI. *Redwald* about 600. But some talk of one *Vuffa* (whence these Kings were called *Vuffings*) to be Author of it near thirty years before. VII. In *Penda* 626. Others will in *Crida* some forty before.	VI. *Eorpwald* 632, although *Redwald* were Christened, for he soon fell to apostasy, by persuasion of his wife, and in the same Chapel made one altar to Christ, another to the Devil. VII. *Peada* King of *Midle-Engle* 653, baptized by *Finna* Bishop of *Lindisfarne,* but enlarged the profession of it in *Vulpher* next King there.
	VII. *Merc-land.*	*Glocester. Hereford. Worcester. Warwick. Leicester. Rutland. Northampton. Lincoln. Hunting-don. Bedford. Bucking-ham. Oxford. Stafford. Derby. Salop. Nottingham Chester.* The *North-ern* part of *Hereford.** But in these the Inhabitants of then *Inlands* were called *Middle-Engles,* and the *Mer-*		

* i.e., *Hertford.*

		Began in	First received the Faith in
Comp. in	cians divided into names of their local quarters.		

Perhaps as good authority may be given against some of my proposed Chronology, as I can justify myself with. But although so, yet I am therefore freed of error, because our old Monks exceedingly in this kind corrupted, or deficient, afford nothing able to rectify. I know the *East-Angles*, by both ancient and later authority, begin above one hundred years before; but if with synchronism you examine it, it will be found most absurd. For, seeing it is affirmed expressly, that *Redwald* was slain by *Ethelfrid* King of *Northumberland*, and being plain by *Bede*[1] (take his story together, and rely not upon syllables and false printed copies) that it must needs be near 600 (for *Edwin* succeeded *Ethelfrid*) and that *Uffa* was some thirty years before: what calculation will cast this into less than five hundred years after Christ? Forget not (if you desire accurate times) my admonition to the Fourth Song, of the twenty-two years' error upon the *Dionysian* account, especially in the beginning of the Kingdoms, because they are for the most part reckoned in old Monks from the coming of the *Saxons*. Where you find different names from these, attribute it to misreading old copies, by such as have published *Carpenwald* for *Eorpenwald*, or *Earpwald*; *Penda* also perhaps for *Wenda*, mistaking the *Saxon* p. for our *P.* and other such, variably both written and printed. How in time they successively came

---

[1] Eccles. Hist. 2. cap. 9. ubi legendum *sexcentesimo* vice τοῦ *quingentesimo*.

THE ELEVENTH SONG.

under the *West-Saxon* rule, I must not tell you, unless I should untimely put on the person of an Historian. Our common Annals manifest it. But know here, that although Seven were, yet but Five had any long continuance of their supremacies:

The Saxons tho in ther power (tho thii were so riue)
Seue Kingdomes made in Engelonde and suthe* but biue,
The King of Northomberlond, and of Eastangle also
Of Kent and of Westsex, and of the March therto,

as *Robert* of *Glocester*, according to truth of Story hath it; for *Estsex* and *Southsex* were not long after their beginnings (as it were) annexed to their ruling neighbour Princes.

388. *A Nation from their first bent naturally* to spoil.

Indeed so were universally the *Germans* (out of whom our *Saxons*) as *Tacitus* relates to us; *Nec arare terram aut exspectare annum tam facilè persuaseris, quam vocare hostes et vulnera mereri. Pigrum quinimò et iners videtur sudore acquirere quod possis sanguine parare,*† and more of that nature we read in him.

400. *Of famous* Cambridge *first* ―――――

About the year 630, *Sigebert* (after death of *Eorpwald*) returning out of *France*, whither his father *Redwald* had banished him, and receiving the *East-angle* Crown, assisted by *Fœlix* a *Burgognone*, and first Bishop of *Dunwich* (then called *Dunmoc*) in *Suffolk*, desiring to imitate what he had seen observable in *France*, for the common good, *Instituit scholam* (read it *scholas*, if you will, as some do, I see no

---

* Afterward.
† You could not so easily persuade them to husbandry, as to martial conflict; nor thought they it better than slothful, to get that by sweat which they might have by blood.

consequence of worth) *in qui pueri literis erudirentur,*[*] as *Bede* writeth. Out of these words thus general, *Cambridge*, being in *Eastangle*, hath been taken for this School, and the School for the University. I will believe it (in so much as makes it then a University) not much sooner than that (I know not what) *Gurguntius* with *Cantaber*, some hundred and fifty years before *Christ*, founded it; or, those Charters of King *Arthur*, Bulls of Pope *Honorius* and *Sergius* sent thither, *Anaximander* or *Anaxagoras* their studies there, with more such pretended and absurd unlikelihoods; unless every Grammar School be an University, as this was, where children were taught by *Pædagogi et Magistri juxta morem Cantuariorum,*[†] as *Bede* hath expressly: which so makes *Canterbury* an University also. But neither is there any touch in authentic and ancient story, which justifies these Schools instituted at *Cambridge*, but generally somewhere in *Eastangle*. Reasons of inducement are framed in multitudes on both sides. But, for my own part, I never saw any sufficiently probable, and therefore most of all rely upon what authorities are afforded. Among them I ever preferred the *Appendix* to the Story of *Crowland* supposed done by *Peter* of *Blois*, affirming that under *Hen*. I. (he lived very near the same time; therefore believe him in a matter not subject to causes of Historians temporizing) *Joffred* Abbot of *Crowland*, with one *Gilbert* his commoigne, and three other Monks, came to his Manor of *Cotenham*, as they used oft-times, to read; and thence daily going to *Cambridge*, *Conducto quodam horreo publico suas scientias palàm profitentes, in brevi temporis excursu grandem discipulorum numerum contraxerunt. Anno verò secundo adventus illorum, tantum accrevit discipulorum numerus, tam ex totâ patriâ quàm ex oppido, quòd quælibet domus*

---

[*] Instituted a School for children.
[†] To Schoolmasters, according to the fashion at *Canterbury*.

maxima, horreum, nec ulla ecclesia sufficeret eorum receptaculo;* and so goes on with an ensuing frequency of Schools. If before this there were an University, I imagine that in it was not professed *Aristotle's* Ethics, which tell us περὶ τῆς Ξενικῆς φιλίας: for, then would they not have permitted learned readers of the Sciences (whom all that hated not the Muses could not but love) to be compelled into a Barn, instead of Schools. Nor is it tolerable in conceit, that for near five hundred years (which interceded twixt this and *Sigebert*) no fitter place of profession should be erected. To this time others have referred the beginning of that famous Seminary of good literature: and, if room be left for me, I offer subscription; but always under reformation of that most honoured Tutress's pupils, which shall (omitting fabulous trash) judiciously instruct otherwise. But the Author here out of *Polydore, Leland,* and others of later time relying upon conjecture, hath his warrant of better credit than *Cantilup*, another relater of that *Arcadian* Original, which some have so violently patronized.

403. *Renownéd* Oxford *built t' Apollo's learned brood.*

So is it affirmed (of that learned King yet knowing not a letter until he was past twelve) by *Polydore, Bale,* and others; grounding themselves upon what *Alfred's* beneficence and most deserving care hath manifested in Royal provision for that sacred Nourice of Learning. But justly it may be doubted, lest they took instauration of what was deficient, for institution: for although you grant that he first founded *University College;* yet it follows not, but there might be common Schools, and Colleges, as at this day in *Leyden, Giesse,* and other places of High and Low *Germany.* If you please, fetch hither that of *Greeklade* (to the Third

---

* Hired a barn to read in, and so continued, till the number of their Scholars exceeded the content of that, or any Church.

Song) which I will not importune you to believe: but without scruple you cannot but credit that of a Monk of S. Dewi's[1] (made Grammar and Rhetoric Reader there by King *Alfred*) in these words of the year 886. [2]*Exorta est pessima ac teterrima Oxonice discordia inter Grimboldum* (this was a great and devout Scholar, whose aid *Alfred* used in his disposition of Lectures) *doctissimosque illos viros secum illuc adduxit, et veteres illos scholasticos quos ibidem invenisset: qui eius adventu, leges, modos, ac prælegendi formulas ab eodem Grimboldo institutas, omni ex parte amplecti recusabant.* And a little after, *Quin etiam probabant et ostendebant idque indubitato veterum annalium testimonio illius loci Ordines ac Instituta, à nonnullis piis et eruditis hominibus, fuisse sancita, ut à Gildà* (*Melkino* he was a great Mathematician, and as *Gildas* also lived between 500 and 600) *Nennio* (the printed book hath falsely *Nemrio*) *Kentigerno* (he lived about 509) *et aliis, qui omnes literis illic consenuerunt, omnia ibidem fœlici pace et concordiâ administrantes;* and affirmed also that Letters had there been happily professed in very ancient time, with frequency of Scholars, until irruptions of Pagans[3] (they meant *Danes*) had brought them to this lately restored deficiency. After this testimony, greater than all exception, what can be more plain than noble worth and fame of this Pillar of the Muses long before King *Alfred's?* Neither make I any great question, but that, where in an old copy of *Gildas* his life (published lately by a *Frenchman*[4]) it is printed, that he studied at *Iren*, which clearly he took for a place in this Land, it should be *Ichen* (and I confess, before me one hath

[1] Asser. Menevens. de Gest. *Alfred*.
[2] A great controversy grew twixt those new Scholars which *Alfred* brought thither, and those which of ancient time were there before, &c.
[3] About *Alfred's* time before his instauration a Grammarian was not found in his Kingdom to teach him. Florent. Wigorn. pag. 309.
[4] Joann. a Bosco Parisiensis. in Bibliothec. Floriacens. Vit. Gild. cap. 6.

well published the conjecture) for 𝕽𝖞𝖉𝖅𝖈𝖍𝖎𝖓 the *Welsh*
name of that City, expressing as much as *Oxenford*. Yet I
would not willingly fall into the extremes of making it
Memprikes, as some do; that were but vain affectation to
dote on my Reverend Mother. But because in those remote
ages, not only Universities and Public Schools (being for a
time prohibited by Pope *Gregory*[1] for fear of breeding *Pela-
gians* and *Arians*) but divers Monasteries and Cloisters
were great Auditories of learning, as appears in *Theodor* and
Adrian's professing at *Canterbury*,[2] *Maldulph* and *Aldelm* at
Malmesbury (this *Aldelm* first taught the *English* to write
Latin prose and verse) *Alcuin* at *Yorke*, *Bede* at *Jarrow*,[3]
and such other more I guess that hence came much obscu-
rity to their name, omitted or suppressed by envious Monks
of those times, than whose traditions descending through
many hands of their like, we have no credible authorities.
But whichsoever of these two Sisters have prerogative of
primogeniture (a matter too much controverted twixt them)
none can give them less attribute, than to be two radiant
Eyes fixed in this Island, as the beauteous face of the earth's
body. To what others have by industrious search communicated, I add concerning *Oxford* out of an ancient MS.[4] (but
since the *Clementines*) what I there read: *Apud Montem
Pessulanum, Parisios, Oxoniam, Colonias, Boloniam, generalia
studia ordinamus. Ad quæ prior Provincialis quilibet possit
mittere duos fratres qui habeant Studentium libertatem;** and
also admonish the reader of an imposture thrust into the
world this last Autumn Mart in a Provincial Catalogue of
Bishoprics, by a professed Antiquary[5] and *Popish* Canon of

[1] Bri. Twin. Apolog. Oxon. 2. §. 84.
[2] Leland ad Cyg. Cant. in Grantâ.   [3] Camd. in Wiltoniâ.
[4] Constitutiones Fratrum. cap. de Studiis et Magist. Student.
* At *Mompelier, Paris, Oxford, Cologne, Bologna* we institute general Studies.
[5] Aubert. Miræus. In Notit. Episcopat. edit. Parisiis, 1610.

Antwerp, telling us, that the MS. Copy of it, found in S. *Victor's* Library at *Paris*, was written five hundred years since, and in the number of *Canterbury* Province, it hath *Oxford;* which being written *Oxoniensis*, I imagined might have been mistaken for *Exoniensis* (as *Exonia* for *Oxonia* sometimes) until I saw *Exoniensis* joined also; by which stood *Petroburgensis*, which bruised all the credit of the monument, but especially of him that published it. For, who knows not that *Peterborough* was no Bishopric till *Hen.* VIII.? nor indeed was *Oxford*, which might be easily thought much otherwise, by incidence of an ignorant eye on that vainly promising title. I abstain from expatiating in matter of our Muses' seats, so largely, and too largely treated of by others.

406. *And into several Shires the Kingdom did divide.*

To those Shires he[1] constituted *Justices* and *Sheriffs*, called ᵹepeꞅas and rhýpᵹeꞅepas, the office of those two being before confounded in *Vice-Domini., i.e. Lieutenants;* but so, that *Vicedominus* and *Vicecomes* remained indifferent words for name of *Sheriff*, as, in a Charter of King *Edred* 950 *Ego Bingulph Vicedominus consului* ✠. *Ego Alfer Vicecomes audivi* ✠. I find together subscribed. The *Justices* were, as I think, no other than those whom they called Ɇolꞅop mannum, being the same with Ɇoples, now *Earls*, in whose disposition and government upon delegation from the King (the title being officiary, not hereditary, except in some particular Shire, as *Leicester*, &c.*) the County was; with the Bishop of the Diocese: the Earl[2] sate in the Scypeᵹemote twice every year, where charge was given touching[3] Ɇoꞅer puhᴛej ᵹerᴄopulb puhᴛe[4]: But by the *Conqueror*, this

[1] Histor. Crowlandensis. * See to Thirteenth Song.
[2] Edgar. Leg. Human. cap. 5.; Edward. cap. 11.; Cannt. cap. 17.
[3] Rot. Chart. 2. Rich. 2. pro Decan. et Capit. Lincoln. transcripsimus in Jano Anglorum, lib. 2. §. 14. et videas apud Fox. Hist. Eccles. 4. [4] *God's* right and the world's.

THE ELEVENTH SONG. 111

meddling of the Bishop in *Turnes* was prohibited. The Sheriff had then his Monthly Court also, as the now *County Court*, instituted by the *Saxon Ed. I.* as that other of the *Turne* by King *Edgar*. The Sheriff is now immediate officer to the King's Court, but it seems that then the Earl (having always the third part of the Shire's profits, both before and since the *Normans**) had charge upon him. For this division of Countries: how many he made, I know not, but *Malmesbury*, under *Ethelred*, affirms, there were thirty-two (*Robert* of *Glocester* thirty-five) about which time *Winchelcomb* was one,[1] but then joined to *Glocestershire*: those thirty-two[2] were

Kent, Sussex, Surrey, Hantshire, Berkshire, Wiltshire, Somerset, Dorset, Devonshire.—Nine, governed by the *West-Saxon* law.

Essex, Middlesex, Suffolke, Norfolke, Hertford, Cambridge, Bedford, Buckingham, Huntingdon, Northampton, Leicester, Derby, Nottingham, Lincolne, Yorke.—Fifteen, governed by the *Danish* law.

Oxford, Warwicke, Glocester, Hereford, Shropshire, Stafford, Cheshire, Worcester.—Eight, governed by the *Mercian* law.

Here was none of *Cornwall, Cumberland* (styled also *Carlileshire*) *Northumberland, Lancaster, Westmerland* (which was since titled *Aplebyshire*) *Durham, Monmouth*, nor *Rutland*, which at this day make our number (beside the twelve in *Wales*) forty. *Cornwall* (because of the *Britons* there planted) until the *Conqueror* gave the County to his brother *Robert* of *Moreton*, continued out of the division. *Cumberland, Northumberland, Westmerland*, and *Durham*, being all Northern, seem to have been then under *Scottish* or *Danish*

* See to the Thirteenth Song.
[1] Codex Wigorniensis apud Cam. in Dobunis.
[2] Polychronicon lib. 1. cap. de Provinciis.

power. But the two first received their division, as it seems, before the Conquest; for *Cumberland* had its particular 'governors,¹ and *Northumberland*² Earls : *Westmerland* perhaps began when King *John* gave it *Robert Vipont*, ancestor to the *Cliffords*, holding by that Patent to this day the inheritance of the Sheriffdom. *Durham* religiously was with large immunities given to the Bishop, since the *Norman* invasion. *Lancaster*, until *Hen.* III. created his younger son *Edmund Crooke-backe* Earl of it, I think, was no County: for, in one of our old Year-Books³ a learned Judge affirms, that, in this *Henry's* time, was the first Sheriff's Tourne held there. Nor until *Edward* (first son to *Edmund* of *Langley* Duke of *Yorke*, and afterward Duke of *Aumerle*) created by *Rich.* II. had *Rutland* any Earls. I know for number and time of those, all authority agrees not with me; but I conjecture only upon selected. As *Alured* divided the Shires first ; so to him is owing the Constitution of *Hundreds, Tithings, Lathes,* and *Wapentakes*, to the end that whosoever were not lawfully, upon credit of his *Boroughes, i.e.*, pledges, admitted in some of them for a good subject, should be reckoned as suspicious of life and loyalty. Some steps thereof remain in our ancient and later Law-books.⁴

416. *Which he an heirloom left unto the* English *Throne.*

The first healing of the *King's Evil* is referred to this *Edward* the *Confessor*⁵ : and, of a particular example in his curing a young married woman, an old monument⁶ is left to

¹ Matth. West. fol. 366.   ² Ingulph. Hist. Crowland.
³ Thorp. 17. *Ed.* 3. fol. 56. b.
⁴ Bract. lib. 3. Tract. de Coronâ, cap. 10. Quàmplurimi casus in annis *Ed.* 3. et 5. Jacob. apud Dom. Ed. Cok. lib. 6. fol. 77. maximè verò hûc faciunt Itinera illa *H.* 3. et *Ed.* 1.
⁵ Polydor. Hist. 8.
⁶ Eilred. Rhivallens. ap. Took. in Charismat. Sanat. cap. 6.

posterity. In *France* such a kind of cure is attributed to their Kings also; both of that and this, if you desire particular inquisition, take Dr. *Tooker's Charisma Sanationis.*

418. *Our Country's* Common Laws *did faithfully produce.*

In *Lambard's Archæonomy* and *Roger* of *Hoveden's Hen.* II. are Laws under name of the *Confessor* and *Conqueror* joined, and deduced for the most part out of their predecessors; but those of the *Confessor* seem to be the same, if *Malmesbury*[1] deceive not, which King *Cnut* collected, of whom his words are, *Omnes leges ab antiquis regibus et maximè antecessore suo Ethelredo latas, sub interminatione Regiæ mulctæ, perpetuis temporibus observari præcepit, in quarum custodiam etiam nunc tempore Bonorum sub nomine Regis Edwardi juratur, non quòd ille statuerit, sed quòd observarerit**: and under this name have they been humbly desired by the subject, granted with qualification, and controverted, as a main and first part of liberty, in the next age, following the *Norman* Conquest.

[1] De Gest. Reg. 2. cap. 11.
* He commanded all laws made by the ancient Kings to be kept, especially those of *Ethelred*, to which the Kings swear under name of King *Edward's* laws, not that he made them, but observed them.

THE TWELFTH SONG.

THE ARGUMENT.

The Muse, that part of Shropshire plies
Which on the East of Severne lies:
Where mighty Wrekin from his height,
In the proud Cambrian Mountains' spite,
Sings those great Saxons ruling here, 5
Which the most famous warriors were.
And as she in her course proceeds,
Relating many glorious deeds,
Of Guy of Warwick's fight doth strain
With Colebrond, that renownéd Dane, 10
And of the famous Battles tried
Twixt Knute and Edmond-Ironside;
To the Staffordian fields doth rove;
Visits the Springs of Trent and Dove;
Of Moreland, Cank, and Needwood sings; 15
An end which to this Canto brings.

THE haughty *Cambrian* Hills enamor'd of their praise
(As they who only sought ambitiously to raise
The blood of god-like *Brute*) their heads do proudly bear:
nd having crown'd themselves sole Regents of the air
\nother war with Heaven as though they meant to make) 5
id seem in great disdain the bold affront to take,[1]

That any petty Hill upon the *English* side,
Should dare, not (with a crouch) to vail unto their pride.
 When *Wrekin*, as a Hill his proper worth that knew,
And understood from whence their insolency grew,   10
For all that they appear'd so terrible in sight,
Yet would not once forego a jot that was his right.
And when they star'd on him, to them the like he gave,
And answer'd glance for glance, and brave again for brave:
That, when some other Hills, which *English* dwellers were, 15
The lusty *Wrekin* saw himself so well to bear
Against the *Cambrian* part, respectless of their power;
His eminent disgrace expecting every hour,
Those Flatterers that before (with many cheerful look)
Had grac'd his goodly site, him utterly forsook,   20
And muffled them in clouds, like mourners veil'd in black,
Which of their utmost hope attend the ruinous wrack:
That those delicious Nymphs, fair *Tearne* and *Rodon* clear
(Two Brooks of him belov'd, and two that held him dear;
He having none but them, they having none but he,   25
Which to their mutual joy might either's object be)
Within their secret breasts conceivéd sundry fears,
And as they mixt their streams, for him so mixt their tears.
Whom, in their coming down, when plainly he discerns,
For them his nobler heart in his strong bosom yearns: 30
But, constantly resolv'd, that (dearer if they were)
The *Britans* should not yet all from the *English* bear;
Therefore, quoth he, brave Flood, though forth by *Cambria*
    brought,[1]
Yet as fair *England's* friend, or mine thou would'st be thought
(O *Severne!*) let thine ear my just defence partake: 35
Which said, in the behalf of th' *English*, thus he spake:
 Wise *Weever* (I suppose) sufficiently hath said
Of those our Princes here, which fasted, watch'd, and pray'd,

[1] Out of *Plinilimon*, in the confines of *Cardigan* and *Montgomery*.

Whose deep devotion went for others' vent'rous deeds:
But in this Song of mine, he seriously that reads, 40
Shall find, ere I have done, the *Britan* (so extoll'd,
Whose height each Mountain strives so mainly to uphold)
Match'd with as valiant men, and of as clean a might,
As skilful to command, and as inur'd to fight.
Who, when their fortune will'd that after they should
    scorse 45
Blows with the big-bon'd *Dane*, eschanging force for force
(When first he put from sea to forage on this shore,
Two hundred years[1] distain'd with either's equal gore;
Now this aloft, now that: oft did the *English* reign,
And oftentimes again depresséd by the *Dane*) 50
The *Saxons*, then I say, themselves as bravely show'd,
As these on whom the *Welsh* such glorious praise bestow'd.

Nor could his angry sword, who *Egbert* overthrew
(Through which he thought at once the *Saxons* to subdue)
His kingly courage quell: but from his short retire, 55
His reinforcéd troops (new forg'd with sprightly fire)
Before them drave the *Dane*, and made the *Britan* run
(Whom he by liberal wage here to his aid had won)
Upon their recreant backs, which both in flight were slain,
Till their huge murtheréd heaps manur'd each neighbouring
    plain. 60

As, *Ethelwolfe* again, his utmost powers that bent
Against those fresh supplies each year from *Denmark* sent
(Which, prowling up and down in their rude *Danish* oars,
Here put themselves by stealth upon the pest'red shores)
In many a doubtful fight much fame in *England* wan. 65
So did the King of *Kent*, courageous *Athelstan*,
Which here against the *Dane* got such victorious days.

So, we the *Wiltshire* men as worthily may praise,
That buckled with those *Danes*, by *Ceorle* and *Osrick* brought.

[1] See to the First Song.

And *Etheldred*, with them nine sundry Fields that fought,
Recorded in his praise, the conquests of one year.   71
You right-nam'd *English* then, courageous men you were
When *Redding* ye regain'd, led by that valiant Lord :
Where *Basrig* ye out-brav'd, and *Halden*, sword to sword ;
The most redoubted spirits that *Denmark* here addrest.   75
    And *Alured*, not much inferior to the rest :
Who having in his days so many dangers past,
In seven brave foughten Fields their Champion *Hubba* chac'd,
And slew him in the end, at *Abington*, that day
Whose like the Sun ne'er saw in his diurnal way :   80
Where those, that from the Field sore wounded sadly fled,
Were well-near overwhelm'd with mountains of the dead.
His force and fortune made the foes so much to fear,
As they the Land at last did utterly forswear.
    And, when proud *Rollo*, next, their former powers repair'd
(Yea, when the worst of all it with the *English* far'd)   86
Whose Countries near at hand, his force did still supply,
And *Denmark* to her drew the strengths of *Normandy*,
This Prince in many a fight their forces still defied.
The goodly River *Lee* he wisely did divide,   90
By which the *Danes* had then their full-fraught Navies
    tew'd :
The greatness of whose stream besiegéd *Harford* row'd.
This *Alfred* whose fore-sight had politicly found
Betwixt them and the *Thames* advantage of the ground,
A puissant hand thereto laboriously did put,   95
§ And into lesser streams that spacious Current cut.
Their ships thus set on shore (to frustrate their desire)
Those *Danish* hulks became the food of *English* fire.
    Great *Alfred* left his life : when *Elflida* up-grew,
That far beyond the pitch of other women flew :   100
Who having in her youth of childing felt the woe,

[1] See to the next Song, of *Rollo*.

THE TWELFTH SONG.

§ Her lord's embraces vow'd she never more would know:
But diff'ring from her sex (as full of manly fire)
This most courageous Queen, by conquest to aspire,
The puissant *Danish* powers victoriously pursu'd,   105
And resolutely here through their thick squadrons hew'd
Her way into the North. Where, *Darby* having won,
And things beyond belief upon the Enemy done,
She sav'd besiegéd *Yorke;* and in the *Danes'* despite,
When most they were upheld with all the Eastern might,   110
More Towns and Cities built out of her wealth and power,
Than all their hostile flames could any way devour.
And, when the *Danish* here the Country most destroy'd,
Yet all our powers on them not wholly were employ'd;
But some we still reserv'd abroad for us to roam,   115
To fetch in foreign spoils, to help our loss at home.
And all the Land, from us, they never clearly wan:
But to his endless praise, our *English Athelstan*,
In the *Northumbrian* fields, with most victorious might
Put *Alaffe* and his powers to more inglorious flight;   120
And more than any King of th' *English* him before,
Each way from North to South, from West to th' Eastern
   shore,
Made all the Isle his own; his seat who firmly fixt,
The *Calidonian* Hills and *Cathnes* point betwixt,
§ And *Constantine* their King (a prisoner) hither brought;   125
Then over *Severne's* banks the warlike *Britans* fought:
Where he their Princes forc'd from that their strong retreat,
In *England* to appear at his Imperial seat.
   But after, when the *Danes*, who never wearied were,
Came with intent to make a general conquest here,   130
They brought with them a man deem'd of so wond'rous
   might,
As was not to be match'd by any mortal wight:
For, one could scarcely bear his axe into the field;

Which as a little wand the *Dane* would lightly wield:
And (to enforce that strength) of such a dauntless spirit, 135
A man (in their conceit) of so exceeding merit,
That to the *English* oft they offer'd him (in pride)
The ending of the war by combat to decide:
Much scandal which procur'd unto the *English* name.
When, some out of their love, and some spurr'd on with
    shame, 140
By envy some provok'd, some out of courage, fain
Would undertake the cause to combat with the *Dane*.
But *Athelstan* the while, in settled judgment found,
Should the Defendant fail, how wide and deep a wound
It likely was to leave to his defensive war. 145
    Thus, whilst with sundry doubts his thoughts perplexéd
    are,
It pleas'd all-powerful Heaven, that *Warwick's* famous *Guy*
(The knight through all the world renown'd for chivalry)
Arriv'd from foreign parts, where he had held him long.
His honourable arms devoutly having hong 150
In a Religious house, the off'rings of his praise,
To his Redeemer *Christ*, his help at all assays
(Those Arms, by whose strong proof he many a Christian
    freed,
And bore the perfect marks of many a worthy deed)
Himself, a palmer poor, in homely russet clad 155
(And only in his hand his hermit's staff he had)
Tow'rds *Winchester* alone (so) sadly took his way,
Where *Athelstan*, that time the King of *England* lay;
And where the *Danish* Camp then strongly did abide,
Near to a goodly mead, which men there call the *Hide*. 160
    The day that *Guy* arriv'd (when silent night did bring
Sleep both on friend and foe) that most religious King
(Whose strong and constant heart, all grievous cares sup-
    prest)

His due devotion done, betook himself to rest.
To whom it seem'd by night an Angel did appear,   165
Sent to him from that God Whom he invok'd by pray'r ;
Commanding him the time not idly to forslow,
But rathe as he could rise, to such a gate to go,
Whereas he should not fail to find a goodly knight
In palmer's poor attire : though very meanly dight,   170
Yet by his comely shape, and limbs exceeding strong,
He eas'ly might him know the other folk among ;
And bad him not to fear, but choose him for the man.
  No sooner brake the day, but uprose *Athelstan ;*
And as the Vision show'd, he such a palmer found,   175
With others of his sort, there sitting on the ground :
Where, for some poor repast they only seem'd to stay,
Else ready to depart each one upon his way :
When secretly the King revealèd to the knight
His comfortable dreams that lately-passèd night :   180
With mild and princely words bespeaking him ; quoth he,
Far better you are known to Heaven (it seems) than me
For this great action fit : by Whose most dread command
(Before a world of men) it's lay'd upon your hand.
Then stout and valiant knight, here to my court repair,   185
Refresh you in my baths, and mollify your care
With comfortable wines and meats what you will ask :
And choose my richest arms to fit you for this task.
  The palmer (grey with age) with countenance lowting low,
His head even to the earth before the King doth bow,   190
Him softly answering thus ; Dread Lord, it fits me ill
(A wretched man) t' oppose high Heaven's eternal will :
Yet my most sovereign Liege, no more of me esteem
Than this poor habit shows, a pilgrim as I seem ;
But yet I must confess, have seen in former days   195
The best knights of the world, and scuffled in some frays.
Those times are gone with me ; and, being agèd now,

Have off'red up my arms, to Heaven and made my vow
Ne'er more to bear a shield, nor my declining age
(Except some palmer's tent, or homely hermitage) 200
Shall ever enter roof: but if, by Heaven and thee,
This action be impos'd great *English* King on me,
Send to the *Danish* Camp, their challenge to accept,
In some convenient place proclaiming it be kept:
Where, by th' Almighty's power, for *England* I'll appear. 205
    The King, much pleas'd in mind, assumes his wonted
      cheer,
And to the *Danish* power his choicest herault sent.
When, both through camp and court, this combat quickly
    went.
Which suddenly divulg'd, whilst every list'ning ear,
As thirsting after news, desirous was to hear, 210
Who for the *English* side durst undertake the day;
The puissant Kings accord, that in the middle way
Betwixt the tent and town, to either's equal sight,
Within a goodly mead, most fit for such a fight,
The Lists should be prepar'd for this material prize. 215
    The day prefixt once com'n, both *Dane* and *English* rise,
And to th' appointed place th' unnumb'red people throng:
The weaker female sex, old men, and children young,
Into the windows get, and up on stalls, to see
The man on whose brave hand their hope that day must be.
In noting of it well, there might a man behold 221
More sundry forms of fear than thought imagine could.
One looks upon his friend with sad and heavy chear,
Who seems in this distress a part with him to bear:
Their passions do express much pity mixt with rage. 225
Whilst one his wife's laments is labouring to assuage,
His little infant near, in childish gibbridge shows
What addeth to his grief who sought to calm her woes.
One having climb'd some roof, the concourse to descry,

THE TWELFTH SONG.

From thence upon the earth directs his humble eye, 230
As since he thither came he suddenly had found
Some danger them amongst which lurk'd upon the ground.
One stands with fixéd eyes, as though he were aghast :
Another sadly comes, as though his hopes were past.
This hark'neth with his friend, as though with him to break
Of some intended act. Whilst they together speak, 236
Another standeth near to listen what they say,
Or what should be the end of this so doubtful day.
One great and general face the gatheréd people seem :
So that the perfect'st fight beholding could not deem 240
What looks most sorrow show'd ; their griefs so equal were.
Upon the heads of two, whose cheeks were join'd so near
As if together grown, a third his chin doth rest :
Another looks o'er his : and others, hardly prest,
Look'd underneath their arms. Thus, whilst in crowds
    they throng 245
(Led by the King himself) the Champion comes along;
A man well-strook in years, in homely palmer's gray,
And in his hand his staff, his reverend steps to stay,
Holding a comely pace : which at his passing by,
In every censuring tongue, as every serious eye, 250
Compassion mixt with fear, distrust and courage bred.

    Then *Colebrond* for the *Danes* came forth in ireful red ;
Before him (from the camp) an ensign first display'd
Amidst a guard of gleaves : then sumptuously array'd
Were twenty gallant youths, that to the warlike sound 255
Of *Danish* brazen drums, with many a lofty bound,
Come with their Country's march, as they to *Mars* should
    dance.
Thus, forward to the fight, both Champions them advance :
And each without respect doth resolutely chuse
The weapon that he brought, nor doth his foe's refuse. 260
The *Dane* prepares his axe, that pond'rous was to feel,

Whose squares were laid with plates, and riveted with steel,
And arméd down along with pikes; whose hard'ned points
(Forc'd with the weapon's weight) had power to tear the
    joints
Of curass or of mail, or whatsoe'er they took: 265
Which caus'd him at the knight disdainfully to look.
  When our stout palmer soon (unknown for valiant *Guy*)
The cord from his straight loins doth presently untie,
Puts off his palmer's weed unto his truss, which bore
The stains of ancient arms, but show'd it had before   270
Been costly cloth of gold; and off his hood he threw:
Out of his hermit's staff his two-hand sword he drew
(The unsuspected sheath which long to it had been)
Which till that instant time the people had not seen;
A sword so often try'd. Then to himself, quoth he,   275
Arms let me crave your aid, to set my Country free:
And never shall my heart your help again require,
But only to my God to lift you up in pray'r.
  Here, *Colebrond* forward made, and soon the Christian
    knight
Encounters him again with equal power and spight: 280
Whereas, betwixt them two, might eas'ly have been seen
Such blows, in public throng as uséd had they been,
Of many there the least might many men have slain:
Which none but they could strike, nor none but they sustain;
The most relentless eye that had the power to awe,   285
And so great wonder bred in those the fight that saw,
As verily they thought, that Nature until then
Had purposely reserv'd the utmost power of men,
Where strength still answer'd strength, on courage courage
    grew.
  Look how two lions fierce, both hungry, both pursue   290
One sweet and selfsame prey, at one another fly,
And with their arméd paws ingrappled dreadfully,

The thunder of their rage, and boist'rous struggling, make
The neighbouring forests round affrightedly to quake :
Their sad encounter, such. The mighty *Colebrond* stroke 295
A cruel blow at *Guy :* which though he finely broke,
Yet (with the weapon's weight) his ancient hilt it split,
And (thereby lessened much) the Champion lightly hit
Upon the reverent brow : immediately from whence
The blood dropp'd softly down, as if the wound had sense 300
Of their much inward woe that it with grief should see.
The *Danes*, a deadly blow supposing it to be,
Sent such an echoing shout that rent the troubled air.
The *English*, at the noise, wax'd all so wan with fear,
As though they lost the blood their agéd Champion shed :
Yet were not these so pale, but th' other were as red ; 306
As though the blood that fell, upon their cheeks had stay'd.
 Here *Guy*, his better spirits recalling to his aid,
Came fresh upon his foe ; when mighty *Colebrond* makes
Another desperate stroke : which *Guy* of *Warwick* takes 310
Undauntedly aloft ; and follow'd with a blow
Upon his shorter ribs, that the excessive flow
Stream'd up unto his hilts : the wound so gap'd withall,
As though it meant to say, ' Behold your Champion's fall
By this proud palmer's hand.' Such claps again and cries 315
The joyful *English* gave as cleft the very skies.
Which coming on along from these that were without,
When those within the town receiv'd this cheerful shout,
They answer'd them with like ; as those their joy that knew.
 Then with such eager blows each other they pursue, 320
As every offer made should threaten imminent death ;
Until, through heat and toil both hardly drawing breath,
They desperately do close. Look how two boars, being set
Together side to side, their threat'ning tusks do whet,
And with their gnashing teeth their angry foam do bite, 325
Whilst still they should'ring seek, each other where to smite :

Thus stood those ireful knights; till flying back, at length
The palmer, of the two the first recovering strength,
Upon the left arm lent great *Colebrond* such a wound,
That whilst his weapon's point fell well-near to the ground,
And slowly he it rais'd, the valiant *Guy* again   331
Sent through his cloven scalp his blade into his brain.
When downward went his head, and up his heels he threw;
As wanting hands to bid his Countrymen adieu.
   The *English* part, which thought an end he would have
      made,   335
And seeming as they much would in his praise have said,
He bade them yet forbear, whilst he pursu'd his fame
That to this passéd King next in succession came;
That great and puissant knight (in whose victorious days
Those knight-like deeds were done, no less deserving praise)
Brave *Edmond, Edward's* son, that *Stafford* having ta'en,   341
With as successful speed won *Darby* from the *Dane.*
From *Lester* then again, and *Lincoln* at the length,
Drave out the *Dacian* Powers by his resistless strength:
And this his *England* clear'd beyond that raging Flood,*   345
Which that proud King of *Hunnes* once christ'ned with his
      blood.
By which, great *Edmond's* power apparantly was shown,
The Land from *Humber* South recovering for his own;
That *Edgar* after him so much disdain'd the *Dane*
Unworthy of a war that should disturb his reign,   350
As generally he seem'd regardless of their hate.
And studying every way magnificence in State,
At *Chester* whilst he liv'd at more than kingly charge,
Eight tributary Kings[1] there row'd him in his barge:
His shores from pirates' sack the King that strongly
      kept: 355
§ A *Neptune,* whose proud sails the *British* Ocean swept.

    * *Humber.*   [1] See to the Tenth Song.

THE TWELFTH SONG.

But after his decease, when his more hopeful son,
§ By cruel stepdame's hate, to death was lastly done,
To set his rightful Crown upon a wrongful head
(When by thy fatal curse, licentious *Etheldred*,   360
Through dissoluteness, sloth, and thy abhorréd life,
As grievous were thy sins, so were thy sorrows rife)
The *Dane*, possessing all, the *English* forc'd to bear
A heavier yoke than first those heathen slaveries were;
Subjected, bought, and sold, in that most wretched plight,   365
As even their thraldom seem'd their neighbours to affright.
Yet could not all their plagues the *English* height abate:
But even in their low'st ebb, and miserablest state,
Courageously themselves they into action put,
§ And in one night, the throats of all the *Danish* cut.   370
And when in their revenge, the most insatiate *Dane*
Unshipp'd them on our shores, under their puissant *Swane :*
And swoll'n with hate and ire, their huge unwieldy force,
Came clust'ring like the *Greeks* out of the Wooden-horse:
And the *Norfolcian* towns, the near'st unto the East,   375
With sacrilege and rape did terriblest infest;
Those *Danes* yet from the shores we with such violence drave,
That from our swords, their ships could them but hardly save.
And to renew the war, that year ensuing, when
With fit supplies for spoil, they landed here again,   380
And all the Southern shores from *Kent* to *Cornwall* spread,
With those disord'red troops by *Alaffe* hither led,
In seconding their *Swane*, which cry'd to them for aid;
Their multitudes so much sad *Ethelred* dismay'd,
As from his Country forc'd the wretched King to fly.   385
An *English* yet there was, when *England* seem'd to lie
Under the heaviest yoke that ever kingdom bore,
Who wash'd his secret knife in *Swane's* relentless gore,
Whilst (swelling in excess) his lavish cups he ply'd.
Such means t' redeem themselves th' afflicted Nation try'd.

And when courageous *Knute*, th' late murther'd *Swanus'* son,
Came in t' revenge that act on his great father done,   392
He found so rare a spirit that here against him rose,
As though ordain'd by Heaven his greatness to oppose :
Who with him foot to foot, and face to face durst stand.   395
When *Knute*, which here alone affected the command,
The Crown upon his head at fair *South-hampton* set :
And *Edmond*, loth to lose what *Knute* desir'd to get,
At *London* caus'd himself inaugurate to be.
King *Knute* would conquer all, King *Edmond* would be free.

The Kingdom is the prize for which they both are prest :
And with their equal powers both meeting in the West,   402
The green *Dorsetian* fields a deep vermilion dy'd :
Where *Gillingham* gave way to their great hosts (in pride)
Abundantly their blood that each on other spent.   405
But *Edmond*, on whose side that day the better went
(And with like fortune thought the remnant to suppress
That *Sarum* then besieg'd, which was in great distress)
With his victorious troops to *Salisbury* retires :
When with fresh bleeding wounds, *Knute*, as with fresh
     desires,   410
Whose might though somewhat maim'd, his mind yet un-
     subdu'd,
His lately conquering Foe courageously pursu'd :
And finding out a way, sent to his friends with speed,
Who him supply'd with aid : and being help'd at need,
Tempts *Edmond* still to fight, still hoping for a day.   415
  Towards *Worstershire* their powers both well upon their way,
There, falling to the field, in a continual fight
Two days the angry hosts still parted were by night :
Where twice the rising sun, and twice the setting, saw
Them with their equal wounds their wearied breath to draw.
Great *London* to surprise, then (next) *Canutus* makes : 421
And thitherward as fast King *Edmond Ironside* takes.

Whilst *Knute* set down his siege before the Eastern gate,
King *Edmond* through the West pass'd in triumphal state.
But this courageous King, that scornéd, in his pride,   425
A town should be besieg'd wherein he did abide,
Into the fields again the valiant *Edmond* goes.
Kanutus, yet that hopes to win what he did lose,
Provokes him still to fight: and falling back where they
Might field-roomth find at large, their ensigns to display,   430
Together flew again: that *Brentford*, with the blood
Of *Danes* and *English* mix'd, discolour'd long time stood,
Let *Edmond*, as before, went victor still away.
    When soon that valiant *Knute*, whom nothing could dismay,
Recall'd his scatter'd troops, and into *Essex* hies,   435
Where (as ill-fortune would) the *Dane* with fresh supplies
Was lately come a-land, to whom brave *Ironside* makes;
But *Knute* to him again as soon fresh courage takes:
And Fortune (as herself) determining to show
That she could bring an ebb on valiant *Edmond's* flow,   440
And eas'ly cast him down from off the top of chance,
By turning of her wheel, *Canutus* doth advance.
Where she beheld that Prince which she had favour'd long
(Even in her proud despite) his murther'd troops among
With sweat and blood besmear'd (Dukes, Earls, and Bishops
    slain,   445
In that most dreadful day, when all went to the *Dane*)
Through worlds of dangers wade; and with his sword and
    shield,
Such wonders there to act as made her in the Field
Ashaméd of herself, so brave a spirit as he
By her unconstant hand should so much wrongéd be.   450
    But, having lost the day, to *Glocester* he draws,
To raise a second power in his slain soldiers' cause.
When late-encourag'd *Knute*, whilst fortune yet doth last,
Who oft from *Ironside* fled, now follow'd him as fast.

Whilst thus in Civil Arms continually they toil, 455
And what th' one strives to make, the other seeks to spoil,
With threat'ning swords still drawn; and with obnoxious
    hands
Attending their revenge, whilst either enemy stands,
One man amongst the rest from this confusion breaks,
And to the ireful Kings with courage boldly speaks: 460
    Yet cannot all this blood your ravenous out-rage fill?
Is there no law, no bound, to your ambitious will,
But what your swords admit? as Nature did ordain
Our lives for nothing else, but only to maintain
Your murthers, sack, and spoil? If by this wasteful war 465
The land unpeopled lie, some nation shall from far,
By ruin of you both, into the Isle be brought,
Obtaining that for which you twain so long have fought.
Unless then through your thirst of empery you mean
Both nations in these broils shall be extinguish'd clean, 470
Select you champions fit, by them to prove your right,
Or try it man to man yourselves in single fight.
    When as those warlike Kings, provok'd with courage high,
It willingly accept in person by and by.
And whilst they them prepare, the shapeless concourse grows
In little time so great, that their unusual flows 476
Surrounded *Severne's* banks, whose stream amazéd stood,
Her *Birlich* to behold, in-isléd with her flood,
That with refulgent Arms then flaméd; whilst the Kings,
Whose rage out of the hate of either's empire springs, 480
Both arméd, *cap-à-pe*, upon their barréd horse
Together fiercely flew; that in their violent course
(Like thunder when it speaks most horribly and loud,
Tearing the full-stuff'd panch of some congealéd cloud)
Their strong hoofs strook the earth: and with the fearful
    shock, 485
Their spears in splinters flew, their bevers both unlock.

Canutus, of the two that furthest was from hope,
Who found with what a foe his fortune was to cope,
Cries, 'Noble *Edmond*, hold ; Let us the Land divide.'
Here th' *English* and the *Danes*, from either equal side 490
Were echoes to his words, and all aloud do cry,
'Courageous Kings divide ; 'twere pity such should die.'
 When now the neighbouring Floods will'd *Wrekin* to suppress
His style, or they were like to surfeit with excess.
And time had brought about, that now they all began 495
To listen to a long-told prophecy, which ran
Of *Moreland*, that she might live prosperously to see
A River born of her, who well might reckon'd be
The third of this large Isle : which saw did first arise
From *Arden*, in those days delivering prophecies. 500
 The *Druids* (as some say) by her instructed were.
In many secret skills she had been conn'd her lere.
The ledden of the birds most perfectly she knew :
And also from their flight strange auguries she drew ;
Supremest in her place : whose circuit was extent 505
From *Avon* to the banks of *Severne* and to *Trent :*
Where Empress-like she sat with Nature's bounties blest,
And serv'd by many a Nymph ; but two, of all the rest,
That *Staffordshire* calls hers, there both of high account.
The eld'st of which is *Canke :* though *Needwood* her surmount, 510
In excellence of soil, by being richly plac'd
Twixt *Trent* and batning *Dove ;* and, equally imbrac'd
By their abounding banks, participates their store ;
Of *Britain's* Forests all (from th' less unto the more)
For fineness of her turf surpassing ; and doth bear 515
Her curlèd head so high, that Forests far and near
Oft grutch at her estate ; her flourishing to see,
Of all their stately tires disrobèd when they be.

9—2

But (as the world goes now) o woful *Canke* the while,
As brave a Wood-Nymph once as any of this Isle;   520
Great *Arden's* eldest child : which, in her mother's ground
Before fair *Feck'nham's* self, her old age might have crown'd ;
When as those fallow deer, and huge-hanch'd stags that graz'd
Upon her shaggy heaths, the passenger amaz'd   524
To see their mighty herds, with high-palm'd heads to threat
The woods of o'ergrown oaks ; as though they meant to set
Their horns to th' others' heights. But now, both those
        and these
Are by vile gain devour'd : So abject are our days.
She now, unlike herself, a neatherd's life doth live,
And her dejected mind to country cares doth give.   530
  But Muse, thou seem'st to leave the *Morelands* too too long :
Of whom report may speak (our mighty wastes among)
She from her chilly site, as from her barren feed,
For body, horn, and hair, as fair a beast doth breed
As scarcely this great Isle can equal : then of her,   535
Why should'st thou all this while the prophecy defer?
Who bearing many springs, which pretty Rivers grew,
She could not be content, until she fully knew
Which child it was of hers (born under such a fate)
As should in time be rais'd unto that high estate.   540
(I fain would have you think, that this was long ago,
When many a River, now that furiously doth flow,
Had scarcely learn'd to creep) and therefore she doth will
Wise *Arden*, from the depth of her abundant skill,
To tell her which of these her Rills it was she meant.   545
To satisfy her will ; the Wizard answers, *Trent.*
For, as a skilful seer, the aged Forest wist,
A more than usual power did in that name consist,
Which thirty doth import[1] ; by which she thus divin'd,
There should be found in her, of Fishes thirty kind ;   550

[1] *Trent signifieth thirty.*

THE TWELFTH SONG.   133

And thirty Abbeys great, in places fat and rank,
Should in succeeding time be builded on her bank;
And thirty several Streams from many a sundry way,
Unto her greatness should their wat'ry tribute pay.
   This, *Moreland* greatly lik'd : yet in that tender love,   555
Which she had ever borne unto her darling *Dove*,
She could have wish'd it his : because the dainty grass
That grows upon his bank, all other doth surpass.
But, subject he must be : as *Sow*, which from her spring,
At *Stafford* meeteth *Penk*, which she along doth bring   560
To *Trent* by *Tixall* grac'd, *the* Astons' *ancient seat;*
Which oft the Muse hath found her safe and sweet retreat.
The noble owners now of which beloved place,
Good fortunes them and theirs with honour'd titles grace:
May Heav'n still bless that House, till happy Floods you see   565
Yourselves more grac'd by it, than it by you can be.
Whose bounty still my Muse so freely shall confess,
As when she shall want words, her signs shall it express.
   So *Blyth* bears eas'ly down tow'rds her dear Sovereign
      Trent:
But nothing in the world gives *Moreland* such content   570
As her own darling *Dove* his confluence to behold
Of Floods in sundry strains : as, crankling *Many-fold*
The first that lends him force : of whose meand'red ways,
And labyrinth-like turns (as in the moors she strays)
She first receiv'd her name, by growing strangely mad,   575
O'ergone with love of *Hanse*, a dapper moorland lad.
Who near their crystal springs as in those wastes they
      play'd,
Bewitch'd the wanton heart of that delicious maid :
Which instantly was turn'd so much from being coy,
That she might seem to dote upon the moorish boy.   580
Who closely stole away (perceiving her intent)
With his dear lord the *Dove*, in quest of princely *Trent*,

With many other Floods (as, *Churnet*, in his train
That draweth *Dunsmore* on, with *Yendon*, then clear *Taine*,
That comes alone to *Dove*) of which, *Hanse* one would be,   585
And for himself he fain of *Many-fold* would free
Thinking this amorous Nymph by some means to beguile)
He closely under earth conveys his head awhile.
But, when the River fears some policy of his,
And her belovéd *Hanse* immediately doth miss,   590
Distracted in her course, improvidently rash,
She oft against the cleeves her crystal front doth dash :
Now forward, then again she backward seems to bear ;
As, like to lose herself by straggling here and there.
   Hanse, that this while suppos'd him quite out of her sight,
No sooner thrusts his head into the cheerful light,   595
But *Many-fold* that still the runaway doth watch,
Him (ere he was aware) about the neck doth catch :
And, as the angry *Hanse* would fain her hold remove,
They struggling tumble down into their lord, the *Dove*.   600
   Thus though th' industrious Muse hath been imploy'd so
      long,
Yet is she loth to do poor little *Smestall* wrong,
That from her *Wilfrune's* spring near *Hampton* plies, to pour
The wealth she there receives, into her friendly *Stowr*.
Nor shall the little *Bourne* have cause the Muse to blame,   605
From these *Staffordian* Heaths that strives to catch the *Tame:*
Whom she in her next Song shall greet with mirthful cheer,
So happily arriv'd now in her native Shire.

ILLUSTRATIONS.

AKING her progress into the land, the Muse comes Southward from *Cheshire* into adjoining *Stafford*, and that part of *Shropshire*, which lies in the *English* side, East from *Severne*.

96. *And into lesser streams the spacious Current cut.*

In that raging devastation over this Kingdom by the *Danes*, they had gotten divers of their ships fraught with provision out of *Thames* into the river *Ley* (which divides *Middlesex* and *Essex*) some twenty miles from *London*; *Alfred* holding his tents near that territory, especially to prevent their spoil of the instant harvest, observed that by dividing the river, then navigable between them and *Thames*, their ships would be grounded, and themselves bereft of what confidence their navy had promised them. He thought it, and did it, by parting the water into three channels. The *Danes* betook themselves to flight, their ships left as a prey to the *Londoners*.

120. *Her lord's imbraces vow'd she never more would know.*

This *Alured* left his son *Edward* successor, and, among other children, this *Elfled*, or *Ethelfled* his daughter, married to *Ethelred* Earl of *Merc-land.* Of *Alfred's* worth and troublous reign, because here the Author leaves him, I offer you these of an ancient *English* wit:

Nobilitas innata tibi probitatis honorem
Armipotens Alfrede *dedit, probitasque laborem*
Perpetuumque labor nomen. Cui mixta dolori
Gaudia semper erant, spes semper mista timori.
Si modo victor eras, ad crastina bella parebas:
Si modo victus eras, ad crastina bella parabas.
Cui restes sudore jugi, cui sicca cruore
Tincta jugi, quantum sit onus regnare probârunt.

Huntingdon cites these as his own; and if he deal plainly with us (I doubted it because his MS. epigrams, which make in some copies the eleventh and twelfth of his History, are of most different strain, and seem made when *Apollo* was either angry, or had not leisure to overlook them) he shows his Muse (as also in another written by him upon *Edgar,* beginning *Auctor opum, vindex scelerum, largitor honorum, &c.*) in that still declining time of learning's state, worthy of much precedence. Of *Ethelfled* in *William* of *Malmesbury,* is the *Latin* of this *English: She was the love of the subject, fear of the enemy, a woman of a mighty heart; having once endured the grievous pains of child-birth, ever afterward denied her husband those sweeter desires; protesting, that, yielding indulgence towards a pleasure, having so much consequent pain, was unseemly in a King's daughter.* She was buried at S. *Peter's* in *Glocester;* her name loaden by Monks with numbers of her excellencies.

125. *And* Constantine *their King, an hostage hither brought.*

After he had taken *Wales* and *Scotland* (as our Historians say) from *Howel, Malmesbury* calls him *Ludwal,* and *Con-*

*stantine**; he restored presently their Kingdoms, affirming, that, *it was more for his majesty to make a King than be one.* The *Scottish* stories[1] are not agreeing here with ours; against whom *Buchanan* storms, for affirming what I see not how he is so well able to confute, as they to justify. And for matter of that nature, I rather send you to the collections in *Ed.* I. by *Thomas* of *Walsingham*, and thence for the same and other to *Edw. Hall's Hen.* VIII.

356. *A* Neptune, *whose proud sails the* British Ocean *swept.*

That flower and delight of the *English* world, in whose birth-time S. *Dunstane* (as is said) at *Glastenbury*, heard this Angelical voice† :

𝕿𝖔 𝖍𝖔𝖑𝖕 𝕮𝖍𝖚𝖗𝖈𝖍 𝖆𝖓𝖉 𝖙𝖔 𝖙𝖍𝖊 𝕷𝖔𝖗𝖉 𝕻𝖆𝖞𝖘 𝖎𝖘 𝖞𝖇𝖔𝖗𝖊 𝖆𝖓𝖉 𝖇𝖑𝖎𝖘
𝕭𝖞 𝖙𝖍𝖚𝖑𝖐𝖊 𝕮𝖍𝖎𝖑𝖉𝖘 𝖙𝖎𝖒𝖊, 𝖙𝖍𝖆𝖙 𝖓𝖔𝖚𝖙𝖍𝖊 𝖞𝖇𝖔𝖗𝖊 𝖎𝖘,

(among his other innumerable benefits, and royal cares) had a Navy of 3600‡ sail; which by tripartite division in the East, West, and Northern coasts, both defended what was subject to pirates' rapine, and so made strong his own nation against the enemies' invasion.

358. *By cruel* stepdame's hate *to death was lastly done.*

Edgar had by one woman (his greatest stains showed themselves in this variety and unlawful obtaining of lustful sensuality, as Stories will tell you, in that of Earl *Ethelwald*, the Nun *Wulfrith*, and the young lass of *Andever*) called *Egelfled*, surnamed *Ened*, daughter to *Odmer* a great nobleman, *Edward;* and by Queen *Elfrith*, daughter to *Orgar* Earl of *Devonshire*, *Ethelred* of some seven years age at his death. That, *Egelfled* was a professed Nun,[2] some have

---

* 926.   [1] Hector. Booth. lib. 11. et Buchanan. Hist. 6. reg. 85.
† Rob. Glocestrens.   ‡ Some say 4000.
[2] Ex Osberno in Vitâ Dunstan. Fox. Eccles. Hist. 4.

argued and so make *Ethelred* the only legitimate heir to the Crown: nor do I think that, except *Alfrith*, he was married to any of the ladies on whom he got children. *Edward* was anointed King (for in those days was that use of Anointing among the *Saxon* Princes,[1] and began in King *Alfred*) but not without disliking grudges of his stepmother's faction, which had nevertheless in substance, what his vain name only of King pretended: but her bloody hate, bred out of womanish ambition, straining to every point of sovereignty, not thus satisfied, compelled in her this cruelty.* King *Edward* not suspecting her dissembled purposes, with simple kindness of an open nature, wearied after the chase in *Purbeck* Isle in *Dorsetshire*, without guard or attendance, visits her at *Corfe Castle;* she, under sweet words and saluting kisses, palliating her hellish design, entertains him: but while he being very hot and thirsty (without imagination of treason) was in pledging her, she, or one of her appointed servants,† stabbed the innocent King. His corpse, within little space expiring its last breath, was buried at *Warham*, thence afterward by *Alfer* Earl of *Merc-land*, translated into *Shaftsbury*, which (as to the Second Song I note) was hereby for a time called S. *Edward's*.[2] Thus did his brother-in-law *Ethelred* (according to wicked *Elfrith's* cruel and traitorous project) succeed him. As, of *Constantine Copronymus*, the *Greeks*, so, of this *Ethelred*, is affirmed, that, in his holy tincture he abused the Font with natural excrements, which made S. *Dunstan*, then Christening him, angrily exclaim, *Per Deum et Matrem Ejus, ignavus homo erit*.‡ Some ten years of age was he, when his brother *Edward* was slain, and, out of childish affection, wept for him bitterly; which his mother extremely disliking, being author of the murther

---

[1] Anointed Princes.　　　　　　　* 978.
† Vide Malmesb. lib. 2. cap. 9. et Huntingdon. Hist. 5.
[2] Malmesb. Lib. de Pontific. 2.
‡ By *God* and His Mother, he will be a slovenly fellow.

only for his sake, most cruelly beat him herself with an handful of wax,[1]

——————————— Candlen long and towe
Heo* ne bileued noght ar he lay at hir bet pswowe:†
War thorn this child afterward such hey mon as he was
Was the worse wan he pscp‡ Candlen bor this cas.

But I have read it affirmed,[2] that *Ethelred* never would endure any wax candles, because he had seen his mother unmercifully with them whip the good S. *Edward*. It's not worth one of the candles, which be the truer; I incline to the first. To expiate all, she afterward built two Nunneries, one at *Werwell*, the other at *Ambresbury;* and by all means of Penitence and Satisfaction (as the doctrine then directed) endeavoured her freedom out of this horrible offence.

370. *And in one night the throats of all the* Danish *cut.*

History, not this place, must inform the reader of more particulars of the *Danes;* and let him see to the First Song. But, for this slaughter, I thus ease his inquisition. *Ethelred* (after multitudes of miseries, long continued through their exactions and devastations, being so large, that sixteen Shires had endured their cruel and even conquering spoils) in the twenty-third of his reign,[3] strengthened with provoking hopes, grounded on alliance, which, by marriage with *Emma*, daughter of *Richard* I. Duke of *Normandy*, he had with his neighbour potentate, sent privy letters into every place of note, where the *Danes* by truce peaceably resided, to the *English*, commanding them, all as one, on the self-same day and hour appointed (the day was S. *Brictius*, that is, the 13th of *November*) suddenly to put them, as re-

[1] Rob. Glocestrensis.   * She.   † Feet in woe.   ‡ Saw.
[2] Vit. S. Edwardi apud Ranulph. Cestrens. lib. 6.   [3] 1002.

spective occasion best fitted, to fire or sword; which was performed.

A Chronological order and descent of the Kings here included in *Wrekin's* Song.

Anno Christi

800   *Egbert* son to *Inegild* (others call him *Alhmund*) grandchild to King *Ine*. After him* scarce any, none long, had the name of King in the Isle, but Governors or Earls; the common titles being *Duces, Comites, Consules*, and such like; which in some writers after the Conquest were indifferent names, and *William* the First is often called Earl of *Normandy*.

836   *Ethelulph* son to *Egbert*.

855   *Ethelbald* and *Ethelbert*, sons to *Ethelulph*, dividing their Kingdom, according to their father's testament.

860   *Ethelbert* alone, after *Ethelbald's* death.

866   *Ethelred*, third son of *Ethelulph*.

871   *Alfred* youngest son to *Ethelulph*, brought up at *Rome;* and there, in *Ethelred's* life-time, anointed by Pope *Leo* IV. as in ominous hope of his future Kingdom.

901   *Edward* I. surnamed in Story *Senior*,† son to *Alfred*.

924   *Athelstan*, eldest son to *Edward*, by *Egwine* a shepherd's daughter; but to whom beauty and noble spirit denied, what base parentage required. She, before the King lay with her,

---

* See to the last Song before. Because in *Westsex* all the rest were at last confounded. These are most commonly written Kings of *Westsex*, although in *Seigniory* (as it were) or, as the Civilians call it, *Direct Property*, all the other Provinces (except some Northern, and what the *Danes* unjustly possessed) were theirs.   † The elder.

THE TWELFTH SONG. 141

Anno Christi

dreamed (you remember that of *Olympias*, and many such like) that out of her womb did shine a Moon, enlightening all *England*, which in her Birth (*Athelstan*) proved true.

940   *Edmund* I. son of *Edward** by his Queen *Edgive*.
946   *Edred* brother to *Edmund*.
955   *Edwy* first son of *Edmund*.
959   *Edgar* (second son of *Edmund*) *Honor ac Deliciæ Anglorum*.†
975   *Edward* II. son to *Edgar* by *Egelfled*, murdered by his stepmother *Alfrith*, and thence called S. *Edward*.
979   *Ethelred* II. son to *Edgar*, by Queen *Alfrith*, daughter to *Orgar* Earl of *Devonshire*.
1016   *Edmund* II. son to *Ethelred* by his first wife *Elfgive*, surnamed *Ironside*.

Between him and *Cnut* (or *Canutus*) the *Dane*, son to *Swaine*, was that intended single combat; so by their own particular fortunes, to end the miseries, which the *English* soil bore recorded in very great characters, written with streams of her children's blood. It properly here breaks off; for (the composition being, that *Edmund* should have his part *Westsex*, *Estsex*, *Estangle*, *Middlesex*, *Surrey*, *Kent*, and *Sussex*; and the *Dane* (who durst not fight it out, but first moved for a treaty) *Merc-land* and the *Northern* territories) *Edmund* died the same year (some report was, that traitorous *Edric Streona* Earl of *Merc-land* poisoned him) leaving sons *Edmund* and *Edward*; but they were, by *Danish* ambition, and traitorous perjury of the unnatural

---

* Malè enim et ineptè Veremundi sequax Hector ille Boeth. lib. II qui Edm. et Eirelum Æthelstano scribit prognatos.
† The M. s. in of his subjects.

English State, disinherited, and all the Kingdom cast under *Cnut*. After him reigned his son *Harold* I. *Lightfoot* a shoemaker's son* (but dissembled, as begotten by him on his Queen *Alfgive*): then, with *Harold*, *Hardcnut*, whom he had by his wife *Emma*, King *Ethelred's* Dowager. So that from *Edmund*, of *Saxon* blood (to whose glory *Wrekin* hath dedicated his endeavour; and therefore should transcend his purpose, if he exceeded their empire) until *Edward* the *Confessor*, following *Hardcnut*, son to *Ethelred*, by the same Queen *Emma*, the Kingdom continued under *Danish* Princes.

* Marian. Scot. et Florent. Wigorn.

THE THIRTEENTH SONG.

THE ARGUMENT.

This Song our Shire of Warwick sounds;
Revives old Arden's ancient bounds.
Through many shapes the Muse here roves;
Now sporting in those shady Groves,
The tunes of Birds oft stays to hear: 5
Then, finding herds of lusty Deer,
She huntress-like the Hart pursues;
And like a Hermit walks, to chuse
The Simples ev'rywhere that grow;
Comes Ancor's glory next to show; 10
Tells Guy of Warwick's famous deeds;
To th' Vale of Red-horse then proceeds,
To play her part the rest among;
There shutteth up her Thirteenth Song.

UPON the Mid-lands[1] now th' industrious Muse doth
    fall ;
That Shire which we the Heart of *England* well
    may call,
As she herself extends (the midst which is decreed)
Betwixt S. *Michael's Mount,* and *Barwick*-bord'ring *Tweed,*

    [1] *Warwickshire,* the middle Shire of *England.*

Brave *Warwick;* that abroad so long advanc'd her Bear,* 5
§ By her illustrious Earls renownéd everywhere;
Above her neighbouring Shires which always bore her head.
   My native Country then, which so brave spirits hast bred,
If there be virtue yet remaining in thy earth,
Or any good of thine thou breath'd'st into my birth, 10
Accept it as thine own whilst now I sing of thee;
Of all thy later Brood th' unworthiest though I be.
   Muse, first of *Arden* tell, whose footsteps yet are found
In her rough wood-lands more than any other ground
§ That mighty *Arden* held even in her height of pride; 15
Her one hand touching *Trent,* the other *Severne's* side.[1]
   The very sound of these, the Wood-Nymphs doth awake:
When thus of her ownself the ancient Forest spake:
   My many goodly sites when first I came to show,
Here opened I the way to mine own overthrow: 20
For, when the world found out the fitness of my soil,
The gripple wretch began immediately to spoil
My tall and goodly woods, and did my grounds inclose:
By which, in little time my bounds I came to lose.
   When *Britain* first her fields with Villages had fill'd, 25
Her people wexing still, and wanting where to build,
They oft dislodg'd the hart, and set their houses, where
He in the broom and brakes had long time made his lair.
Of all the Forests here within this mighty Isle,
If those old *Britans* then me Sovereign did instyle, 30
I needs must be the great'st; for greatness 'tis alone
That gives our kind the place: else were there many a one
For pleasantness of shade that far doth me excell.
But, of our Forests' kind the quality to tell,
We equally partake with wood-land as with plain, 35
Alike with hill and dale; and every day maintain

   * The ancient Coat of that Earldom.
   [1] Divers Towns expressing her name: as *Henly* in *Arden, Hampton* in *Arden,* &c.

The sundry kinds of beasts upon our copious wastes,
That men for profit breed, as well as those of chase.
   Here *Arden* of herself ceas'd any more to show ;
And with her sylvan joys the Muse along doth go.   40
   When *Phœbus* lifts his head out of the Winter's wave,
No sooner doth the earth her flowery bosom brave,
At such time as the year brings on the pleasant Spring,
But Hunts-up to the Morn the feath'red *Sylvans* sing :
And in the lower grove, as on the rising knole,   45
Upon the highest spray of every mounting pole,
Those Quiristers are perch'd with many a speckled breast.
Then from her burnish'd gate the goodly glitt'ring East
Gilds every lofty top, which late the humorous Night
Bespangled had with pearl, to please the Morning's sight :   50
On which the mirthful Quires, with their clear open throats,
Unto the joyful Morn so strain their warbling notes,
That hills and valleys ring, and even the echoing air
Seems all compos'd of sounds, about them everywhere.
The *Throstell*, with shrill sharps ; as purposely he song   55
T' awake the lustless Sun ; or chiding, that so long
He was in coming forth, that should the thickets thrill :
The *Woosell* near at hand, that hath a golden bill ;
As Nature him had mark'd of purpose, t' let us see
That from all other birds his tunes should different be :   60
For, with their vocal sounds, they sing to pleasant May ;
Upon his dulcet pipe the *Merle* doth only play.[1]
When in the lower brake, the *Nightingale* hard-by,
In such lamenting strains the joyful hours doth ply,
As though the other birds she to her tunes would draw.   65
And, but that Nature (by her all-constraining law)
Each bird to her own kind this season doth invite,
They else, alone to hear that Charmer of the Night
(The more to use their ears) their voices sure would spare,

    [1] Of all Birds, only the *Blackbird* whistleth.

That moduleth her tunes so admirably rare, 70
As man to set in parts, at first had learn'd of her.
  To *Philomell* the next, the *Linnet* we prefer;
And by that warbling bird, the *Wood-Lark* place we then,
The *Reed-sparrow*, the *Nope*, the *Red-breast*, and the *Wren*,
The *Yellow-pate*: which though she hurt the blooming tree, 75
Yet scarce hath any bird a finer pipe than she.
And of these chanting fowls, the *Goldfinch* not behind,
That hath so many sorts descending from her kind.
The *Tydie* for her notes as delicate as they,
The laughing *Hecco*, then the counterfeiting *Jay*, 80
The softer, with the shrill (some hid among the leaves,
Some in the taller trees, some in the lower greaves)
Thus sing away the Morn, until the mounting sun,
Through thick exhaléd fogs, his golden head hath run,
And through the twisted tops of our close covert creeps 85
To kiss the gentle shade, this while that sweetly sleeps.
  And near to these our thicks, the wild and frightful herds,
Not hearing other noise but this of chatt'ring birds,
Feed fairly on the launds; both sorts of seasonéd *Deer*:
Here walk, the stately *Red*, the freckled *Fallow* there: 90
The *Bucks* and lusty *Stags* amongst the *Rascalls* strew'd,
As sometime gallant spirits amongst the multitude.
  Of all the beasts which we for our venerial name,*
The *Hart* amongst the rest, the hunter's noblest game:
Of which most princely chase sith none did e'er report, 95
Or by description touch, t' express that wond'rous sport
(Yet might have well beseem'd th' ancients' nobler songs)
To our old *Arden* here, most fitly it belongs:
Yet shall she not invoke the Muses to her aid;
But thee *Diana* bright, a Goddess and a maid: 100
In many a huge-grown wood, and many a shady grove,
Which oft hast borne thy bow (great Huntress) us'd to rove

* Of hunting, or Chase.

At many a cruel beast, and with thy darts to pierce
The *Lion*, *Panther*, *Ounce*, the *Bear*, and *Tiger* fierce ;
And following thy fleet game, chaste mighty forest's Queen,
With thy dishevell'd Nymphs attir'd in youthful green,   105
About the launds hast scour'd, and wastes both far and near,
Brave Huntress : but no beast shall prove thy quarries here ;
Save those the best of chase, the tall and lusty *Red*,
The *Stag* for goodly shape, and stateliness of head,   110
Is fitt'st to hunt at force.* For whom, when with his hounds
The labouring hunter tufts the thick unbarbéd grounds
Where harbour'd is the *Hart;* there often from his feed
The dogs of him do find ; or thorough skilful heed,
The huntsman by his slot,† or breaking earth, perceives,   115
Or ent'ring of the thick by pressing of the greaves
Where he hath gone to lodge. Now when the *Hart* doth hear
The often-bellowing hounds to vent his secret lair,
He rousing rusheth out, and through the brakes doth drive,
As though up by the roots the bushes he would rive.   120
And through the cumb'rous thicks, as fearfully he makes,
He with his branchéd head the tender saplings shakes,
That sprinkling their moist pearl do seem for him to weep ;
When after goes the cry, with yellings loud and deep,
That all the forest rings, and every neighbouring place :   125
And there is not a hound but falleth to the chase.
Rechating¹ with his horn, which then the hunter chears,
Whilst still the lusty *Stag* his high-palm'd head up-bears,
His body showing state, with unbent knees upright,
Expressing (from all beasts) his courage in his flight.   130
But when th' approaching foes still following he perceives,
That he his speed must trust, his usual walk he leaves ;
And o'er the champain flies : which when th' assembly find,

* A description of hunting the *Hart*. † The tract of the foot.
¹ One of the Measures in winding the horn.

Each follows, as his horse were footed with the wind.
But being then imbost, the noble stately deer   135
When he hath gotten ground (the kennel cast arere)
Doth beat the brooks and ponds for sweet refreshing soil :
That serving not, then proves if he his scent can foil,
And makes amongst the herds, and flocks of shag-wooll'd
    sheep,
Them frighting from the guard of those who had their keep.
But when as all his shifts his safety still denies,   141
Put quite out of his walk, the ways and fallows tries.
Whom when the plow-man meets, his team he letteth stand
T' assail him with his goad : so with his hook in hand,
The shepherd him pursues, and to his dog doth hallow : 145
When, with tempestuous speed, the hounds and huntsmen
    follow ;
Until the noble deer through toil bereav'd of strength,
His long and sinewy legs then failing him at length,
The villages attempts, enrag'd, not giving way
To anything he meets now at his sad decay.   150
The cruel rav'nous hounds and bloody hunters near,
This noblest beast of chase, that vainly doth but fear,
Some bank or quick-set finds : to which his haunch oppos'd,
He turns upon his foes, that soon have him inclos'd.
The churlish-throated hounds then holding him at bay,   155
And as their cruel fangs on his harsh skin they lay,
With his sharp-pointed head he dealeth deadly wounds.
    The hunter, coming in to help his wearied hounds,
He desp'rately assails ; until oppress'd by force,
He who the mourner is to his own dying corse,   160
Upon the ruthless earth his precious tears lets fall.[1]
    To Forests that belongs ; but yet this is not all :
With solitude what sorts, that here's not wondrous rife ?

[1] The *Hart* weepeth at his dying : his tears are held to be precious in medicine.

Whereas the Hermit leads a sweet retiréd life,
From villages replete with ragg'd and sweating clowns, 165
And from the loathsome airs of smoky citied towns.
Suppose twixt noon and night, the sun his halfway wrought[1]
(The shadows to be large, by his descending brought)
Who with a fervent eye looks through the twyring glades,
And his dispersèd rays commixeth with the shades, 170
Exhaling the milch dew, which there had tarried long,
And on the ranker grass till past the noon-sted hong;
When as the Hermit comes out of his homely Cell,
Where from all rude resort he happily doth dwell:[2]
Who in the strength of youth, a man-at-arms hath been; 175
Or one who of this world the vileness having seen,
Retires him from it quite: and with a constant mind
Man's beastliness so loths, that flying human kind,
The black and darksome nights, the bright and gladsome days
Indiff'rent are to him, his hope on God that stays. 180
Each little village yields his short and homely fare:
To gather wind-fall'n sticks, his great'st and only care;
Which every aged tree still yieldeth to his fire.
 This man, that is alone a King in his desire,
By no proud ignorant lord is basely over-aw'd, 185
Nor his false praise affects, who grossly being claw'd,
Stands like an itchy moyle; nor of a pin he weighs
What fools, abused Kings, and humorous ladies raise.
His free and noble thought, ne'er envies at the grace
That often-times is given unto a bawd most base, 190
Nor stirs it him to think on the impostor vile,
Who seeming what he's not, doth sensually beguile
The sottish purblind world: but absolutely free,
His happy time he spends the works of God to see,

---

[1] A description of the afternoon.
[2] Hermits have oft had their abodes by ways that lie through forests.

In those so sundry herbs which there in plenty grow : 195
Whose sundry strange effects he only seeks to know.
And in a little maund, being made of osiers small,
Which serveth him to do full many a thing withall,
He very choicely sorts his simples got abroad.
Here finds he on an oak rheum-purging *Polipode ;* 200
And in some open place that to the sun doth lie,
He *Fumitorie* gets, and *Eye-bright* for the eye :
The *Yarrow*, wherewithal he stops the wound-made gore :
The healing *Tutsan* then, and *Plantan* for a sore.
And hard by them again he holy *Vervaine* finds, 205
Which he about his head that hath the megrim binds.
The wonder-working *Dill* he gets not far from these,
Which curious women use in many a nice disease.
For them that are with newts, or snakes, or adders stong,
He seeketh out an herb that's calléd *Adders-tong ;* 210
As Nature it ordain'd, its own like hurt to cure,
And sportive did herself to niceties inure.
Valerian then he crops, and purposely doth stamp,
T' apply unto the place that's ailéd with the cramp.
As *Century*, to close the wideness of a wound : 215
The belly hurt by birth, by *Mugwort* to make sound.
His *Chickweed* cures the heat that in the face doth rise.

   For physick, some again he inwardly applies.
For comforting the spleen and liver, gets for juice,
Pale *Hore-hound*, which he holds of most especial use. 220
So *Saxifrage* is good, and *Hart's-tongue* for the stone,
With *Agrimony*, and that herb we call S. *John*.
To him that hath a flux, of *Shepherd's-purse* he gives ;
And *Mouse-ear* unto him whom some sharp rupture grieves.
And for the labouring wretch that's troubled with a cough,
Or stopping of the breath, by fleagm that's hard and tough,
Campana here he crops, approvéd wondrous good : 227
As *Comfrey* unto him that's bruiséd, spitting blood ;

And from the falling-ill, by *Five-leaf* doth restore;
And melancholy cures by sovereign *Hellebore*. 230
   Of these most helpful herbs yet tell we but a few,
To those unnumb'red sorts of simples here that grew.
Which justly to set down, even *Dodon*[1] short doth fall;
Nor skilful *Gerard*,[1] yet, shall ever find them all.
   But from our Hermit here the Muse we must inforce, 235
And zealously proceed in our intended course:
How *Arden* of her Rills and Riverets doth dispose;
By *Alcester* how *Alne* to *Arro* eas'ly flows;
And mildly being mix'd, to *Avon* hold their way:
And likewise tow'rd the North, how lively-tripping *Rhea*, 240
T' attend the lustier *Tame*, is from her fountain sent:
So little *Cole* and *Blyth* go on with him to *Trent*.
His *Tamworth* at the last, he in his way doth win:
There playing him awhile, till *Ancor* should come in,
Which trifleth 'twixt her banks, observing state, so slow, 245
As though into his arms she scorn'd herself to throw:
Yet *Arden* will'd her *Tame* to serve her* on his knee;
For by that Nymph alone, they both should honour'd be.
The Forest so much fall'n from what she was before,
That to her former height Fate could her not restore; 250
Though oft in her behalf, the *Genius* of the Land
Importunéd the Heavens with an auspicious hand.
Yet granted at the last (the aged Nymph to grace)
They by a Lady's birth would more renown that place
Than if her Woods their heads above the Hills should seat;
And for that purpose, first made *Coventry* so great 255
(A poor thatch'd village then, or scarcely none at all,
That could not once have dream'd of her now stately wall),
§ And thither wisely brought that goodly Virgin-band,
Th' Eleven thousand maids, chaste *Ursula's* Command, 260
Whom then the *Britan* Kings gave her full power to press,

[1] The Authors of two famous Herbals.   * *Ancor*.

For matches to their friends in *Brittany* the less.
At whose departure thence, each by her just bequest
Some special virtue gave, ordaining it to rest
With one of their own sex, that there her birth should have,
Till fulness of the time which Fate did choicely save ;   266
Until the *Saxons'* reign, when *Coventry* at length,
From her small mean regard, recovered state and strength,
§ By *Leofric* her Lord yet in base bondage held,
The people from her marts by tollage who expell'd :   270
Whose Duchess, which desir'd this tribute to release,
Their freedom often begg'd. The Duke, to make her cease,
Told her that if she would his loss so far inforce,
His will was, she should ride stark nak'd upon a horse
By daylight through the street: which certainly he thought,
In her heroic breast so deeply would have wrought,   276
That in her former suit she would have left to deal.
But that most princely Dame, as one devour'd with zeal,
Went on, and by that mean the City clearly freed.

    The first part of whose name, Godiva, *doth foreread*   280
Th' first syllable of hers, and Goodere *half doth sound;*
For by agreeing words, great matters have been found.
But further than this place the mystery extends.
What Arden *had begun, in* Ancor *lastly ends:*
For in the British *tongue, the* Britans *could not find,*   285
Wherefore to her that name of Ancor *was assign'd:*
Nor yet the Saxons *since, nor times to come had known,*
But that her being here, was by this name foreshown,
As prophesying her. For, as the first did tell
Her Sirname, so again doth Ancor *lively spell*   290
Her Christen'd title Anne. *And as those Virgins there*
Did sanctify that place: so holy Edith *here*
A Recluse long time liv'd, in that fair Abbey plac'd
Which Alured *enrich'd, and* Powlesworth *highly grac'd.*
A Princess being born, and Abbess, with those Maids,   295

All noble like herself, in bidding of their beads
Their holiness bequeath'd, upon her to descend
Which there should after live: in whose dear self should end
Th' intent of Ancor's *name, her coming that decreed,*
As hers (her place of birth) fair Coventry *that freed.* 300

But whilst about this tale smooth *Ancor* trifling stays,
Unto the lustier *Tame* as loth to come her ways,
The Flood intreats her thus: Dear Brook, why dost thou wrong
Our mutual love so much, and tediously prolong
Our mirthful marriage-hour, for which I still prepare? 305
Haste to my broader banks, my joy and only care.
For as of all my Floods thou art the first in fame;
When frankly thou shalt yield thine honour to my name,
I will protect thy state: then do not wrong thy kind. 309
What pleasure hath the world that here thou may'st not find?

Hence, Muse, divert thy course to *Dunsmore*, by that Cross[1]
Where those two mighty ways,[2] the *Watling* and the *Fosse*,
Our Centre seem to cut. (The first doth hold her way,
From *Dover*, to the farth'st of fruitful *Anglesey:*
The second South and North, from *Michael's* utmost Mount,
To *Cathnesse*, which the furth'st of *Scotland* we account.) 316
And then proceed to show, how *Avon* from her spring,
By *Newnham's** Fount is blest; and how she, blandishing,
By *Dunsmore* drives along. Whom *Sow* doth first assist,
Which taketh *Shirburn* in, with *Cune*, a great while miss'd;
Though *Coventry*[3] from thence her name at first did raise, 321
Now flourishing with fanes, and proud pyramidés;
Her walls in good repair, her ports so bravely built,
Her halls in good estate, her cross so richly gilt,
As scorning all the Towns that stand within her view: 325
Yet must she not be griev'd, that *Cune* should claim her due.

[1] The *High-cross*, supposed to be the midst of *England*.
[2] See to the Sixteenth Song.   * *Newnham Wells*.
[3] Otherwise, *Cune-tre:* that is, the Town upon *Cune*.

Tow'rds *Warwick* with this train as *Avon* trips along,
To *Guy-cliffe* being come, her Nymphs thus bravely song;
To thee renownèd Knight, continual praise we owe,
And at thy hallowed Tomb thy yearly *Obiits* show;   330
Who, thy dear *Phillis'* name and Country to advance,
Left'st *Warwick's* wealthy seat: and sailing into *France*,
At tilt, from his proud steed, Duke *Otton* threw'st to ground:
And with th' invalu'd prize of *Blanch* the beauteous crown'd
(The *Almaine* Emperor's heir) high acts didst there achieve:
As *Loraine* thou again didst valiantly relieve.   336
Thou in the *Soldan's* blood thy worthy sword imbru'dst;
And then in single fight, great *Amerant* subdu'dst.
'Twas thy *Herculian* hand, which happily destroy'd
That Dragon, which so long *Northumberland* annoy'd;   340
And slew that cruel Boar, which waste our wood-lands laid,
Whose tusks turn'd up our tilths, and dens in meadows made:
Whose shoulder-blade remains at *Coventry* till now;
And, at our humble suit, did quell that monstrous Cow
The passengers that us'd from *Dunsmore* to affright.   345
Of all our *English* (yet) O most renownèd Knight,
That *Colebrond* overcam'st: at whose amazing fall
The *Danes* remov'd their camp from *Winchester's* sieg'd wall.
Thy statue *Guy-cliffe* keeps, the gazer's eye to please;
Warwick, thy mighty arms (thou *English Hercules*)   350
Thy strong and massy sword, that never was controll'd:
Which, as her ancient right, her Castle still shall hold.

Scarce ended they their Song, but *Avon's* winding stream,
By *Warwick*, entertains the high-complection'd *Leame:*
And as she thence along to *Stratford* on doth strain,   355
Receiveth little *Heile* the next into her train:
Then taketh in the *Stour*, the Brook, of all the rest
Which that most goodly Vale of *Red-horse* loveth best;
A Valley that enjoys a very great estate,
Yet not so famous held as smaller, by her fate: 360

Now, for report had been too partial in her praise,
Her just conceivéd grief, fair *Red-horse* thus bewrays:
   Shall every Vale be heard to boast her wealth? and I,
The needy countries near that with my corn supply
As bravely as the best, shall only I endure 365
The dull and beastly world my glories to obscure;
Near way-less *Arden's* side, sith my retir'd abode
Stood quite out of the way from every common road?
Great *Eusham's* fertile glebe, what tongue hath not extoll'd?
As though to her alone belong'd the garb[1] of gold. 370
Of *Bever's* batfull earth, men seem as though to feign,
Reporting in what store she multiplies her grain:
And folk such wondrous things of *Alsburie* will tell,
As though aboundance strove her burthen'd womb to swell.
Her room amongst the rest, so *White-horse* is decreed: 375
She wants no setting forth: her brave *Pegasian* Steed
(The wonder of the West) exalted to the skies:
My *Red-horse* of you all contemnéd only lies.
The fault is not in me, but in the wretched time:
On whom, upon good cause, I well may lay the crime: 380
Which as all noble things, so me it doth neglect.
But when th' industrious Muse shall purchase me respect
Of countries near my site, and win me foreign fame
(The *Eden* of you all deservedly that am)
I shall as much be prais'd for delicacy then, 385
As now in small account with vile and barbarous men.
For, from the lofty *Edge*[2] that on my side doth lie,
Upon my spacious earth who casts a curious eye,
As many goodly seats shall in my compass see,
As many sweet delights and rarities in me 390
As in the greatest Vale: from where my head I couch

[1] The Sheaf.
[2] The *Edge-hill.*

At *Cotswold's* country's foot, till with my heels I touch
The *North-hamptonian* fields,[1] and fatt'ning pastures; where
I ravish every eye with my inticing cheer.
As still the year grows on, that *Ceres* once doth load
The full earth with her store; my plenteous bosom strow'd
With all aboundant sweets: my frim and lusty flank
Her bravery then displays, with meadows hugely rank.
The thick and well-grown fog doth mat my smoother
    slades,
And on the lower leas, as on the higher hades
The dainty clover grows (of grass the only silk)
That makes each udder strout abundantly with milk.

  As an unlett'red man,[2] at the desiréd sight
Of some rare beauty mov'd with infinite delight,
Not out of his own spirit, but by that power divine,
Which through a sparkling eye perspicuously doth shine,
Feels his hard temper yield, that he in passion breaks,
And things beyond his height, transported strangely speaks:
So those that dwell in me, and live by frugal toil,
When they in my defence are reasoning of my soil,
As rapted with my wealth and beauties, learnéd grow,
And in well-fitting terms, and noble language, show
The lordships in my lands, from *Rolright* (which remains
§ A witness of that day we won upon the *Danes*)
To *Towcester* well-near: twixt which, they use to tell
Of places which they say do *Rumney's* self excell.
Of *Dasset*[3] they dare boast, and give *Wormlighton*[3] prize,
As of that fertile Flat by *Bishopton*[3] that lies.

  For showing of my bounds, if men may rightly guess,
By my continued form which best doth me express,
On either of my sides and by the rising grounds,

---

[1] The bounds of the Vale of *Red-horse*.
[2] A Simile of the place and people.
[3] Wondrous fruitful places in the Vale.

Which in one fashion hold, as my most certain mounds,
In length near thirty miles I am discern'd to be.
   Thus *Red-horse* ends her tale; and I therewith agree
To finish here my Song: the Muse some ease doth ask,   425
As wearied with the toil in this her serious task.

ILLUSTRATIONS.

INTO the heart of *England* and *Wales*, the Muse here is entered, that is, *Warwickshire* her Native Country; whose territory you might call *Middle-Engle* (for here was that part of *Mercland*, spoken of in Story) for equality of distance from the inarming Ocean.

6. *By her* illustrious Earls *renownéd everywhere*.

Permit to yourself credit of those, loaden with antique fables, as *Guy* (of whom the Author in the Twelfth Song, and here presently) *Morind* and such like, and no more testimony might be given, to exceed. But, more sure justification hereof is, in those great princes *Henry Beauchamp* Earl of *Warwick*, and *Præcomes Angliæ** (as the Record calls him) under *Hen.* VI.[1] and *Richard Nevill* making it (as it were) his gain to crown and depose Kings in that bloody dissension twixt the White and Red Roses.

15. *That mighty* Arden *held*———

What is now the *Woodland* in *Warwickshire*, was heretofore part of a larger Weald or Forest, called *Arden*. The relics of whose name in *Dene* of *Monmouthshire*, and that

* Chief Earl of *England*.   [1] Parl. Rot. 23. *Hen.* 6. ap. Cam.

Ardvenna or *La Forest d'Ardenne*, by *Henault* and *Luxembourg*, shows likelihood of interpretation of the yet used *English* name of *Woodland*. And, whereas, in old inscriptions,[1] *Diana Nemorensis*,* with other additions, hath been found among the *Latins*, the like seems to be expressed in an old Marble, now in *Italy*,[2] graven under *Domitian*, in part thus:

DIS. MANIBVS.
Q. CAESIVS. Q. F. CLAVD.
ATILIANVS. SACERDOS.
DEANAE. ARDVINNAE.†

That comprehensive largeness which this *Arden* once extended (before ruin of her woods) makes the Author thus limit her with *Severn* and *Trent*. By reason of this her greatness, joined with antiquity, he also made choice of this place for description of the Chase, the *English* Simples, and Hermit, as you read in him.

259. *And thither wisely brought that goodly* Virgin band.

Sufficient justification of making a poem, may be from tradition, which the Author here uses; but see to the Eighth Song, where you have this incredible number of Virgins, shipped at *London;* nor skills it much on which you bestow your faith, or if on neither. Their request (as the *Genius'* prayer) are the Author's own fictions, to come to express the worth of his native soil's City.

260. *By* Leofrique *her Lord yet in base* bondage *held*.

The ensuing Story of this *Leofrique* and *Godiva*, was under the Confessor.[3] I find it reported in *Matthew* of *West-*

---

[1] Hubert. Goltz. Thesaur. in *Aris*.   * *Diana* of the wood.
[2] Jul. Jacobon. ap. Paul. Merul. Cosmog. part. 2. lib. 3. cap. 11.
† To the separated souls, Q. *Caesius*, &c., Priest of *Diana* of *Arden*, or surnamed *Arden*.   [3] About 1050.

minster, that *Nuda, equum ascendens, crines capitis et tricas dissolvens, corpus suum totum, præter crura candidissima, inde relavit.** This *Leofrique* (buried at *Coventry*) was Earl of *Leicester*, not *Chester* (as some ill took it by turning *Legecestra*, being indeed sometimes for *Chester*, of old called *Urbs Legionum*, as to the Eleventh Song already) which is without scruple showed in a Charter,[1] of the Manor of *Spalding* in *Lincolnshire*, made to *Wulgat* Abbot of *Crowland*, beginning thus: *Ego Thoroldus De* Buckenhale *coram Nobilissimo Domino meo* Leofrico Comite Leicestriæ, *et Nobilissimâ Comitissâ suâ Dominâ* Godivâ *sorore meâ, et cum consensu et bonâ voluntate Domini et Cognati mei* Comitis Algari, *primogeniti et hæredis eorum, donari, &c.* This *Algar* succeeded him; and, as a special title, government, and honour, this Earldom was therein among the *Saxons* so singular, that it was hereditary with a very long pedigree, till the Conquest, from King *Ethelbald's* time, above three hundred years. In *Malmesbury*, he is styled Earl of *Hereford;* and indeed, as it seems, had large dominion over most part of *Mercland*, and was a great Protector of good King *Edward*, from ambitious *Godwin's* faction. You may note in him, what power[2] the Earls of those times had for granting, releasing, or imposing liberties and exactions, which since only the Crown hath, as unseparably annexed to it. Nay, since the *Normans*, I find that *William Fitz-Osbern*,[3] Earl of *Hereford*, made a law in his County, *ut nullus miles pro qualicûnque commisso plus septem solidis solvat*,† which was observed without controversy, in *Malmesbury's* time; and I have seen original letters of Protection (a perfect and uncommunicable power Royal) by that great Prince *Richard* Earl of *Poiters* and *Cornwall*, brother to *Hen.* III. sent to the Sheriff of *Rutland*, for and

---

* As she was on horseback, her hair loose hung so long, that it covered all her body, to her thighs.   [1] Ingulphus Hist. fol. 519.
[2] Power of Earls anciently.   [3] Malmesb. de Gest. Reg. 3.
† That no Knight should be amerced above seven shillings.

in behalf of a Nunnery about *Stanford:* and it is well
known, that his successor *Edmund* left no small tokens of
such supremacy in constitutions, liberties, and imposed
subsidies in the Stannaries of *Cornwall;* with more such
like extant in monuments. But whatsoever their power
heretofore was, I think it ceased with that custom[1] of their
having the third part of the King's profit in the county,
which was also in the *Saxon* times usual, as appears in
that, [2]*In* Ipswich *Regina Edera duas partes habuit et Comes
Guert tertiam;* Norwich *reddebat XX. libras Regi, et Comiti
X. libras:* of the Borough of *Lewes,* its profits *erant II.
partes Regis, tertia Comitis*[3]*: et* Oxford *reddebat Regi XX.
libras, et sex sextarios mellis, Comiti verò* Algaro *X. libras.*[4]
And under King *John, Geffrey Fitz-Peter,* Earl of *Essex,* and
William le Marshall Earl of *Striguil,* **administrationem suorum
Comitatuum habebant,* saith *Hoveden.* But Time hath, with
other parts of Government, altered all this to what we now
use.

414. *A witness of that day we won upon the* Danes.

He means *Rollritch Stones* in the confines of *Warwick* and
Oxfordshire; of which the vulgar there have a fabulous tradition, that they are an army of men, and I know not what
great general amongst them, converted into stones: a tale
not having his superior in the rank of untruths. But (upon
the conceit of a most learned man) the Muse refers it to
some battle of the *Danes,* about time of *Rollo's* piracy and
incursion, and for her Country takes the better side (as
justifiable as the contrary) in affirming the day to the *Eng-*

---

[1] Lib. vetust. Monast. de Bello ap. Camd.
[2] Lib. 𝔇𝔬𝔪𝔢𝔰𝔇𝔞𝔶 in Scaccario.
[3] Third part of the Counties' profits to the Earl.
[4] See to the Eleventh Song.
[5] Had rule of their Counties. Et v. Jo. Carnotens. Epist. 263.
Nicol. Vice-comiti *Essexiæ.*

lish. But, to suppose this a Monument of that battle, fought at *Hochnorton*, seems to me in matter of certainty not very probable: I mean, being drawn from *Rollo's* name: of whose story, both for a passage in the last Song, and here, permit a short examination.[1] The *Norman*[2] tradition is, that he, with divers other *Danes* transplanting themselves, as well for dissension twixt him and his King, as for new seat of habitation, arrived here, had some skirmishes with the *English* defending their territories; and soon afterward being admonished in a dream, aided and advised by King *Athelstan*, entered *Seine* in *France;* wasted and won part of it about *Paris, Baieux*, elsewhere; returned upon request by embassage to assist the *English* King against rebels; and afterward in the year 911 or 912 received his Dukedom of *Normandy*, and Christianity, his name of *Robert*, with *Ægidia* or *Gilla* (for wife) daughter to *Charles*, surnamed the Simple; as to the Fourth Song I have, according to the credit of the story, touched it. But how came such habitude twixt *Athelstan* and him, before this 912, when, as it is plain, that *Athelstan* was not King till 924, or near that point? Neither is any concordance twixt *Athelstan* and this *Charles*, whose Kingdom was taken from him by *Rodulph* Duke of *Burgundy*, two years before our King *Edward* I. (of the *Saxons*) died. In the ninth year of whose reign, falling under 906, was that battle of *Hochnorton;* so that, unless the name of *Athelstan* be mistook for this *Edward*, or, be wanting to the Dominical year of those twenty-two of the *Dionysian* calculation (whereof to the Fourth Song) I see no means to make their story stand with itself, nor our Monks; in whom (most of them writing

---

[1] Inquisition in the *Norman* Story, partly touched to the Fourth Canto.
[2] Guil. Gemeticens. de Ducib. Norm. 2. cap. 4. et seqq. *Thom. de Walsingham* in Hypodig. Neust. secundum quos, in quantum ad chronologicam rationem spectat, plerique alii.

about the *Norman* times) more mention would have been
of *Rollo*, ancestor to the Conqueror, and his acts here, had
they known any certainty of his name or wars: which I
rather guess to have been in our maritime parts, than inlands, unless when (if that were at all) he assisted King
Athelstan. Read *Frodoard*, and the old Annals of *France*,
written nearer the supposed times, and you will scarce find
him to have been, or else there under[1] some other name;
as *Godfrey*, which some have conjectured, to be the same
with *Rollo*. You may see in *Æmilius* what uncertainties, if
not contrarieties, were, in *Norman* traditions of this matter;
and, I make no question, but of that unknown Nation so
much mistaking hath been of names and times, that scarce
any undoubted truth therein now can justify itself. For,
observe but what is here delivered, and compare it with
them[2] which say in 998 *Rollo* was overthrown at *Chartres* by
Richard Duke of *Burgundy*, and *Ebal* Earl of *Poiters*, assisting *Walzelm* Bishop of that city; and, my question is,
Where have you hope of reconciliation? Except only in
equivocation of name; for plainly *Hastings*, *Godfrey*, *Hroruc*
and others (if none of these were the same) all *Danes*, had
to do, and that with dominion in *France* about this age;
wherein it is further reported, that *Robert* Earl of *Paris*,[3]
and in some sort a King twixt *Charles* and *Rodulph*, gave to
certain *Normans* that had entered the land at *Loire* (they
first entered there in 853[4]) all Little *Bretagne* and *Nants*,
and this in 922, which agrees with that gift of the same
tract to *Rollo* by *Charles*, little better than harshest discords.
And so doth that of *Rollo's* being aided by the *English*
King, and in league with him against the *French*, with
another received truth: which is, that *Charles* was (by mar-

[1] Ita quidam apud P. Emilium Hist. Franc. 3. quem. de hac re
vide, et Polydor. ejusdem sequacem Hist. 5.
[2] Floren. Wigorn. pag. 335. et Roger Hoveden. part. 1. fol. 241.
[3] Frodoard. Presbyt. Annal. Franc.   [4] Reicherspergens.

riage with *Edgith** of the *English* King's loins) son-in-law to *Edward*, and brother-in-law to *Athelstan*, in whose[1] protection here *Lewes* (afterwards the Fourth) was, while *Rodulph* of *Burgundy* held the Crown. For that unmannerly homage also, spoken of to the Fourth Song, by one of *Rollo's* knights, it is reported by *Malmesbury* and others, to be done by *Rollo* himself; and, touching that *Egidia* wife to *Rollo*, the judicious *French* historiographer *P. Emilius* (from whom the *Italian Polydore* had many odd pieces of his best contexts) tells clearly, that she was daughter to *Lothar* King of *Romans*, and given by his cousin *Charles* the *Gross*, to *Godfrey* King of *Normans*, with 𝔚𝔢𝔰𝔱𝔯𝔦𝔠𝔥 (that is *Neustria*) about 886, and imagines that the *Norman* historians were deceived by equivocation of name, mistaking *Charles* the *Simple* for *Charles* the *Gross*, living near one time; as also that they finding *Egidia* a King's daughter (being indeed *Lothar's*) supposed her *Charles* the *Simple's*. This makes me think also that of *Godfrey* and *Rollo*, hath been like confusion of name. But both times, reigns, and persons are so disturbed in the stories, that being insufficient to rectify the contrarieties, I leave you to the liberty of common report.

* *Oginia* dicta P. Æmilio.
[1] Membran. vetust. Cœnob. Floriacens. edit. a P. Pithæo.

THE FOURTEENTH SONG.

THE ARGUMENT.

Her sundry strains the Muse to prove,
Now sings of homely country love;
What moan th' old herdsman Clent *doth make,*
For his coy Wood-Nymph Feck'nham's *sake;*
And, how the Nymphs each other greet, 5
When Avon *and brave* Severn *meet.*
The Vale of Eusham *then doth tell,*
How far the Vales do Hills excell.
Ascending, next, fair Cotswold's *Plains,*
She revels with the shepherds swains; 10
And sends the dainty Nymphs away,
'Gainst Tame *and* Isis' *Wedding-day.*

T length, attain'd those lands that South of *Severn* lie,
As to the varying earth the Muse doth her apply,
Poor sheep-hook and plain goad, she many times doth sound:
Then in a buskin'd strain she instantly doth bound.
Smooth as the lowly stream, she softly now doth glide: 5
And with the Mountains straight contendeth in her pride.
Now back again I turn, the land with me to take,
From the *Staffordian* heaths as *Stour** her course doth make.

* Running by *Sturbridge* in *Worstershire*, towards *Severn*.

Which *Clent*, from his proud top, contentedly doth view:
But yet the agéd Hill, immoderately doth rue   10
His lovéd *Feck'nham's* fall, and doth her state bemoan;
To please his amorous eye, whose like the world had none.
For, from her very youth, he (then an agéd Hill)
Had to that Forest-Nymph a special liking still:
The least regard of him who never seems to take,   15
But suff'reth in herself for *Salwarp's* only sake;
And on that River dotes, as much as *Clent* on her.

Now, when the Hill perceiv'd, the Flood she would prefer,
All pleasure he forsakes; that at the full-bagg'd cow,
Or at the curl-fac'd bull, when venting he doth low,   20
Or at th' unhappy wags, which let their cattle stray,
At Nine-holes on the heath whilst they together play,
He never seems to smile; nor ever taketh keep
To hear the harmless swain pipe to his grazing sheep:
Nor to the carter's tune, in whistling to his team;   25
Nor lends his list'ning ear (once) to the ambling stream,
That in the evening calm against the stones doth rush
With such a murmuring noise, as it would seem to hush
The silent meads asleep; but, void of all delight,
Remedilessly drown'd in sorrow day and night,   30
Nor *Licky* his ally and neighbour doth respect:
And therewith being charg'd, thus answereth in effect;
That *Lickey*[1] to his height seem'd slowly but to rise,
And that in length and breadth he all extended lies,
Nor doth like other hills to sudden sharpness mount,   35
That of their kingly kind they scarce can him account;
Though by his swelling soil set in so high a place,
That *Malvern's* mighty self he seemeth to out-face.

Whilst *Clent* and *Licky* thus, do both express their pride,
As *Salwarpe* slips along by *Feck'nham's* shady side,   40

[1] The *Lickey*, supposed to be the highest ground of this Isle not being a Mountain.

That Forest him affects in wand'ring to the *Wych*:[1]
But he, himself by salts there seeking to enrich,
His *Feck'nham* quite forgets; from all affection free.
  But she, that to the Flood most constant means to be,
More prodigally gives her woods to those strong fires   45
Which boil the source to salts. Which *Clent* so much admires,
That love, and her disdain, to madness him provoke:
When to the Wood-Nymph thus the jealous Mountain spoke:
   Fond Nymph, thy twisted curls, on which were all my
      care,
   Thou lett'st the furnace waste; that miserably bare   50
   I hope to see thee left, which so dost me despise;
   Whose beauties many a morn have blest my longing eyes
   And, till the weary sun sunk down unto the West,
   Thou still my object wast, thou once my only best.
   The time shall quickly come, thy groves and pleasant springs,
   Where to the mirthful merle the warbling mavis sings,   56
   The painful labourer's hand shall stock the roots, to burn;
   The branch and body spent, yet could not serve his turn.
   Which when, most wilful Nymph, thy chance shall be to see,
   Too late thou shalt repent thy small regard of me.   60
  But *Salwarpe* down from *Wycke* his nimbler feet doth ply,
Great *Severn* to attend, along to *Tewksbury*,
With others to partake the joy that there is seen,
When beauteous *Avon* comes unto her sovereign Queen.[2]
Here down from *Eusham's* Vale, their greatness to attend,   65
Comes *Swilliat* sweeping in, which *Cotswold* down doth send:
And *Garran* there arrives, the great recourse to see.
Where thus together met, with most delightful glee,
The cheerful Nymphs that haunt the Valley rank and low
(Where full *Pomona* seems most plenteously to flow,   70
And with her fruitery swells by *Pershore*, in her pride)
Amongst the batfull meads on *Severn's* either side,

[1] The Salt Fountain of *Worcestershire*.   [2] *Severn*.

To these their confluent Floods, full bowls of perry brought:
Where, to each other's health pass'd many a deep-fetch'd
    draught,
And many a sound carouse from friend to friend doth go 75
Thus whilst the mellowed earth with her own juice doth flow,
Inflaméd with excess the lusty pamp'red Vale,
In praise of her great self, thus frames her glorious tale:
  I doubt not but some Vale enough for us has said,
To answer them that most with baseness us upbraid; 80
Those high presumptuous Hills, which bend their utmost
Us only to deject, in their inveterate spite: [might,
But I would have them think, that I (which am the Queen
Of all the *British* Vales, and so have ever been
Since *Gomer's* giant-brood inhabited this Isle, 85
And that of all the rest, myself may so enstyle)
Against the highest Hill dare put myself for place,
That ever threat'ned Heaven with the austerest face. [forth
And for our praise, then thus; What Fountain send they
(That finds a River's name, though of the smallest worth) 90
But it invales itself, and on it either side   [pride
Doth make those fruitful meads, which with their painted
Imbroder his proud bank? whilst in lascivious gyres
He swiftly sallieth out, and suddenly retires
In sundry works and trails, now shallow, and then deep, 95
Searching the spacious shores, as though it meant to sweep
Their sweets with it away, with which they are replete.
And men, first building towns, themselves did wisely seat
Still in the bounteous Vale: whose burthenéd pasture bears
The most aboundant swathe, whose glebe such goodly ears,
As to the weighty sheaf with scythe or sickle cut, 101
When as his hard'ned hand the labourer comes to put,
Sinks him in his own sweat, which it but hardly wields:
And on the corn-strew'd lands, then in the stubble fields,
There feed the herds of neat, by them the flocks of sheep, 105

Seeking the scatt'red corn upon the ridges steep:
And in the furrow by (where *Ceres* lies much spill'd)
Th' unwieldy larding swine his maw then having fill'd,
Lies wallowing in the mire, thence able scarce to rise.
When as those monstrous Hills so much that us despise 110
(The Mountain, which forsooth the lowly Valley mocks)
Have nothing in the world upon their barren rocks,
But greedy clamb'ring goats, and conies, banish'd quite
From every fertile place; as rascals, that delight
In base and barren plots, and at good earth repine. 115
And though in winter we to moisture much incline,
Yet those that be our own, and dwell upon our land,
When twixt their burly stacks, and full-stuff'd barns they
Into the softer clay as eas'ly they do sink,   [stand,
Pluck up their heavy feet, with lighter spirits, to think 120
That autumn shall produce, to recompense their toil,
A rich and goodly crop from that unpleasant soil.
And from that envious foe which seeks us to deprave,
Though much against his will this good we clearly have,
We still are highly prais'd, and honour'd by his height. 125
For, who will us survey, their clear and judging sight
May see us thence at full: which else the searching'st eye,
By reason that so flat and levelléd we lye,
Could never throughly view, ourselves nor could we show.

   Yet more; what lofty Hills to humble Valleys owe, 130
And what high grace they have which near to us are plac'd,
In *Breedon** may be seen, being amorously imbrac'd
In cincture of mine arms. Who though he do not vaunt
His head like those that look as they would Heaven sup-
    plant:
Yet let them wisely note, in what excessive pride 135
He in my bosom sits; while him on every side
With my delicious sweets and delicates I trim.

    * A Hill invironed on every side with the Vale of *Evsham*.

And when great *Malvern* looks most terrible and grim,
He with a pleaséd brow continually doth smile.
　Here *Breedon*, having heard his praises all the while, 140
Grew insolently proud; and doth upon him take
Such state, as he would seem but small account to make
Of *Malvern*, or of *Mein*. So that the wiser Vale,
To his instruction turns the process of her tale.
T' avoid the greater's wrath, and shun the meaner's hate, 145
Quoth she, take my advice, abandon idle state;
And by that way I go, do thou thy course contrive:
Give others leave to vaunt, and let us closely thrive.
Whilst idly but for place the lofty Mountains toil,
Let us have store of grain, and quantity of soil. 150
To what end serve their tops (that seem to threat the sky)
But to be rent with storms? whilst we in safety lie.
Their rocks but barren be, and they which rashly climb,
Stand most in Envy's sight, the fairest prey for Time.
And when the lowly Vales are clad in summer's green, 155
The grisled winter's snow upon their heads is seen.
Of all the Hills I know, let *Mein* thy pattern be:
Who though his site be such as seems to equal thee,
And destitute of nought that *Arden* him can yield;
Nor of th' especial grace of many a goodly field; 160
Nor of dear *Clifford's* seat (the place of health and sport)
Which many a time hath been the Muse's quiet port.
Yet brags not he of that, nor of himself esteems
The more for his fair site; but richer than he seems,
Clad in a gown of grass, so soft and wondrous warm, 165
As him the summer's heat, nor winter's cold can harm.
Of whom I well may say, as I may speak of thee;
From either of your tops, that who beholdeth me,
To Paradise may think a second he had found,
If any like the first were ever on the ground. 170
　Her long and zealous speech thus *Eusham* doth conclude:

When straight the active Muse industriously pursu'd
This noble Country's praise, as matter still did rise.
For *Gloster* in times past herself did highly prize,
When in her pride of strength she nourish'd goodly vines, 175
§ And oft her cares repress'd with her delicious wines.
But, now th' all-cheering sun the colder soil deceives,
§ And us (here tow'rds the pole) still falling South-ward
  leaves :
So that the sullen earth th' effect thereof doth prove ;
According to their books, who hold that he doth move 180
From his first zenith's point ; the cause we feel his want.
But of her vines depriv'd, now *Gloster* learns to plant
The pear-tree everywhere : whose fruit she strains for juice,
That her pur'st perry is, which first she did produce
From *Worstershire*, and there is common as the fields ; 185
Which naturally that soil in most aboundance yields.
 But the laborious Muse, which still new work assays,
Here sallieth through the slades, where beauteous *Severn*
  plays,
Until that River gets her *Gloster's* wishéd sight :
Where, she her stream divides, that with the more delight 190
She might behold the Town, of which she's wondrous proud :
Then takes she in the *Frome*, then *Cam*, and next the *Strowd*,
As thence upon her course she wantonly doth strain.
Supposing then herself a Sea-god by her train,
She *Neptune*-like doth float upon the bracky marsh. 195
Where, lest she should become too combersome and harsh,
Fair *Micklewood* (a Nymph, long honour'd for a Chase,
Contending to have stood the high'st in *Severn's* grace,
Of any of the *Dryads* there bord'ring on her shore)
With her cool amorous shades, and all her sylvan store, 200
To please the goodly Flood imploys her utmost powers,
Supposing the proud Nymph might like her woody bowers.
 But *Severn* (on her way) so large and headstrong grew,

That she the Wood-Nymph scorns, and *Avon* doth pursue;
A River with no less than goodly *Kings-wood* crown'd,   205
A Forest and a Flood by either's fame renown'd;
And each with other's pride and beauty much bewitch'd;
Besides, with *Bristowe's* state both wondrously enrich'd.
Which soon to *Severn* sent th' report of that fair Road[1]
(So burthened still with barks, as it would overload   210
Great *Neptune* with the weight) whose fame so far doth ring.
When as that mighty Flood, most bravely flourishing,
Like *Thetis'* goodly self, majestically glides;
Upon her spacious breast tossing the surgefull tides,
To have the River see the state to which she grows,   215
And how much to her Queen the beauteous *Avon* owes.
But, noble Muse, proceed immediately to tell
How *Eusham's* fertile Vale at first in liking fell   [site
With *Cotswold*, that great King of Shepherds: whose proud
When that fair Vale first saw, so nourish'd her delight,   220
That him she only lov'd: for wisely she beheld
The beauties clean throughout that on his surface dwell'd:
Of[2] just and equal height two banks arising, which
Grew poor (as it should seem) to make some Valley rich:
Betwixt them thrusting out an elbow of such height,   225
As shrouds the lower soil; which, shadowed from the light,
Shoots forth a little grove, that in the summer's day
Invites the flocks, for shade that to the covert stray.
A Hill there holds his head, as though it told a tale,
Or stooped to look down, or whisper with a Vale;   230
Where little purling winds like wantons seem to dally,
And skip from bank to bank, from valley trip to valley.
Such sundry shapes of soil where Nature doth devise,
That she may rather seem fantastical than wise.
T' whom *Sarum's* Plain gives place; though famous for
   her flocks,   235

[1] *King's Road.*   [2] A nice description of *Cotswold*.

THE FOURTEENTH SONG.

Yet hardly doth she tithe our *Cotswold's* wealthy locks.
Though *Lemster* him exceed for fineness of her ore,
Yet quite he puts her down for his aboundant store.
A match so fit as he, contenting to her mind,
Few Vales (as I suppose) like *Eusham* hapt to find: 240
Nor any other Wold, like *Cotswold* ever sped
So fair and rich a Vale by fortuning to wed.
He hath the goodly wool, and she the wealthy grain:
Through which they wisely seem their household to maintain.
He hath pure wholesome air, and dainty crystal springs. 245
To those delights of his, she daily profit brings:
As to his large expense, she multiplies her heaps:
Nor can his flocks devour th' aboundance that she reaps;
As th' one with what it hath, the other strove to grace.
   And, now that everything may in the proper place 250
Most aptly be contriv'd, the sheep our Wold doth breed
(The simplest though it seem) shall our description need,
And shepherd-like, the Muse thus of that kind doth speak:
No brown, nor sullied black the face or legs doth streak,
Like those of *Moreland*, *Cank*, or of the *Cambrian* Hills 255
That lightly laden are: but *Cotswold* wisely fills
Her with the whitest kind: whose brows so woolly be,
As men in her fair sheep no emptiness should see.
The staple deep and thick, through, to the very grain,
Most strongly keepeth out the violentest rain: 260
A body long and large, the buttocks equal broad;
As fit to undergo the full and weighty load.
And of the fleecy face, the flank doth nothing lack,
But everywhere is stor'd; the belly, as the back.
The fair and goodly flock, the shepherd's only pride, 265
As white as winter's snow, when from the river's side
He drives his new-wash'd sheep; or on the Shearing-day,
When as the lusty ram, with those rich spoils of May

His crooked horns hath crown'd; the bell-wether, so brave
As none in all the flock they like themselves would have.

But Muse, return to tell, how there the Shepherds' King,
Whose flock hath chanc'd that year the earliest lamb to
    bring,
In his gay bauldric sits at his low grassy board,   [stor'd :
With flawns, curds, clouted-cream, and country dainties
And, whilst the bag-pipe plays, each lusty jocund swain
Quaffs sillibubs in cans, to all upon the Plain,
And to their country-girls, whose nosegays they do wear,
Some roundelays do sing : the rest, the burthen bear.

    But *Cotswold*,[1] be this spoke to th' only praise of thee,
That thou of all the rest, the chosen soil should'st be,
Fair *Isis* to bring forth (the Mother of great *Tames*)
With those delicious Brooks, by whose immortal streams,
Her greatness is begun : so that our Rivers' King,
When he his long descent shall from his bel-sires bring,
Must needs (Great Pastures' Prince) derive his stem by thee,
From kingly *Cotswold's* self, sprung of the third degree :
As th' old world's Heroes wont, that in the times of yore,
On *Neptune*, *Jove*, and *Mars*, themselves so highly bore.

    But eas'ly from her source as *Isis* gently dades;
Unto her present aid, down through the deeper slades,
The nimbler-footed *Churne*, by *Cisseter* doth slide;
And first at *Greeklade* gets pre-eminence, to guide
Queen *Isis* on her way, ere she receive her train.
Clear *Colne*, and lively *Leech*, so down from *Cotswold's* Plain,
At *Leechlade* linking hands, come likewise to support
The Mother of great *Tames*. When, seeing the resort,
From *Cotswold Windrush* scours; and with herself doth cast
The train to overtake, and therefore hies her fast
Through the *Oxfordian* fields; when (as the last of all
Those Floods, that into *Tames* out of our *Cotswold* fall,

---

[1] The fountain of *Thames*, rising in the South of *Cotswold*.

And farth'st unto the North) bright *Enload* forth doth bear,
For, though it had been long, at length she came to hear
That *Isis* was to *Tame* in wedlock to be tied;
And therefore she prepar'd t' attend upon the Bride;
Expecting, at the feast, past ordinary grace.   305

And being near of kin to that most spring-full place,
Where out of *Blockley's* banks so many Fountains flow,
That clean throughout his soil proud *Cotswold* cannot show
The like : as though from far, his long and many Hills,
There emptied all their veins, wherewith those Founts he
    fills,   310
Which in the greatest drought so brimfull still do float,
Sent through the rifted rocks with such an open throat,
As though the cleeves consum'd in humour; they alone,
So crystalline and cold, as hard'neth stick to stone.

But whilst this while we talk, the fardivulgéd fame   315
Of this great Bridal tow'rd, in *Phœbus'* mighty name
Doth bid the Muse make haste, and to the Bride-house
    speed;
Of her attendance there least they should stand in need.

ILLUSTRATIONS.

SOMEWHAT returning now near the way you descended from the Northern parts, the Muse leads you through that part of *Worcestershire*, which is on this side *Severn*, and the neighbouring *Stafford*, viewing also *Cotteswold*, and so *Glocester*. The fictions of this Song are not so covert, nor the allusions so difficult, but that I presume your conceit, for the most part, willingly discharges my labour.

176. *And oft her cares repress'd with her delicious wines.*

In this tract of *Glocestershire* (where to this day many places are styled *Vineyards*) was of ancient time among other fruits of a fertile soil, great store of vines, and more than in any other place of the Kingdom. Now in many parts of this realm we have some: but what comes of them in the press is scarce worth respect. Long since, the Emperor *Probus*,[1] *Gallis omnibus et Hispanis ac Britannis permisit ut vites haberent vinumque conficerent:** but *Tacitus*,[2] before that, speaking of this Island, commends it with *Solum præter oleam vitemque et cætera calidioribus* terris oriri

---

[1] Flav. Vopiscus in ejusd. vitâ.
* Permitted Vines to the *Gauls*, *Spaniards*, and *Britons*, and leave to make Wines.   [2] In Jul. Agricola.

sueta, patiens frugum, fæcundum.* Long since *Probus*, England had its vineyards also, and some store of wine, as appears by that in 𝔇𝔬𝔪𝔢𝔰𝔡𝔞𝔶, *Unus et Parcus et VI. Arpenni Vineæ* (that is between five and six acres; *arpent* in *French* signifying a content of ground of one hundred rods square, every rod eighteen feet) *et reddit XX. modios vini si benè procedit*,† being recorded of a place[1] by *Ralegh* in *Essex*. This was under *William* I.: and since him in time of *Hen.* I.[2] much wine was made here in *Gloccstershire*. That now the Isle enjoys not frequency of this benefit, as in old time, whether it be through the soil's old age, and so like a woman growing sterile (as[3] in another kind *Tremellius* many hundred years since thought) or by reason of the earth's change of place, as upon difference in astronomical observation *Stadius* guessed, or that some part of singular influence, whereon Astrology hangs most of inferior qualities, is altered by that slow course (yet of great power in alteration of Heaven's System) of the eighth Sphere (or præcession of the Æquinoctial) or by reason of industry wanting in the husbandman, I leave it to others' examination.

177. ——————— *still falling Southward leaves.*

He alludes to the difference of the Zodiac's obliquity from what it was of old. For, in *Ptolemy's* time about 1460 years since the utmost declination of the sun in the first of *Cancer* (where she is nearest to our vertical point) was 23 Gr. and about 52 Minut. since that, *Albategni* (about *Charlemaine's* time) observed it some 15 Scruples less: after him (near 1000th year of *Christ*) *Arzachel* found it 23 Gr. 34 Scr.,

---

* A soil fruitful enough, except of *olives* and *vines*, which are for hotter climates.

† One park and six arpens of vineyard, and brings forth some twenty firkins of wine, if the year prove well.

[1] Camd. in Trinobantibus.   [2] Malmesb. de Pontificum Gestis, 4.
[3] Ap. Columell. de re Rustic. 2. cap. 1.

and in this later age *John* of *Conigsburg* and *Copernicus*[1] brought it to 23 Gr. 28 Scrup., which concords also with the *Prutenic* accompt, and as many as thence traduce their *Ephemerides*. So that (by this calculation) about 24 minutes the sun comes not now so near our *Zenith*, as it did in *Ptolemy's* time. But in truth (for in these things I accompt that truth, which is warranted by most accurate observation; and those learned mathematicians, by omitting of parallax and refractions, deceived themselves and posterity) the declination in this age is 23 Gr. $31\frac{1}{2}$ Scrup. as that noble *Dane*, and most honoured restorer of astronomical motions, *Tycho Brahe*, hath taught us: which, although it be greater than that of *Copernicus* and his followers, yet is much less than what is in *Ptolemy;* and by two scruples different from *Arzachel's*, so justifying the Author's conceit, supposing the cause of our climate's not now producing wines, to be the sun's declination from us, which for every scruple answers in earth, about one of our miles; but a far more large distance in the celestial globe. I can as well maintain this high-fetched cause, being upon difference of so few minutes in one of the slowest motions, and we see that greatest effects are always attributed to them, as upon the old conceit of the *Platonic* year, abridged into near his half by *Copernicus*, those consequents foretold upon the change of eccentrics[2] out of one sign into another, the Equinoctial præcession, and such like; as others may their conversion of a planet's state into *Fortunate*, *Opprest*, or *Combust.* by measuring or missing their 16 Scruples of *Cazimi*, their *Orbes moities*, and such curiosities. Neither can you salve the effect of this declination by the sun's much nearer

[1] Copernic. Re. 3. cap. 3.
[2] Cardan. ad 2. Tetrabibl. et de Varietat. Rer. 2. qui prophanè nimiùm, à motibus octavæ Sphæræ, iis scilicet quos circa 1800 contrario velut fieri modo supponit sacrosanctæ Religionis mutationem inceptè simul et impiè prædixit, et hujus generis sexcenta.

approach to the earth, upon that decrease of his eccentricity which *Copernicus* and his followers have published. For, admitting that were true, yet judicial astrology relies more upon aspect and beams falling on us with angles (which are much altered by this change of obliquity in the Zodiac) than distance of every singular star from the earth. But indeed, upon mistaking the pole's altitude, and other error in observation, *Copernicus** was deceived, and in this present age the sun's eccentricity (in *Ptolemy*, being the 24th of the eccentric's semidiameter, divided into 60) hath been found[1] between the 27th and 28th P. which is far greater than that in *Copernicus*, erroneously making it but near the 31st. But this is too heavenly a language for the common reader; and perhaps too late I leave it.

* Cui, hoc nomine, gravitèr minitatus est Jul. Scalig. Exercitat. 90. sect. 2.

[1] Tycho Brahe in Progymnasm.

THE FIFTEENTH SONG.

THE ARGUMENT.

The guests here to the Bride-house hie.
The goodly Vale of Alsbury
*Sets her son (*Tame*) forth, brave as* May,
Upon the joyful Wedding-day:
Who deck'd up, tow'rd's his Bride is gone.   5
So lovely Isis *coming on,*
At Oxford *all the Muses meet her,*
And with a Prothalamion *greet her.*
The Nymphs are in the Bridal Bowers,
Some strowing sweets, some sorting flowers: 10
Where lusty Charwell *himself raises,*
And sings of Rivers, and their praises.
Then Tames *his way tow'rd* Windsor *tends.*
Thus, with the Song, the Marriage ends.

OW Fame had through this Isle divulg'd, in every ear,
The long-expected day of Marriage to be near,
That *Isis, Cotwold's* heir, long woo'd was lastly won,
And instantly should wed with *Tame,*[1] old *Chiltern's* son.

[1] *Tame,* arising in the Vale of *Alsbury,* at the foot of the *Chiltern.*

And now that Wood-mans wife, the mother of the Flood, 5
The rich and goodly Vale of *Alsbury*, that stood
So much upon her *Tame*, was busied in her bowers,
Preparing for her son, as many suits of flowers,
As *Cotswold* for the Bride, his *Isis*, lately made;
Who for the lovely *Tame*, her Bridegroom, only stay'd. 10
 Whilst every crystal Flood is to this business prest,
The cause of their great speed and many thus request:
O! whither go ye Floods? what sudden wind doth blow,
Than other of your kind, that you so fast should flow?
What business is in hand, that spurs you thus away? 15
Fair *Windrush* let me hear, I pray thee *Charwell* say:
They suddenly reply, What lets you should not see
That for this Nuptial feast we all preparéd be?
Therefore this idle chat our ears doth but offend:
Our leisure serves not now these trifles to attend. 20
 But whilst things are in hand, old *Chiltern* (for his life)
From prodigal expense can no way keep his wife;
Who feeds her *Tame* with marl, in cordial-wise prepar'd,
And thinks all idly spent, that now she only spar'd
In setting forth her son: nor can she think it well, 25
Unless her lavish charge do *Cotswold's* far excell.
For, *Alsbury's* a Vale[1] that walloweth in her wealth,
And (by her wholesome air continually in health)
Is lusty, frim, and fat, and holds her youthful strength.
Besides her fruitful earth, her mighty breadth and length, 30
Doth *Chiltern* fitly match: which mountainously high,
And being very long, so likewise she doth lie;
From the *Bedfordian* fields, where first she doth begin,
To fashion like a Vale, to th' place where *Tame* doth win
His *Isis'* wishéd bed; her soil throughout so sure, 35
For goodness of her glebe, and for her pasture pure,

[1] The richness of the Vale of *Alsbury*.

That as her grain and grass, so she her sheep doth breed,
For burthen and for bone all other that exceed :
And she, which thus in wealth aboundantly doth flow,
Now cares not on her Child what cost she do bestow.   40
Which when wise *Chiltern* saw (the world who long had try'd,
And now at last had laid all garish pomp aside :
Whose hoar and chalky head descry'd him to be old,
His beechen woods bereft[1] that kept him from the cold)
Would fain persuade the Vale to hold a steady rate ;   45
And with his curious wife, thus wisely doth debate :

Quoth he, you might allow what needeth, to the most :
But where as less will serve, what means this idle cost !
Too much, a surfeit breeds, and may our Child annoy :
These fat and luscious meats do but our stomachs cloy.   50
The modest comely mean, in all things likes the wise,
Apparel often shews us womanish precise.
And what will *Cotswold* think when he shall hear of this ?
He'll rather blame your waste, than praise your cost, I wiss.

But, women wilful be, and she her will must have,   55
Nor cares how *Chiltern* chides, so that her *Tame* be brave.
Alone which tow'rds his Love she eas'ly doth convey :
For the *Oxonian Ouze*[2] was lately sent away
From *Buckingham*, where first he finds his nimbler feet ;
Tow'rds *Whittlewood* then takes : where, past the noblest Street,*   60
He to the Forest gives his farewell, and doth keep
His course directly down into the *German* Deep,
To publish that great day in mighty *Neptune's* Hall,
That all the Sea-gods there might keep it festivall.

As we have told how *Tame* holds on his even course,   65
Return we to report, how *Isis* from her source

[1] The *Chiltern*-country beginning also to want wood.
[2] That *Ouze* arising near *Brackley*, running into the *German* Sea.
* *Watling*

Comes tripping with delight, down from her daintier
    springs;
And in her princely train, t'attend her Marriage, brings
Clear *Churnet, Colne,* and *Leech,*[1] which first she did retain,
With *Windrush:* and with her (all outrage to restrain   70
Which well might off'red be to *Isis* as she went)
Came *Yenloud* with a guard of Satyrs, which were sent
From *Whichwood,* to await the bright and god-like Dame.
So, *Bernwood* did bequeath his Satyrs to the *Tame,*
For sticklers in those stirs that at the Feast should be.   75

    These preparations great when *Charwell* comes to see,
To *Oxford* got before, to entertain the Flood,
Apollo's aid he begs, with all his sacred brood,
To that most learnéd place to welcome her repair.
Who in her coming on, was wax'd so wondrous fair,   80
That meeting, strife arose betwixt them, whether they
Her beauty should extol, or she admire their bay.[2]
On whom their several gifts (to amplify her dower)
The Muses there bestow; which ever have the power
Immortal her to make. And as she pass'd along,   85
Those modest *Thespian* Maids[3] thus to their *Isis* song:

    Ye Daughters of the Hills, come down from every side,
And due attendance give upon the lovely Bride:
Go strew the paths with flowers by which she is to pass.
For be ye thus assur'd, in *Albion* never was   90
A beauty (yet) like hers: where have ye ever seen
So absolute a Nymph in all things, for a Queen?
Give instantly in charge the day be wondrous fair,
That no disorder'd blast attempt her braided hair.
Go, see her state prepar'd, and every thing be fit,   95
The Bride-chamber adorn'd with all beseeming it.

---

[1] Rivers arising in *Cotswold,* spoke of in the former Song.
[2] Laurel for learning.   [3] The Muses.

And for the princely Groom, who ever yet could name
A Flood that is so fit for *Isis* as the *Tame?*
Ye both so lovely are, that knowledge scarce can tell,
For feature whether he, or beauty she excell : 100
That ravishéd with joy each other to behold,
When as your crystal waists you closely do enfold,
Betwixt your beauteous selves you shall beget a Son,
That when your lives shall end, in him shall be begun.
The pleasant *Surryan* shores shall in that Flood delight, 105
And *Kent* esteem herself most happy in his sight.
The Shire that *London* loves, shall only him prefer,
And give full many a gift to hold him near to her.
The *Skeld*, the goodly *Mose*, the rich and viny *Rhine*,[1]
Shall come to meet the *Thames* in *Neptune's* wat'ry plain. 110
And all the *Belgian* Streams and neighbouring Floods of
    Gaul,
Of him shall stand in awe, his tributaries all.

As of fair *Isis* thus, the learnéd Virgins spake,
A shrill and sudden bruit this *Prothalamion*[2] brake ;
That *White-horse*, for the love she bare to her ally, 115
And honour'd sister Vale, the bounteous *Alsbury*,
Sent presents to the *Tame* by *Ock* her only Flood,
Which for his Mother Vale, so much on greatness stood.

From *Oxford, Isis* hastes more speedily, to see
That River like his birth might entertainéd be : 120
For, that ambitious Vale, still striving to command,
And using for her place continually to stand,
Proud *White-horse* to persuade, much business there hath
    been
T' acknowledge that great Vale of *Eusham* for her Queen.

[1] They all three, rivers of greatest note in the *Lower Germany*, cast themselves into the ocean, in the coast opposite to the mouth of *Thames*.
[2] Marriage Song.

And but that *Evsham* is so opulent and great, 125
That thereby she herself holds in the sovereign seat,
This *White-horse*¹ all the Vales of *Britain* would o'erbear,
And absolutely sit in the imperial Chair;
And boasts as goodly herds, and numerous flocks to feed;
To have as soft a glebe, as good increase of seed; 130
As pure and fresh an air upon her face to flow,
As *Evsham* for her life: and from her Steed doth show,
Her lusty rising Downs, as fair a prospect take
As that imperious Wold*: which her great Queen doth make
So wondrously admir'd, and her so far extend. 135
But, to the Marriage, hence, industrious Muse descend.

The *Naïads*, and the Nymphs extremely overjoy'd,
And on the winding banks all busily imploy'd,
Upon this joyful day, some dainty chaplets twine:
Some others chosen out, with fingers neat and fine, 140
Brave anadems² do make: some bauldricks up do bind:
Some garlands: and to some, the nosegays were assign'd;
As best their skill did serve. But, for that *Tame* should be
Still man-like as himself, therefore they will that he
Shall not be drest with flowers, to gardens that belong, 145
(His Bride that better fit) but only such as sprong
From the replenish'd meads, and fruitful pastures near.
To sort which flowers, some sit; some making garlands were;
The *Primrose*³ placing first, because that in the spring
It is the first appears, then only flourishing; 150
The azur'd *Hare-bell* next, with them, they neatly mixt:
T' allay whose luscious smell, they *Woodbind* plac'd betwixt.
Amongst those things of scent, there prick they in the *Lilly*,
And near to that again, her sister *Daffadilly*.

¹ *White-horse* striveth for sovereignty with all the Vales of *Britain*.
* *Cotswold*. ² Crowns of flowers.
³ Flowers of the meadows and pastures.

To sort these flowers of show, with th' other that were
    sweet,   155
The *Cowslip* then they couch, and th' *Oxslip*, for her meet:
The *Columbine* amongst they sparingly do set,
The yellow *King-cup*, wrought in many a curious fret,
And now and then among, of *Eglantine* a spray,
By which again a course of *Lady-smocks* they lay: 160
The *Crow-flower*, and thereby the *Clover-flower* they stick,
The *Daisy*, over all those sundry sweets so thick,
As Nature doth herself; to imitate her right:
Who seems in that her pearl* so greatly to delight,
That every Plain therewith she powd'reth to behold: 165
The crimson *Darnell Flower*, the *Blue-bottle*, and *Gold:*
Which though esteem'd but weeds; yet for their dainty hues,
And for their scent not ill, they for this purpose choose.
    Thus having told you how the Bridegroom *Tame* was
    drest,
I'll show you, how the Bride, fair *Isis*, they invest;   170
Sitting to be attir'd under her Bower of State,
Which scorns a meaner sort, than fits a princely rate.
In anadems for whom they curiously dispose
The *Red*,[1] the dainty *White*, the goodly *Damask Rose*,
For the rich *Ruby*, *Pearl*, and *Amatist*, men place   175
In Kings' emperial crowns, the circle that enchase.
The brave *Carnation* then, with sweet and sovereign power
(So of his colour call'd, although a *July-flower*)
With th' other of his kind, the speckled and the pale:
Then th' odoriferous *Pink*, that sends forth such a gale   180
Of sweetness; yet in scents, as various as in sorts.
The purple *Violet* then, the *Pansy* there supports:
The *Mary-gold* above t' adorn the archéd bar:
The double *Daisy*, *Thrift*, the *Button-batcheler*,
Sweet William, *Sops in Wine*, the *Campion:* and to these,   185

* *Margarita* is both a pearl and a daisy.   [1] Flowers of gardens.

Some *Lavander* they put, with *Rosemary* and *Bays:*
Sweet *Marjoram*, with her like, sweet *Basil* rare for smell,
With many a flower, whose name were now too long to tell:
And rarely with the rest, the goodly *Flower-delice.*
 Thus for the nuptial hour, all fitted point-device,   190
Whilst some still busied are in decking of the Bride,
Some others were again as seriously imploy'd
In strewing of those herbs,[1] at Bridals us'd that be;
Which everywhere they throw with bounteous hands and free.
The healthful *Balme* and *Mint*, from their full laps do fly, 195
The scent-full *Camomill*, the verdurous *Costmary.*
They hot *Muscado* oft with milder *Maudlin* cast:
Strong *Tansey*, *Fennell* cool, they prodigally waste:
Clear *Isop*, and therewith the comfortable *Thyme*,
Germander with the rest, each thing then in her prime; 200
As well of wholesome herbs, as every pleasant flower,
Which Nature here produc'd, to fit this happy hour.
Amongst these strewing kinds, some other wild that grow,
As *Burnet*, all abroad, and *Meadow-wort* they throw.
 Thus all things falling out to every one's desire,   205
The ceremonies done that Marriage doth require,
The Bride and Bridegroom set, and serv'd with sundry cates,
And every other plac'd, as fitted their estates;
Amongst this confluence great, wise *Charwell* here was thought
The fitt'st to cheer the guests; who throughly had been taught
In all that could pertain to courtship, long agon,   211
As coming from his sire, the fruitful *Helidon*,*
He travelleth to *Tames;* where passing by those Towns
Of that rich Country near, whereas the mirthful clowns,
With taber and the pipe, on holydays do use,   215
Upon the May-pole Green, to trample out their shoes:
And having in his ears the deep and solemn rings,†

[1] Strewing herbs.
* A Hill betwixt *Northamptonshire* and *Warwick.*
† Famous rings of bells in *Oxfordshire*, called the *Cross-ring.*

Which sound him all the way, unto the learnéd Springs,*
Where he, his Sovereign *Ouze* most happily doth meet,
And him, the thrice-three maids, *Apollo's* offspring, greet 220
With all their sacred gifts: thus, expert being grown
In music; and besides, a curious maker† known:
This *Charwell* (as I said) the fitt'st these Floods among,
For silence having call'd, thus to th' assembly song:

    Stand fast ye higher Hills: low Valleys easily lie: 225
And Forests that to both you equally apply
(But for the greater part, both wild and barren be);
Retire ye to your wastes; and Rivers only we,
Oft meeting let us mix: and with delightful grace,
Let every beauteous Nymph, her best-lov'd Flood imbrace,
An alien be he born, or near to her own spring, 231
So from his native fount he bravely flourishing,
Along the flow'ry fields, licentiously do strain,
Greeting each curléd grove, and circling every plain;
Or hasting to his fall, his shoaly gravel scours, 235
And with his crystal front, then courts the climbing tow'rs.

    Let all the world be judge, what Mountain hath a name,
Like that from whose proud foot, there springs some Flood
    of fame:
And in the earth's survey, what seat like that is set,
Whose streets some ample Stream, aboundantly doth wet?
Where is there Haven found, or Harbour, like that Road, 241
Int' which some goodly Flood, his burthen doth unload?
By whose rank swelling Stream, the far-fetch'd foreign
    fraught,
May up to inland towns conveniently be brought.
Of any part of earth, we be the most renown'd; 245
That countries very oft, nay, empires oft we bound.
As *Rubicon*, much fam'd, both for his fount and fall,

---

    * *Oxford.*
    † A fine poet.

The ancient limit held, twixt *Italy* and *Gaul.**
Europe and *Asia* keep on *Tanais*' either side.
Such honour have we Floods, the world (even) to divide. 250
Nay : Kingdoms thus we prove are christ'ned oft by us;
Iberia takes her name of crystal *Iberus*.
Such reverence to our kind the wiser ancients gave,
As they suppos'd each Flood a Deity to have :
   But with our fame at home return we to proceed. 255
In *Britain* here we find, our *Severn*, and our *Tweed*,
The tripartited *Isle* do generally divide,
To *England, Scotland, Wales,* as each doth keep her side.
Trent cuts the Land in two, so equally, as tho'
Nature it pointed-out, to our great *Brute* to show 260
How to his mighty sons the Island he might share.
A thousand of this kind, and nearer, I will spare ;
Where if the state of Floods, at large I list to show,
I proudly could report how *Pactolus* doth throw
Up grains of perfect gold ; and of great *Ganges* tell, 265
Which when full *India's* showers inforceth him to swell,
Gilds with his glistering sands the over-pampered shore :
How wealthy *Tagus* first by tumbling down his ore,
The rude and slothful *Moors* of old *Iberia* taught,
To search into those hills, from which such wealth be
   brought. 270
Beyond these if I pleas'd, I to your praise could bring,
In sacred *Tempe*, how (about the hoof-plow'd Spring)
The *Heliconian* Maids, upon that hallowed ground,
Recounting heavenly hymns eternally are crown'd.
And as the earth doth us in her own bowels nourish ; 275
So everything, that grows by us, doth thrive and flourish.
To godly virtuous men, we wisely likened are :
To be so in themselves, that do not only care ;

   * That which was called *Gallia Cisalpina*, and is **Lombardy, Romagna**, and the Western part of *Italy*.

But by a sacred power, which goodness doth await,
Do make those virtuous too, that them associate. 280
   By this, the Wedding ends, and brake up all the show:
And *Tames*, got, born, and bred, immediately doth flow,
To *Windsor*-ward amain (that with a wond'ring eye,
The Forest might behold his awful empery)
And soon becometh great, with waters wax'd so rank, 285
That with his wealth he seems to retch his widened bank:
Till happily attain'd his grandsire *Chiltern's* grounds,
Who with his beechen wreaths this King of Rivers crowns,
Amongst his holts and hills, as on his way he makes,
At *Reading* once arriv'd, clear *Kennet* overtakes: 290
Her lord the stately *Tames*, which that great Flood again,
With many signs of joy doth kindly entertain.
Then *Loddon* next comes in, contributing her store;
As still we see, "The much runs ever to the more."
Set out with all this pomp, when this emperial Stream, 295
Himself establish'd sees, amidst his wat'ry realm,
His much-lov'd *Henly* leaves, and proudly doth pursue
His Wood-nymph *Windsor's* seat, her lovely site to view.
Whose most delightful face when once the River sees,
Which shows herself attir'd in tall and stately trees, 300
He in such earnest love with amorous gestures wooes,
That looking still at her, his way was like to lose;
And wand'ring in and out so wildly seems to go,
As headlong he himself into her lap would throw.
   Him with the like desire the Forest doth imbrace, 305
And with her presence strives her *Tames* as much to grace.
No Forest, of them all, so fit as she doth stand.
When Princes, for their sports, her pleasures will command,
No Wood-nymph as herself such troops hath ever seen,
Nor can such quarries boast as have in *Windsor* been. 310

Nor any ever had so many solemn days;
So brave assemblies view'd, nor took so rich assays.*

   Then, hand in hand, her *Tames* the Forest softly brings,
To that supremest place of the great *English* Kings,
§ The *Garter's* Royal seat, from him who did advance   315
That Princely Order first, our first that conquered *France;*
The Temple of *Saint George*, whereas his honoured Knights,
Upon his hallowed day, observe their ancient rites:
Where *Eaton* is at hand to nurse that learnéd brood,
To keep the Muses still near to this princely Flood: 320
That nothing there may want, to beautify that seat,
With every pleasure stor'd: And here my Song complete.

    * Breaking up of Deer brought into the quarry.

ILLUSTRATIONS.

SHALL here be shorter than in the last before. The Muse is so full in herself, employed wholly about the Nuptials of *Tame* and *Isis*. In the girlands of *Tame* are wreathed most of our *English field-flowers:* in them of *Isis*, our more sweet and those of the *Garden;* Yet upon that,

315. *The* Garter's *Royal seat, from him who did advance.*

I cannot but rememver the institution (touched to the Fourth Song) of his most honourable Order, dedicated to S. *George* (in 24 *Ed.* III.) it is yearly at this place celebrated by that Noble Company of Twenty-six. Whether the cause were upon the word of *Garter* given in the *French* wars among the *English*, or upon the Queen's, or Countess of *Salisbury's*, Garter fallen from her leg, or upon different and more ancient original whatsoever, know clearly (without unlimited affectation of your Country's glory) that it exceeds in majesty, honour, and fame, all Chivalrous Orders in the world; and (excepting those of *Templars*, S. *James*, *Calatrava*, *Alcantara*, and such like other, which were more Religious than Military) hath precedence of antiquity before the eldest rank of honour, of that kind anywhere established. The *Anunciada* (instituted[1] by *Amades* VI. Earl of *Savoy*, about 1409, although others have it by *Amades* IV. and so create it before this of the Garter) and that of the *Golden Fleece*, by *Philip* Duke of *Burgundy*, 1429, of S. *Michael* by *Lewes* XI., *Della Banda* by *Alfonso* of *Spain*, and such like, ensued it, as imitating Institutions, after a regard of the far extended fame, worth, and glory of S. *George's* Knights.

[1] V. Aubert. Mir. Orig. Equest. 2. cap. 4. et Sansouin. Orig. de Cavalieri.

THE SIXTEENTH SONG.

THE ARGUMENT.

Old Ver, near to Saint Albans, brings
Watling to talk of ancient things;
What Verlam was before she fell,
And many more sad ruins tell.
Of the four old Emperial Ways, 5
The course they held, and to what Seas;
Of those Seven Saxon Kingdoms here,
Their sites, and how they bounded were.
Then Pure-vale vaunts her rich estate:
And Lea bewrays her wretched fate. 10
The Muse, led on with much delight,
Delivers London's happy site;
Shows this loose Age's lewd abuse:
And for this time there stays the Muse.

HE Bridal of our *Tame* and princely *Isis* past:
And *Tamesis* their son, begot, and waxing fast,
Inviteth crystal *Colne*[1] his wealth on him to lay,
Whose beauties had intic'd his Sovereign *Tames* to
    stay,
Had he not been inforc'd by his unruly train. 5
For *Brent*, a pretty Brook, allures him on again,
Great *London* to salute, whose high-rear'd turrets throng
To gaze upon the Flood, as he doth pass along.

---
[1] The river running by *Uxbridge* and *Colbrooke*.

Now, as the *Tames* is great, so most transparent *Colne*,
Feels, with excessive joy, her amorous bosom swolne,　10
That *Ver* of long esteem'd, a famous ancient Flood
(Upon whose aged bank old *Verlamchester* stood,
Before the *Roman* rule) here glorified of yore,
Unto her clearer banks contributed his store;
Enlarging both her stream, and strengthening his renown, 15
Where the delicious meads her through her course do crown.
This *Ver*[1] (as I have said) *Colne's* tributary brook,
On *Verlam's* ruin'd walls as sadly he doth look,
Near holy *Alban's* Town, where his rich shrine was set,
Old *Watling* in his way the Flood doth over-get.　20
Where after reverence done, *Ver*, quoth the ancient Street,
'Tis long since thou and I first in this place did meet.
And so it is, quoth *Ver*, and we have liv'd to see
Things in far better state than at this time they be:
But He that made, amend: for much there goes amiss. 25
Quoth *Watling*, Gentle Flood, yea so in truth it is:
And sith of this thou speak'st; the very sooth to say,
Since great *Melmutius*, first, made me the noblest Way,
The soil is altered much; the cause I pray thee show.
The time that thou hast liv'd, hath taught thee much to know. 30
I fain would understand, why this delightful place,
In former time that stood so high in Nature's grace,
(Which bare such store of grain, and that so wondrous great,
That all the neighbouring coast was call'd the soil of wheat*)
Of later time is turn'd a hot and hungry sand,　35
Which scarce repays the seed first cast into the land.
At which the silent Brook shrunk in his silver head,
And feign'd as he away would instantly have fled;
Suspecting, present speech might passéd grief renew.
Whom *Watling* thus again doth seriously pursue:　40

[1] The little clear river by *Saint Albans*.　　* *Whethamstead*.

I pray thee be not coy, but answer my demand :
The cause of this (dear Flood) I fain would understand.
§ Thou saw'st when *Verlam* once her head aloft did bear
(Which in her cinders now lies sadly buried here)
With alablaster, tuch, and porphery adorn'd,   45
When (well near) in her pride great *Troynovant* she scorn'd.
§ Thou saw'st great-burthen'd ships through these thy
    valleys pass,
Where now the sharp-edg'd scythe sheers up the spiring
    grass :
That where the ugly seal and porpoise us'd to play,
The grasshopper and ant now lord it all the day :   50
Where now *Saint Albans* stands was called *Holme-hurst* then;
Whose sumptuous Fane we see neglected now again.
    This rich and goodly Fane which ruin'd thou dost see,
Quoth *Ver*, the motive is that thou importun'st me:
But to another thing thou cunningly dost fly,   55
And reason seem'st to urge of her sterility.
With that he fetch'd a sigh, and ground his teeth in rage ;
Quoth *Ver* even for the sin of this accursed Age.
Behold that goodly Fane, which ruin'd now doth stand,
To holy *Alban*[1] built, first Martyr of the Land ;   60
Who in the faith of Christ from *Rome* to *Britain* came,
And dying in this place, resign'd his glorious name.
In memory of whom, (as more than half-divine)
Our English *Offa* rear'd a rich and sumptuous shrine
And monastery here : which our succeeding kings,   65
From time to time endow'd with many goodly things.
And many a Christian knight was buried here, before
The Norman set his foot upon this conquered shore ;
And after those brave spirits in all those baleful stowers,
That with Duke *Robert*[2] went against the Pagan powers,   70

[1] Look before to the Eleventh Song.
[2] With the eldest son of the *Conqueror* into the Holy Land.

And in their Country's right at *Cressy* those that stood,
And that at *Poyters* bath'd their bilbowes in French blood ;
Their valiant Nephews next at *Agincourt* that fought,
Whereas rebellious France upon her knees was brought :
In this Religious House at some of their returns, 75
When Nature claim'd her due, here plac'd their hallowed
    urns :
Which now devouring Time, in his so mighty waste,
Demolishing those walls, hath utterly defac'd.
So that the earth to feel the ruinous heaps of stones,
That with the burth'nous weight now press their sacred
    bones, 80
Forbids this wicked brood, should by her fruits be fed ;
As loathing her own womb, that such loose children bred.
Herewith transported quite, to these exclaims he fell :
Lives no man, that this world her grievous crimes dare tell ?
Where be those noble spirits for ancient things that stood ?
When in my prime of youth I was a gallant Flood ; 86
In those free golden days, it was the satire's use
To tax the guilty times, and rail upon abuse :
But soothers find the way preferment most to win ;
Who serving great men's turns, become the bawds to sin. 90
    When *Watling* in his words that took but small delight,
Hearing the angry Brook so cruelly to bite ;
As one that fain would drive these fancies from his mind,
Quoth he, I'll tell thee things that suit thy gentler kind.
My song is of myself, and my three sister Streets, 95
Which way each of us run, where each her fellow meets,
    § Since us, his kingly Ways, *Mulmutius* first began,
From sea, again to sea, that through the Island ran.
Which that in mind to keep posterity might have,
Appointing first our course, this privilege he gave, 100
That no man might arrest, or debtor's goods might seize
In any of us four his military Ways.

And though the *Fosse* in length exceed me many a mile,
That holds from shore to shore the length of all the Isle,
From where rich *Cornwall* points to the *Iberian* seas,   105
Till colder *Cathnes* tells the scattered *Orcades*,
I measuring but the breadth, that is not half his gait;
Yet, for that I am grac'd with goodly *London's* state,[1]
And *Tames* and *Severn* both since in my course I cross,
And in much greater trade; am worthier far than *Fosse*.   110
But O, unhappy chance! through time's disastrous lot,
Our other fellow Streets lie utterly forgot:
As *Icning*, that set out from *Yarmouth* in the East,
By the *Iceni* then being generally possest,
Was of that people first term'd *Icning* in her race,   115
Upon the *Chiltern*[2] here that did my course imbrace:
Into the dropping South and bearing then outright,
Upon the *Solent* Sea stopt on the *Isle*-of-*Wight*.
 And *Rickneld*, forth that raught from *Cambria's* farther shore,
Where *South-Wales* now shoots forth *Saint David's* promontore.   120
And, on his mid-way near, did me in *England* meet;
Then in his oblique course the lusty straggling Street
Soon overtook the *Fosse;* and toward the fall of *Tine*,
Into the *German* Sea dissolv'd at his decline.   124
 Here *Watling* would have ceas'd, his tale as having told:
But now this Flood that fain the Street in talk would hold,
Those ancient things to hear, which well old *Watling* knew,
With these enticing words, her fairly forward drew.
 Right noble Street, quoth he, thou hast liv'd long, gone far,
Much traffic had in peace, much travailéd in war;   130

---

[1] *Watling*, the chiefest of the four great Ways.
[2] Not far from *Dunstable*.

And in thy larger course survey'st as sundry grounds
(Where I poor Flood am lock'd within these narrower
    bounds,
And like my ruin'd self these ruins only see,
And there remains not one to pity them or me) '
On with thy former speech : I pray thee somewhat say.   135
For, *Watling*, as thou art a military Way,
Thy story of old Streets likes me so wondrous well,
That of the ancient folk I fain would hear thee tell.
    With these persuasive words, smooth *Ver* the *Watling* wan:
Stroking her dusty face, when thus the Street began ;   140
    When once their Seven-fold Rule the *Saxons* came to rear,
And yet with half this *Isle* sufficed scarcely were,
Though from the *inland* part the *Britans* they had chas'd,
Then understand how here themselves the *Saxons* plac'd.
    Where in Great *Britain's* state four people of her own   145
Were by the several names of their abodes well known
(As, in that horn which juts into the sea so far,
Wherein our *Devonshire* now, and furthest *Cornwall* are,
The old *Danmonii* dwelt : so hard again at hand,
The *Durotriges* sat on the *Dorsetian* sand ;   150
And where from sea to sea the *Belgæ* forth were let,
Even from *Southhampton's* shore through *Wilts* and *Somerset*
The *Attrebates* in *Bark* unto the bank of *Tames*
Betwixt the *Celtic* sleeve and the *Sabrinian* streams)
The *Saxons* there set down one Kingdom : which install'd,
And being West, they it their Western Kingdom call'd.   156
So Eastward where by *Tames* the *Trinobants* were set,
To *Trinovant* their town, for that their name in debt,
That *London* now we term, the *Saxons* did possess
And their East Kingdom call'd, as *Essex** doth express ;   160

¹ For a more plain division of the English kingdoms see to the
Eleventh Song.
* So called of the *East-Saxons*.

The greatest part thereof, and still their name doth bear;
Though *Middlesex* therein, and part of *Hartford* were;
From *Colne* upon the West, upon the East to *Stour*,*
Where mighty *Tames* himself doth into *Neptune* pour.
    As to our farthest rise, where forth those Fore-lands lean,
Which bear their chalky brows into the *German* Main,   166
The *Angles* which arose out of the *Saxon* race,
Allur'd with the delights and fitness of that place,
Where the *Iceni* liv'd did set their Kingdom down,
From where the wallowing seas those queachy Washes drown
That *Ely* do in-isle, to martyred *Edmond's* Ditch,   171
Till those *Norfolcian* shores vast *Neptune* doth inrich :
Which (farthest to the East of this divided *Isle*)
Th' East *Angles*' Kingdom, then, those *English* did instyle.
    And *Sussex* seemeth still, as with an open mouth,   175
Those *Saxons*' Rule to show that of the utmost South
The name to them assum'd, who rigorously expell'd
The *Kentish Britans* thence, and those rough wood-lands held
From where the goodly *Tames* the *Surrian* grounds doth sweep,
Until the smiling Downs salute the *Celtic* Deep.   180
    Where the *Dobuni* dwelt, their neighbouring *Cateuclani*,
Cornavii more remote, and where the *Coritani*,
Where *Dee* and *Mersey* shoot into the *Irish* Sea ;
(Which well-near o'er this part, now called *England*, lay,
From *Severn* to the Ditch that cuts *New-Market* Plain,   185
And from the banks of *Tames* to *Humber*, which contain
So many goodly Shires, of *Mersey Mercia* hight)
Their mightier Empire, there, the middle *English* pight.
Which farthest though it raught, yet there it did not end :
But *Offa*, King thereof, it after did extend   190
Beyond the bank of *Dee ;* and by a Ditch he cut
Through *Wales* from North to South, into wide *Mercia* put

* A River upon the confines of *Suffolk* and *Essex*.

Well-near the half thereof: and from three peoples there,
To whom three special parts divided justly were
(The *Ordovices*, now which *North-Wales* people be, 195
From *Cheshire* which of old divided was by *Dee:*
And from our *Marchers* now, that were *Demetæ* then;
And those *Silures* call'd, by us the *South-Wales* men)
Beyond the *Severn*, much the *English Offa* took,
To shut the *Britans* up, within a little nook. 200
 From whence, by *Mersey's* banks, the rest a Kingdom made:
Where, in the *Britans'* rule (before) the *Brigants* sway'd;
The powerful *English* there establish'd were to stand:
Which, North from *Humber* set, they term'd *North-humber-*
 land; [stall'd.
Two Kingdoms which had been, with several thrones in-
Bernitia hight the one; *Diera* th' other call'd. 206
The first from *Humber* stretch'd unto the bank of *Tine:*
Which river and the *Frith* the other did confine.
Diera beareth through the spacious *Yorkish* bounds,
From *Durham* down along to the *Lancastrian* Sounds,* 210
With *Mersey* and clear *Tine* continuing to their fall,
To *England*-ward within the *Pict's* renownéd Wall,
And did the greater part of *Cumberland*† contain:
With whom the *Britans'* name for ever shall remain;
Who there amongst the rocks and mountains livéd long, 215
When they *Loegria* left, inforc'd through powerful wrong.
Bernitia over *Tine*, into *Albania* lay,
To where the *Frith*‡ falls out into the *German* Sea.
 This said, the aged Street sagg'd sadly on alone:
And *Ver* upon his course now hasted to be gone, 220
T' accompany his *Colne:* which as she gently glides,
Doth kindly him imbrace: whom soon this hap betides:
As *Colne* come on along, and chanc'd to cast her eye

---

* Sea-depths near the shores.   † The *Cymbries'* Land.
‡ A river running by *Edenbrough* into the sea.

THE SIXTEENTH SONG.

Upon that neighbouring Hill where *Harrow* stands so high,
She *Peryvale*[1] perceiv'd prank'd up with wreaths of wheat,   225
And with exulting terms thus glorying in her seat:
Why should not I be coy, and of my beauties nice,
Since this my goodly grain is held of greatest price?
No manchet can so well the courtly palate please,
As that made of the meal fetch'd from my fertile leaze.   230
Their finest of that kind, compared with my wheat,
For whiteness of the bread, doth look like common cheat.
What barley is there found, whose fair and bearded ear
Makes stouter *English* ale, or stronger *English* beer?
The oat, the bean, and pease, with me but pulses are;   235
The coarse and browner rye, no more than fitch and tare.
What seed doth any soil, in *England* bring, that I
Beyond her most increase yet cannot multiply?
Besides, my sure abode next goodly *London* is,
To vent my fruitful store, that me doth never miss.   240
And those poor baser things, they cannot put away,
Howe'er I set my price, ne'er on my chap-men stay.
    When presently the Hill, that maketh her a Vale,
With things he had in hand, did interrupt her tale,
With *Hampsted* being fall'n and *High-gate* at debate;   245
As one before them both, that would advance his state,
From either for his height to bear away the praise,
Besides that he alone rich *Peryvale* surveys.
But *Hampsted* pleads, himself in simples to have skill,[2]
And therefore by desert to be the noblest Hill;   250
As one, that on his worth, and knowledge doth rely,
In learnéd physic's use, and skilful surgery;[3]
And challengeth, from them, the worthiest place her own,
Since that old *Watling* once, o'er him, to pass was known.

---

[1] *Peryvale*, or *Pure-vale*, yieldeth the finest meal of *England*.
[2] *Hampsted* excellent for simples.
[3] *Hampsted* hill, famous for simples.

Then *High-gate* boasts his Way; which men do most fre-
    quent; 255
His long-continued fame; his high and great descent;
Appointed for a Gate of *London* to have been,
When first the mighty *Brute* that City did begin.
And that he is the Hill, next *Enfield* which hath place,
A Forest for her pride, though titled but a Chace. 260
Her purlewes, and her parks, her circuit full as large,
As some (perhaps) whose state requires a greater charge.
Whose holts* that view the East, do wistly stand to look
Upon the winding course of *Lee's* delightful Brook.
Where *Mimer* coming in, invites her sister *Beane*, 265
Amongst the chalky banks t' increase their Mistress' train;
Whom by the dainty hand, obsequiously they lead
(By *Hartford* gliding on, through many a pleasant mead.
And coming in her course, to cross the common fare,
For kindness she doth kiss that hospitable *Ware*) 270
Yet scarcely comfort *Lee* (alas!) so woe-begone,
Complaining in her course, thus to herself alone:
How should my beauty now give *Waltham* such delight,
Or I poor silly Brook take pleasure in her sight?
Antiquity (for that it stands so far from view, 275
And would her doting dreams should be believ'd for true)
Dare loudly lie for *Colne*, that sometimes ships did pass,
To *Verlam* by her stream, when *Verlam* famous was;
But, by these later times, suspected but to feign,
She planks and anchors shows, her error to maintain; 280
Which were, indeed, of boats, for pleasure there to row
Upon her (then a Lake) the *Roman* Pomp to show,
When *Rome*, her forces here did every year supply,
And at old *Verlam* kept a warlike colony.
But I distressèd *Lee*, whose course doth plainly tell, 285
That what of *Colne* is said, of me none could refell,

* High woody banks.

Whom *Alfred** but too wise (poor River) I may say
(When he the cruel *Danes* did cunningly betray,
Which *Hartford* then besieg'd, whose Navy there abode,
And on my spacious breast, before the Castle rode)   290
By vantage of my soil, he did divide my stream,
That they might ne'er return to *Neptune's* wat'ry realm
And, since, distresséd *Lee* I have been left forlorn,
A by-word to each Brook, and to the world a scorn.
 When *Sturt*, a Nymph of hers (whose faith she oft had
  prov'd,   295
And whom, of all her train, *Lee* most intirely lov'd)
Lest so excessive grief, her Mistress might invade,
Thus (by fair gentle speech) to patience doth persuade:
 Though you be not so great to others as before,
Yet not a jot for that dislike yourself the more.   300
Your case is not alone, nor is (at all) so strange ;
Sith everything on earth subjects itself to change.
Where rivers sometime ran, is firm and certain ground :
And where before were hills, now standing lakes are found.
And that which most you urge, your beauty to dispoil,   305
Doth recompense your bank, with quantity of soil,
Beset with ranks of swans ; that, in their wonted pride,
Do prune their snowy plumes upon your pleasant side.
And *Waltham* woos you still, and smiles with wonted cheer:
And *Tames* as at the first, so still doth hold you dear.   310
 To much belovéd *Lee*, this scarcely *Sturt* had spoke,
But goodly *London's* sight their further purpose broke :
When *Tames*, his either banks adorn'd with buildings fair,
The City to salute doth bid the Muse prepare.
Whose turrets, fanes, and spires, when wistly she beholds,
Her wonder at the sight, thus strangely she unfolds :   316
 At thy great builder's wit, who's he but wonder may ?
Nay, of his wisdom, thus ensuing times shall say :

   * See to the Twelfth Song.

O more than mortal man, that did this Town begin!
Whose knowledge found the plot, so fit to set it in.   320
What God, or heavenly power was harbour'd in thy breast,
From whom with such success thy labours should be blest?
Built on a rising bank, within a vale to stand,[1]
And for thy healthful soil, chose gravel mix'd with sand.
And where fair *Tames* his course into a crescent casts   325
(That, forcéd by his tides, as still by her he hastes,
He might his surging waves into her bosom send)
Because too far in length, his Town should not extend.
   And to the North and South, upon an equal reach,
Two hills their even banks do somewhat seem to stretch,   330
Those two extremer winds* from hurting it to let;
And only level lies, upon the rise and set.
Of all this goodly *Isle*, where breathes most cheerful air,
And every way thereto the ways most smooth and fair;
As in the fittest place, by man that could be thought,   335
To which by land, or sea, provision might be brought.
And such a road for ships scarce all the world commands,
As is the goodly *Tames*, near where *Brute's* City stands.
Nor any haven lies to which is more resort,
Commodities to bring, as also to transport: 340
Our kingdom that enrich'd (through which we flourish'd long)
Ere idle gentry up in such aboundance sprong.
Now pestring all this Isle: whose disproportion draws
The public wealth so dry, and only is the cause
Our gold goes out so fast, for foolish foreign things,   345
Which upstart gentry still into our country brings;
Who their insatiate pride seek chiefly to maintain
By that, which only serves to uses vile and vain:
Which our plain fathers erst would have accounted sin,
Before the costly coach, and silken stock came in;   350

[1] The goodly situation of *London.*
* The North and South winds.

THE SIXTEENTH SONG. 207

Before that *Indian* weed* so strongly was imbrac'd ;
Wherein, such mighty sums we prodigally waste ;
That merchants long train'd up in gain's deceitful school,
And subtly having learn'd to sooth the humorous fool,
Present their painted toys unto this frantic gull,   355
Disparaging our tin, our leather, corn, and wool ;
When foreigners, with ours them warmly clothe and feed,
Transporting trash to us, of which we ne'er had need.
  But whilst the angry Muse, thus on the Time exclaims,
Sith everything therein consisteth in extremes ;   360
Lest she inforc'd with wrongs, her limits should transcend,
Here of this present Song she briefly makes an end.

* Tobacco.

ILLUSTRATIONS.

 N wandering passage the Muse returns from the Wedding, somewhat into the land, and first to *Hartford*; whence, after matter of description, to *London*.

43. *Thou saw'st when* Verlam *once her head aloft did bear.*

For, under *Nero*, the *Britons* intolerably loaden with weight of the *Roman* government, and especially the *Icens* (now *Norfolk* and *Suffolk* men) provoked by that cruel servitude, into which, not themselves only, but the wife also and posterity of their King *Prasutagus* were, even beyond right of victory, constrained: at length breathing for liberty (and in a further continuance of war having for their general Queen *Boudicea, Bunduica,* or as the difference of her name is) rebelled against their foreign conqueror, and in martial opposition committing a slaughter of no less than 80,000, (as *Dio* hath, although *Tacitus* miss 10,000 of this number,) ransacked and spoiled *Maldon* (then *Camalodunum*) and also this *Verulam* (near S. *Albans*, which were the two chief towns of the Isle[1]; The first a Colony (whereof the Eighth

[1] Sueton. lib. 6. cap. 39.

THE SIXTEENTH SONG.

Song :) this a *Municipal* City,* called expressly in a Catalogue at the end of *Nennius, Caer-Municip.* Out of *A. Gellius*[1] I thus note to you its nature : *Municipes sunt Cives Romani ex municipiis suo jure et legibus suis utentes, Muneris tantùm cum Pop. Rom. honorarii participes, à quo Munere capessendo appellati videntur : nullus aliis necessitatibus neque ullâ Pop. Rom. lege astricti, quùm nunquam Pop. Rom. eorum fundus factus esset.*† It differed from a *Colony*, most of all in that a *Colony* was a progeny of the City, and this of such as were received into State-favour and friendship by the *Roman*. Personating the *Genius* of *Verlam*, that ever-famous *Spenser*[2] sung,

*I was that Citie, which the Garland wore
Of* Britaine's *Pride, delivered unto me
By* Romane *Victors, which it wonne of yore ;
Though nought at all but Ruines now I bee,
And lye in mine owne ashes, as ye see :*
Verlam *I was ; what bootes it that I was,
Sith now I am but weedes and wastfull gras ?*

As under the *Romans*, so in the *Saxon*‡ times afterward it endured a second ruin : and, out of its corruption, after the Abbey erected by King *Offa*, was generated that of Saint *Albans ;* whither, in later times most of the stone-works and whatsoever fit for building was by the Abbots translated.[3] So that,

——— *Now remaines no memorie,
Nor anie little moniment to see,
By which the travailer, that fares that way,
This once was shee, may warned be to say.*[4]

* *Municipium* Tacit. Annal. 14.   [1] Noct. Attic. 16. cap. 13.
† Such as lived in them were free of *Rome*, but using their own laws, capable only of honorary titles in the *Roman* state, and thence had their name.   [2] In his Ruines of Time.
‡ 795.   [3] Leland. ad Cyg. Cant.   [4] Spens. ubi suprà.

The name hath been thought from the river there running called *Ver*, and *Humfrey Lhuid*[1] makes it, as if it were **Uer=lhan**, *i.e.*, a Church upon *Ver*.

17. *Thou saw'st great* burthen'd ships *through these thy valleys pass.*

Lay not here unlikelihoods to the Author's charge; he tells you more judiciously towards the end of the Song. But the cause why some have thought so, is, for that, *Gildas*,[2] speaking of S. *Alban's* martyrdom and his miraculous passing through the river at *Verlamcestre*, calls it *iter ignotum trans Thamesis fluvii alveum** :* so by collection they guessed that *Thames* had then his full course this way, being thereto further moved by anchors and such like here digged up. This conjecture hath been followed by that noble Muse[3] thus in the person of *Verlam :*

> *And where the christall* Thamis *wont to slide*
> *In silver channell downe along the lee,*
> *About whose flowrie bankes on either side*
> *A thousand Nymphes, with mirthfull jollitee,*
> *Were wont to play, from all annoyance free :*
> *There now no river's course is to be scene,*
> *But moorish fennes, and marshes ever greene.*
>
> *There also, where the winged ships were seene,*
> *In liquid waves to cut their fomie waie ;*
> *A thousand Fishers numbred to have been,*
> *In that wide lake looking for plenteous praie*
> *Of fish, with baits which they usde to betraie,*
> *Is now no lake, nor any Fishers store,*
> *Nor ever ship shall saile there anie more.*

But, for this matter of the *Thames*, those two great anti-

[1] In Brev. Brit.   [2] In Epist. de Excid. Britan.
* An unknown passage over Thames.   [3] Spenser.

THE SIXTEENTH SONG. 211

quaries, *Leland* and *Camden*, have joined in judgment against it : and for the anchors, they may be supposed of fish-boats in large pools, which have here been; and yet are left relics of their name.

97. *Since us his* Kingly Ways Molmutius *first began.*

Near 500 years before our Saviour, this King *Molmutius* (take it upon credit of the *British* story) constituted divers laws; especially that *Churches, Ploughs,* and *High-ways* should have liberties of Sanctuary, by no authority violable. That *Churches* should be free and enjoy liberty for refuge, consenting allowance of most nations have tolerated, and in this kingdom (it being affirmed also by constitution of King *Lucius*[1] a Christian,) every Churchyard was a Sanctuary, until by Act of Parliament[2] under *Hen.* VIII. that licence, for protection of offences, being too much abused, was taken away; but, whether now restored in the last Parliament,[3] wherein all Statutes concerning *Abjuration* or *Sanctuary* made before 35 *Eliz.* are repealed, I examine not. The *Plough* and Husbandmen have by our Statutes[4] and especially by *Civil*[5] and *Persian*[6] law, great freedom. *High-ways*, being without exception necessary, as well for peace as war, have been defended in the *Roman*[7] laws, and are taken in ours, to be in that respect (as they are by implication of the name) *the King's High-ways,*[8] and *res sacræ: et qui aliquid inde occupaverit excedendo fines et terminos terræ suæ dicitur fecisse Purpresturam super ipsum Regem.** According to this privilege of *Mulmutius* in the Statute of

[1] Florilegus. [2] 22 *Hen.* 8. cap. 14.
[3] Jacob. Sess. 1. cap. 25.
[4] West. 2. cap. 20. et 21. *Ed.* 1. District. Scaccarii.
[5] C. Quæ res pignori oblig. 1. 7. Executores et alibi.
[6] Xenoph. Cyropæd. *t.*   [7] ff. de viâ publica.
[8] Bract. lib. 4. tract. Assis. Nov. Diss. c. 11, §. 8.
* Privileged places, and he which trespasses there commits purpresture upon the King.

Marlebridge[1] it is enacted, that none should distrain in the King's High-way, or the common Street, but the King and his Ministers, *specialem authoritatem ad hæc habentibus;* which I particularly transcribe, because the printed books are therein so generally corrupted by addition of this here cited in Latin; You see it alters the Law much, and we have divers judgments, that in behalf of the King by common Bailiffs without special authority 𝕯𝖎𝖘𝖙𝖗𝖊𝖘𝖘 may be taken,[2] as for an amerciament in the Sheriff's Torne or Leet, or for Parliament Knights' fees. But the old rolls of the Statute (as I have seen in a fair MS. examined by the exemplification, for the Record itself is with many other lost) had not those words, as the Register[3] also specially admonishes, nor is any part of that Chapter in some MSS. which I marvel at, seeing we have a formal writ grounded upon it. Not much amiss were it here to remember a worse fault, but continually received, in the *Charter of the Forest, Art. VII.* where you read *Nullus Forestarius etc. aliquam collectam faciat nisi per Visum et Sacramentum XII. Regardatorum quando faciunt Regardum. Tot Forestarii, etc.,* the truth of the best copies (and so was the Record) being in this digestion, *Nullus Forestarius, etc. aliquam collectam faciat. Et per visum Sacramentum XII. Regardatorum quando faciunt Regardum tot Forestarii ponantur, etc.,* as beside authentic MSS. it is expressly in the like Charter, almost word for word, given first by King *John,* and printed in *Mathew Paris;* twixt which, and that of ours commonly read, may be made a time-deserving comparison. Were it not for digression, I would speak of the senseless making of *Boniface* Archbishop of *Canterbury* witness to the grand Charter in 9

---

[1] 52 *Hen.* 3. cap. 16. et vid. Artic. Cler. cap. 9. Statutum *Marlbridge* sibi restitutum.
[2] 34 *Ed.* 1. 𝔄𝔲𝔬𝔲𝔯𝔶 232. 8. *Rich.* 2. ibid. 194. 11 *Hen.* 4. fol. 1, 19 *Ed.* 2. 𝔄𝔲𝔬𝔲𝔯𝔶 221. et 225. alibi. [3] Original. fol. 97. b.
[4] Charta de Foresta ad MS. emendata.

Hen. III. When as it is plain that he was not Archbishop until 25. The best copy that ever I saw had *Simon* Archbishop of *Canterbury:* which indeed was worse, there being no such prelate of that See in those times; but the mistaking was by the transcriber turning the single *S.* (according to the form of writing in that age) into *Simon* for *Stephen*, who was (*Stephen* of *Langton*) Archbishop at that time. But I forget myself in following matter of my more particular study, and return to *Molmutius.* His constitution being general for liberty of Highways, controversy grew about the course and limits of them: whereupon his son, King *Belin*, to quit the subject of that doubt, caused more specially these four, here presently spoken of, to be made, which might be for interrupted passage, both in war and peace; and hence by the Author, they are called *Military*, (a name given by the *Romans* to such High-ways, as were for their marching armies) and indeed by more polite conceit[1] and judicious authority these our Ways have been thought a work of the *Romans* also. But their courses are differently reported, and in some part their names also. The Author calls them *Watling-street*, the *Fosse*, *Ikinild* and *Rickeneld.* This name of *Rickeneld* is in *Randall* of *Chester*, and by him derived from S. *Dewies* in *Pembroke* into *Hereford*, and so through *Worcester*, *Warwick*, *Derby*, and *York*-shires to *Tinmouth*, which (upon the Author's credit reporting it to me) is also justifiable by a very ancient deed of lands, bounded near *Bermingham* in *Warwickshire* by *Rickeneld.* To endeavour certainty in them, were but to obtrude unwarrantable conjecture, and abuse time and you. Of *Watling* (who is here personated, and so much the more proper because *Verlam* was called also by the English,[2] *Watlingchester*,) it is said that it went from

[1] V. Camden Roman.   [2] Lhuid. Brevior. Brit.

Dover in *Kent*, and so by West of *London* (yet part of the name seems to this day left in the middle of the City) to this place, and thence in a crooked line through *Shropshire* by *Wrekin* Hill into *Cardigan*[1]; but others[2] say from *Verlam* to *Chester;* and where all is referred to *Belin* by *Geffrey* ap *Arthur*, and *Polychronicon*, another[3] tells you that the sons of (I know not what) King *Wethle* made, and denominated it. The *Fosse* is derived by one consent out of *Cornwall* into *Devonshire*, through *Somerset*, over *Cotes-wold* by *Teukesburie*, along near *Coventry* to *Leicester*, through *Lincoln* to *Berwick*, and thence to *Cathness* the utmost of *Scotland*. Of restitution of the other you may be desperate; *Rickeneld* I have told you of. In *Henry* of *Huntingdon*, no such name is found, but with the first two, *Ickenild* and *Ermingstreet*. *Ickenild*, saith he, goes from East to West; *Ermingstreet* from South to North. Another tells me that *Ermingstreet* begins at S. *Dewies*, and conveys itself to *Southampton;* which the Author hath attributed to *Ichning*, begun (upon the word's community with *Icens*) in the Eastern parts. It's not in my power to reconcile all these, or elect the best; I only add, that *Ermingstreet* (which being of English idiom, seems to have had its name from Iᵽmunꝛull in that signification, whereby it interprets[4] an universal pillar worshipped for *Mercury*, President of Ways,) is like enough (if *Huntingdon* be in the right, making it from South to North) to have left its part in *Stanstreet* in *Surrey*, where a way made with stones and gravel in a soil on both sides very different, continues near a mile; and thence towards the Eastern shore in *Sussex* are some places seeming as other relics of it. But I here determine nothing.

[1] Polychronic. lib. 1. cap. de Plat. reg.
[2] Henric. Huntingd. Hist. 1.
[3] Roger Hoveden. part 1. fol. 248.
[4] Adam Bremens. Hist. Eccles. cap. 5. And see to the Third Song.

THE SEVENTEENTH SONG.

THE ARGUMENT.

To Medway, Tames a suitor goes;
But fancies Mole, as forth he flows
Her Mother, Homesdale, holds her in:
She digs through earth, the Tames to win.
Great Tames, as King of Rivers, sings   5
The Catalogue of th' English Kings.
Thence the light Muse, to th' Southward soars,
The Surrian and Sussexian shores;
The Forests and the Downs surveys,
With Rillets running to those Seas;   10
This Song of hers then cutteth short,
For things to come, of much import.

T length it came to pass, that *Isis* and her *Tame*
Of *Medway* understood, a Nymph of wondrous fame;
And much desirous were, their princely *Tames* should
   prove
If (as a wooer) he could win her maiden-love;
That of so great descent, and of so large a dower,   5
Might well-ally their House, and much increase his power:
And striving to prefer their Son, the best they may,
Set forth the lusty Flood, in rich and brave array,
Bank'd with imbrodered meads, of sundry suits of flowers,
His breast adorn'd with swans, oft wash'd with silver showers;

A train of gallant Floods, at such a costly rate 11
As might beseem their care, and fitting his estate.
  Attended and attir'd magnificently thus,
They send him to the Court of great *Oceanus*,
The world's huge wealth to see; yet with a full intent, 15
To woo the lovely Nymph, fair *Medway*, as he went.
Who to his Dame and Sire his duty scarce had done,
And whilst they sadly wept at parting of their Son,
See what the *Tames* befell, when 'twas suspected least.
  As still his goodly train yet every hour increast, 20
And from the *Surrian* shores clear *Wey* came down to meet
His greatness, whom the *Tames* so graciously doth greet,
That with the fern-crown'd Flood* he minion-like doth play:
Yet is not this the Brook, enticeth him to stay.
But as they thus, in pomp, came sporting on the shoal, 25
'Gainst *Hampton-Court* he meets the soft and gentle *Mole*.
Whose eyes so pierc'd his breast, that seeming to foreslow
The way which he so long intended was to go,
With trifling up and down, he wand'reth here and there;
And that he in her sight, transparent might appear, 30
Applies himself to fords, and setteth his delight
On that which most might make him gracious in her sight.
  Then *Isis* and the *Tame* from their conjoinèd bed,
Desirous still to learn how *Tames* their son had sped
(For greatly they had hop'd, his time had so been spent, 35
That he ere this had won the goodly heir of *Kent*)
And sending to enquire, had news return'd again
(By such as they imploy'd, on purpose in his train)
How this their only heir, the *Isle's* emperial Flood,
Had loiterèd thus in love, neglectful of his good. 40
  No marvel (at the news) though *Ouse*† and *Tame* were sad,
More comfort of their son expecting to have had. [show'd:
Nor blame them, in their looks much sorrow though they

* Coming by *Fernham*, so called of *fern* there growing.   † *Isis*.

Who fearing lest he might thus meanly be bestow'd,
And knowing danger still increaséd by delay,   45
Employ their utmost power, to hasten him away.
But *Tames* would hardly on : oft turning back to show,
From his much-lovéd *Mole* how loth he was to go.
   The mother of the *Mole*, old *Homesdale*,* likewise bears
Th' affection of her child, as ill as they do theirs :   50
Who nobly though deriv'd, yet could have been content,
T' have match'd her with a Flood, of far more mean descent.
But *Mole* respects her words, as vain and idle dreams,
Compar'd with that high joy, to be belov'd of *Tames :*
And head-long holds her course, his company to win.   55
But, *Homesdale* raiséd hills, to keep the straggler in ;
That of her daughter's stay she need no more to doubt :
(Yet never was there help, but love could find it out.)
§ *Mole* digs herself a path, by working day and night
(According to her name, to show her nature right)   60
And underneath the earth, for three miles' space doth creep :
Till gotten out of sight, quite from her mother's keep,
Her fore-intended course the wanton Nymph doth run ;
As longing to imbrace old *Tame* and *Isis'* son.   [take,
   When *Tames* now understood, what pains the *Mole* did
How far the loving Nymph adventur'd for his sake ;   65
Although with *Medway* match'd, yet never could remove
The often quick'ning sparks of his more ancient love.
So that it comes to pass, when by great Nature's guide
The *Ocean* doth return, and thrusteth-in the tide ;   70
Up tow'rds the place, where first his much-lov'd *Mole* was
      seen,
§ He ever since doth flow, beyond delightful *Sheene*.[1]
   Then *Wandal* cometh in, the *Mole's* belovéd mate,
So amiable, fair, so pure, so delicate,

* A very woody Vale in *Surry.*
[1] *Tames* ebbs and flows beyond *Richmond.*

So plump, so full, so fresh, her eyes so wondrous clear: 75
And first unto her Lord, at *Wandsworth* doth appear,
That in the goodly Court, of their great sovereign *Tames*,
There might no other speech be had amongst the Streams,
But only of this Nymph, sweet *Wandal*, what she wore;
Of her complexion, grace, and how herself she bore. 80
  But now this mighty Flood, upon his voyage prest,
(That found how with his strength, his beauties still increast,
From where, brave *Windsor* stood on tip-toe to behold
The fair and goodly *Tames*, so far as ere he could,
With kingly houses crown'd, of more than earthly pride, 85
Upon his either banks, as he along doth glide)
With wonderful delight, doth his long course pursue,
Where *Otlands*, *Hampton-Court*, and *Richmond* he doth view,
Then *Westminster* the next great *Tames* doth entertain;
That vaunts her Palace large, and her most sumptuous Fane:
The Land's Tribunal seat that challengeth for hers, 91
The Crowning of our Kings, their famous Sepulchres.
Then goes he on along by that more beauteous Strand,
Expressing both the wealth and brav'ry of the Land.
(So many sumptuous Bowers, within so little space, 95
The all-beholding sun scarce sees in all his race.)
And on by *London* leads, which like a crescent lies,[1]
Whose windows seem to mock the star-befreckled skies;
Besides her rising spires, so thick themselves that show,
As do the bristling reeds, within his banks that grow. 100
There sees his crowded wharfs, and people-pestred shores,
His bosom over-spread, with shoals of labouring oars:
With that most costly Bridge, that doth him most renown,[2]
By which he clearly puts all other Rivers down.
  Thus furnished with all that appertain'd to State, 105
Desired by the Floods (his greatness which await)

---

[1] *London* lying like a half-moon.
[2] *London-bridge* the Crown of *Tames*.

That as the rest before, so somewhat he would sing,
Both worthy of their praise, and of himself their King;
A Catalogue of those, the Sceptre here that sway'd,
The princely *Tames* recites, and thus his Song he laid :   110
   As *Bastard William* first, by Conquest hither came,
And brought the *Norman* Rule, upon the *English* name :
So with a tedious war, and almost endless toils,
Throughout his troubled reign, here held his hard-got spoils.
Deceasing at the last, through his unsettled State,   115
§ Left (with his ill-got Crown) unnatural debate.
For, dying at his home, his eldest son abroad,
(Who, in the Holy-war, his person then bestow'd)
His second *Rufus* next usurp'd the wrongéd reign :
§ And by a fatal dart, in his *New Forest* slain,   120
Whilst in his proper right religious *Robert* slept,
Through craft into the Throne the younger *Beau-cleark* crept.
From whom his Sceptre, then, whilst *Robert* strove to wrest,
The other (of his power that amply was possest)
With him in battle join'd : and, in that dreadful day   125
(Where Fortune show'd herself all human power to sway)
Duke *Robert* went to wrack ; and taken in the flight,
§ Was by that cruel King deprivéd of his sight,
And in close prison put ; where miserably he died :
   But *Henry's* whole intent was by just heaven denied.   130
For, as of light, and life, he that sad Lord bereft ;
So his, to whom the Land he purpos'd to have left,
The raging seas devour'd,* as hitherward they sail'd.
   When, in this Line direct, the *Conqueror's* issue fail'd,
Twixt *Henry's* daughter *Mauld,* the *Almayne* Emperour's
      Bride   135
(Which after to the Earl of *Anjou* was affi'd)
And *Stephen* Earl of *Bloys,* the *Conqueror's* Sister's son,
A fierce and cruel war immediately begun ;

* See the last note to the Fourth Song.

Who with their several powers, arrivéd here from *France*,
By force of hostile arms, their titles to advance. 140
But, *Stephen*, what by coin, and what by foreign strength,
Through worlds of danger gain'd the glorious goal at length.
  But, left without an heir, the Empress' issue next,
No title else on foot; upon so fair pretext,
The Second *Henry* soon upon the throne was set, 145
(Which *Mauld* to *Jeffrey* bare) the first *Plantagenet*.
Who held strong wars with *Wales*, that his subjection spurn'd:
Which oftentimes he beat; and, beaten oft, return'd:
With his stern children vex'd: who (whilst he strove t' advance
His right within this *Isle*) rais'd war on him in *France*. 150
With his high fame in fight, what cold breast was not fir'd?
Through all the Western world, for wisdom most admir'd.
  Then *Richard* got the Rule, his most renownéd son;
Whose courage, him the name of *Cure De Lion* won. [born,
With those first earthly Gods, had this brave Prince been
His daring hand had from *Alcides*' shoulders torn 155
The *Nemean Lion's* hide: who in the Holy-land
So dreadful was, as though from *Jove* and *Neptune's* hand,
The thund'ring three-fork'd fire, and trident he had reft,
And him to rule their charge they only then had left. 160
Him *John* again succeeds; who, having put-away
Young *Arthur* (*Richard's* son) the Sceptre took to sway.
Who, of the common-wealth first havoc having made,
§ His sacrilegious hands upon the Churches laid,
In cruelty and rape continuing out his reign; 165
That his outrageous lust and courses to restrain,
§ The Baronage were forc'd defensive arms to raise,
Their daughters to redeem, that he by force would seize.
Which the first Civil War in *England* here began.
And for his sake such hate his son young *Henry* won, 170
That to depose their Prince, th' revengeful people thought;
And from the Line of *France* young *Lewis* to have brought,

THE SEVENTEENTH SONG.

To take on him our Rule : but, *Henry* got the throne,
By his more forceful friends : who, wise and puissant grown,
§ The general Charter seiz'd ; that into slavrey drew   175
The freest-born *English* blood. Of which such discord grew,
And in the Barons' breasts so rough combustions rais'd,
With much expense of blood as long was not appeas'd,
By strong and tedious gusts held up on either side,
Betwixt the Prince and Peers, with equal power and pride.   180
He knew the worst of war, match'd with the Barons strong;
Yet victor liv'd, and reign'd both happily and long.

    This long-liv'd Prince expir'd : the next succeeded ; he,
Of us, that for a God might well related be.
Our *Long-shanks*, *Scotland's* scourge: who to the *Orcads* raught
His Sceptre, and with him from wild *Albania* brought   186
The reliques of her crown (by him first placéd here)
§ The seat on which her Kings inaugurated were.
He tam'd the desperate *Welsh*, that out so long had stood,
And made them take* a Prince, sprung of the English blood.
This *Isle*, from sea to sea, he generally controll'd,   190
And made the other parts of *England* both to hold.

    This *Edward*, First of ours, a Second then ensues ;
Who both his name and birth, by looseness, did abuse :
Fair *Ganymeds* and fools who rais'd to princely places ;   195
And chose not men for wit, but only for their faces.
In parasites and knaves, as he repos'd his trust,
Who sooth'd him in his ways apparantly unjust ;
For that preposterous sin wherein he did offend,
In his posterior parts had his preposterous end.   200

    A Third then, of that name, amends for this did make :
Who from his idle sire seem'd nought at all to take.
But as his grand-sire did his Empire's verge advance :
So led he forth his powers, into the heart of *France*.

       * See before to the Ninth Song.

And fast'ning on that right, he by his mother had,   205
Against the *Salique* law, which utterly forbad
§ Their women to inherit; to propagate his cause,
At *Cressey* with his sword first cancelléd those laws:
Then like a furious storm, through troubled *France* he ran;
And by the hopeful hand of brave *Black Edward* wan   210
Proud *Poytiers*, where King *John* he valiantly subdu'd,
The miserable French and there in mammocks hew'd;
Then with his battering rams made earth-quakes in their
Till trampled in the dust herself she yielded ours. [towers,

As mighty *Edward's* heir, to a Second *Richard* then   215
(Son to that famous Prince *Black Edward*, Man of Men,
Untimely that before his conquering father died)
Too soon the Kingdom fell: who his vain youth applied
To wantonness and spoil, and did to favour draw
Unworthy ignorant sots, with whose dull eyes he saw: 220
Who plac'd their like in Court, and made them great in State,
(Which wise and virtuous men, beyond all plagues, might
To whom he blindly gave: who blindly spent again, [hate.)
And oft oppress'd his Land, their riot to maintain.
He hated his allies, and the deserving sterv'd;   225
His minions and his will, the Gods he only serv'd:
And, finally, depos'd, as he was ever friend
To ribalds, so again by villains had his end.

Henry the Son of *Gaunt*, supplanting *Richard*, then
Ascended to the Throne: when discontented men,   230
Desirous first of change, which to that height him brought,
Deceivéd of their ends, into his actions sought;
And, as they set him up, assay'd to pluck him down:
From whom he hardly held his ill-achievéd Crown;
That, treasons to suppress which oft he did disclose,   235
And raising public arms, against his powerful foes,
His usurpation still being troubled to maintain,
His short disquiet days scarce raught a peaceful reign.

A Fifth succeeds the Fourth : but how his father got
The Crown, by right or wrong, the son respecteth not.   240
Nor further hopes for that e'er leaveth to pursue ;
But doth his claim to *France* courageously renew ;
Upon her wealthy shores un-lades his warlike fraught ;
And, showing us the fields where our brave fathers fought,
First drew his sun-bright sword, reflecting such a light,   245
As put sad guilty *France* into so great a fright,
That her pale *Genius* sank ; which trembling seem'd to stand,
When first he set his foot on her rebellious land.
That all his grand-sire's deeds did over, and thereto
Those high achievements add the former could not do :   250
At *Agincourt's* proud fight, that quite put *Poytiers* down ;
Of all, that time who liv'd, the King of most renown.
Whose too untimely end, the Fates too soon did haste :
Whose nine years noble acts, nine worlds deserve to last.

A Sixth in name succeeds, born great, the mighty son   255
Of him, in *England's* right that spacious *France* had won.
Who coming young to reign, protected by the Peers
Until his non-age out : and grown to riper years,
Prov'd upright, soft, and meek, in no wise loving war ;
But fitter for a cowl, than for a crown by far.   260
Whose mildness over-much, did his destruction bring :
A wondrous godly man, but not so good a King.
Like whom yet never man tried fortune's change so oft ;
So many times thrown-down, so many times aloft   264
(When with the utmost power, their friends could them afford,
The Yorkists, put their right upon the dint of sword)
As still he lost and won, in that long bloody war,
§ From those two Factions styl'd, of *York* and *Lancaster*.
But by his foes inforc'd to yield him to their power,
His wretched reign and life, both ended in the Tower.   270

Of th' *Edwards'* name the Fourth put on the Regal Wreath :
Whom furious bloody war (that seem'd awhile to breath)

Not utterly forsook. For, *Henry's* Queen and heir
(Their once possessèd reign still seeking to repair) ☆
Put forward with their friends, their title to maintain.   275
Whose blood did *Barnet's* streets and *Teuksbury's* distain,
Till no man left to stir. The Title then at rest,
The old *Lancastrian* Line being utterly supprest,
Himself the wanton King to amorous pleasures gave ;
§ Yet jealous of his right descended to his grave.   280
  His son an infant left : who had he liv'd to reign,
Edward the Fifth had been. But justly see again,
As he a King and Prince before had caus'd to die
(The father in the Tower, the son at *Teuksbury*)
So were his children young, being left to be protected   285
By *Richard ;* who nor God, nor human laws respected.
This *Viper*, this most vile devourer of his kind
(Whom his ambitious ends had strook so grossly blind)
From their dear mother's lap, them seizing for a prey
(Himself in right the next, could they be made away)   290
Most wrongfully usurp'd, and them in prison kept ;
Whom cruelly at last he smothered as they slept.
As his unnatural hands, were in their blood imbru'd :
So (guilty in himself) with murther he pursu'd
Such, on his heinous acts as look'd not fair and right ;   295
Yea, such as were not his expressly, and had might
T' oppose him in his course ; till (as a monster loth'd,
The man, to hell and death himself that had betroth'd)
They brought another in, to thrust that tyrant down ;
In battle who at last resign'd both life and crown.   300
  A Seventh *Henry*, then, th' imperial seat attain'd,
In banishment who long in *Britanne* had remain'd,
What time the Yorkists sought his life to have bereft,
Of the *Lancastrian* House then only being left
(Deriv'd from *John* of *Gaunt*) whom *Richmond* did beget,   305
§ Upon a daughter born to *John* of *Somerset*.

THE SEVENTEENTH SONG.

Elizabeth of *York* this noble Prince affi'd,
To make his Title strong thereby on either side.
And grafting of the *White* and *Red Rose* firm together,
Was first that to the Throne advanc'd the name of *Tether*.
In *Bosworth's* fatal Field, who having *Richard* slain, 311
Then in that prosperous peace of his successful reign,
Of all that ever rul'd, was most precise in State,
And in his life and death a King most fortunate.
   This Seventh, that was of ours, the Eighth succeeds in
     name :
Who by Prince *Arthur's* death (his elder brother) came 316
Unto a Land with wealth aboundantly that flow'd :
Aboundantly again, so he the same bestow'd,
In Banquets, Masks, and Tilts, all pleasures prone to try,
Besides his secret scapes who lov'd polygamy. 320
The Abbeys he supprest ; a thousand ling'ring year,
Which with revenues large the world had sought to rear.
And through his awful might, for temporal ends did save,
To other uses erst what frank devotion gave ;
And here the Papal power, first utterly deny'd, 325
§ *Defender of the Faith*, that was instyl'd and dy'd.
   His son the Empire had, our *Edward* Sixth that made ;
Untimely as he sprang, untimely who did fade.
A Protestant being bred ; and in his infant reign,
Th' religion then receiv'd, here stoutly did maintain : 330
But ere he raught to man, from his sad people reft,
His Sceptre he again unto his Sisters left.
   Of which the eldest of two, Queen *Mary*, mounts the Chair:
The ruin'd *Roman* State who striving to repair,
With persecuting hands the Protestants pursu'd, 335
Whose martyred ashes oft the wond'ring streets bestrew'd.
She match'd herself with *Spain*, and brought King *Philip*
     hither,
Which with an equal hand, the Sceptre sway'd togither.

But issueless she dy'd ; and under six years' reign,
To her wise Sister gave the Kingdom up again.   340
  Elizabeth, the next, this falling Sceptre hent ;
Digressing from her sex, with man-like government
This Island kept in awe, and did her power extend
Afflicted *France* to aid, her own as to defend ;
Against th' *Iberian* rule, the *Flemings*' sure defence :   345
Rude *Ireland's* deadly scourge ; who sent her navies hence
Unto the nether *Inde*, and to that shore so green,
Virginia which we call, of her a Virgin Queen :
In *Portugal* 'gainst *Spain*, her *English* ensigns spread ;
Took *Cales*, when from her aid the brav'd *Iberia* fled.   350
Most flourishing in State : that, all our Kings among,
Scarce any rul'd so well : but two,* that reign'd so long.
  Here suddenly he stay'd : and with his kingly Song,
Whilst yet on every side the City loudly rong,
He with the eddy turn'd, a space to look about :   355
The tide, retiring soon, did strongly thrust him out.
And soon the pliant Muse, doth her brave wing advance,
Tow'rds those sea-bord'ring shores of ours, that point at
    France ;
The harder *Surrian* Heath, and the *Sussexian* Down.
Which with so great increase though Nature do not crown,
As many other Shires, of this inviron'd *Isle :*   361
Yet on the Wether's head,† when as the sun doth smile,
Nurs'd by the Southern winds, that soft and gently blow,
Here doth the lusty sap as soon begin to flow ;
The Earth as soon puts on her gaudy summer's suit ;   365
The woods as soon in green, and orchards great with fruit.
  To sea-ward, from the seat where first our Song begun,
Exhaled to the South by the ascending sun,
Four stately Wood-Nymphs stand on the *Sussexian* ground,

    * *Henry* III. and *Edward* III. ; the one reigned fifty-six, the
other, fifty.   † The Sun in *Aries*.

§ Great *Andredsweld's** sometime: who, when she did abound,
In circuit and in growth, all other quite suppress'd: 371
But in her wane of pride, as she in strength decreas'd,
Her Nymphs assum'd them names, each one to her delight.
As, *Water-downe*, so call'd of her depressèd site:
And *Ash-Downe*, of those trees that most in her do grow, 375
Set higher to the Downs, as th' other standeth low.
Saint Leonard's, of the seat by which she next is plac'd,
And *Whord* that with the like delighteth to be grac'd.
These Forests as I say, the daughters of the *Weald*
(That in their heavy breasts, had long their griefs conceal'd)
Foreseeing their decay each hour so fast came on, 381
Under the axe's stroke, fetch'd many a grievous groan,
When as the anvil's weight, and hammer's dreadful sound,
Even rent the hollow woods, and shook the queachy ground.
So that the trembling Nymphs, oppress'd through ghastly fear,
Ran madding to the Downs, with loose dishevell'd hair. 386
The *Sylvans* that about the neighbouring woods did dwell,
Both in the tufty frith and in the mossy fell,
Forsook their gloomy bow'rs, and wand'red far abroad,
Expell'd their quiet seats, and place of their abode, 390
When labouring carts they saw to hold their daily trade,
Where they in summer wont to sport them in the shade.
Could we, say they, suppose, that any would us cherish,
Which suffer (every day) the holiest things to perish?
Or to our daily want to minister supply? 395
These iron times breed none, that mind posterity.
'Tis but in vain to tell, what we before have been,
Or changes of the world, that we in time have seen;
When, not devising how to spend our wealth with waste,
We to the savage swine let fall our larding mast. 400
But now, alas, ourselves we have not to sustain,
Nor can our tops suffice to shield our roots from rain.

* A Forest, containing most part of *Kent, Sussex*, and *Surrey*.

Jove's Oak, the warlike Ash, vein'd Elm, the softer Beech,
Short Hazel, Maple plain, light Aspe, the bending Wych,
Tough Holly, and smooth Birch, must altogether burn : 405
What should the builder serve, supplies the forger's turn ;
When under public good, base private gain takes hold,
And we poor woeful Woods, to ruin lastly sold.   [spoke,
   This utter'd they with grief : and more they would have
But that the envious Downs, int' open laughter broke ; 410
As joying in those wants, which Nature them had given,
Sith to as great distress the Forests should be driven.
Like him that long time hath another's state envy'd,
And sees a following ebb, unto his former tide ;
The more he is depress'd, and bruis'd with fortune's might,
The larger rein his foe doth give to his despight :   416
So did the envious Downs ; but that again the Floods
(Their fountains that derive from those unpitied Woods,
And so much grace thy Downs, as through their dales they
            creep,
Their glories to convey unto the *Celtick* deep)   420
It very hardly took, much murmuring at their pride.
Clear *Larant*, that doth keep the *Southamptonian* side
(Dividing it well-near from the *Sussexian* lands
That *Selsey* doth survey, and *Solent's* troubled sands)
To *Chichester* their wrongs impatiently doth tell :   425
§ And *Arun* (which doth name the beauteous *Arundell*)
As on her course she came, it to her Forest told.
Which, nettled with the news, had not the power to hold :
But breaking into rage, wish'd tempests them might rive ;
And on their barren scalps, still flint and chalk might thrive,
The brave and nobler Woods which basely thus upbraid. 431
§ And *Adur* coming on, to *Shoreham* softly said,
The Downs did very ill, poor Woods so to debase.
But now, the *Ouse*, a Nymph of very scornful grace,
So touchy wax'd therewith, and was so squeamish grown, 435

That her old name she scorn'd should publicly be known.
Whose haven* out of mind when as it almost grew,
The lately passéd times denominate, the New.
So *Cucmer* with the rest put to her utmost might:
As *Ashburne* undertakes to do the Forests right   440
(At *Pemsey*, where she pours her soft and gentler flood)
And *Asten* once distain'd with native *English* blood:
(Whose soil, when yet but wet with any little rain,
§ Doth blush; as put in mind of those there sadly slain,
When *Hastings* harbour gave unto the *Norman* powers,   445
Whose name and honours now are denizen'd for ours)
That boding ominous Brook, it through the Forests rung:
Which echoing it again the mighty *Weald* along,
Great stir was like to grow; but that the Muse did charm
Their furies, and herself for nobler things did arm.   450

* *New-haven.*

ILLUSTRATIONS.

AFTER your travels (thus led by the Muse) through the Inlands, out of the *Welsh* coast maritime, here are you carried into *Surrey* and *Sussex;* the Southern shires from *London* to the Ocean: and *Thames*, as King of all our Rivers, summarily sings the Kings of *England*, from *Norman William* to yesterday's age.

50. Mole *digs herself a path, by working day and night.*

This *Mole* runs into the earth, about a mile from *Darking* in *Surrey*, and after some two miles sees the light again, which to be certain hath been affirmed by inhabitants thereabout reporting trial made of it. Of the River *Deverill* near *Warmister* in *Wiltshire* is said as much; and more of *Alpheus* running out of *Elis* (a part of the now *Morea*, anciently *Peloponnesus* in *Greece*) through the vast Ocean to *Arethusa* in a little isle (close by *Syracuse* of *Sicily*) called *Ortygia*, and thither thus coming unmixed with the sea, which hath been both tried by a cup,[1] lost in *Elis*, and other stuff of the *Olympian* sacrifices there cast up, and is justified also by express assertion of an old Oracle[2] to *Archias*, a *Corinthian*, advising him he should hither deduce a Colony.

[1] Strab. Geograph. 6.   [2] Pausan. Eliac. *t.*

THE SEVENTEENTH SONG. 231

——————— Ἰν' Ἀλφειοῦ στόμα βλύζει
Μισγόμενον πηγαῖς Εὐριπείης Ἀρεθούσης.*

Like this, *Pausanias* reckons more; *Erasin*[1] in *Greece*, *Lycus*[2] that runs into *Meander*, *Tiger*,[3] and divers others, some remember for such quality. And *Gaudiana* (the ancient limit of *Portugal* and the *Bœtique Spain*) is specially famous for this form of subterranean course; which although hath been thought fabulous, yet by some[4] learned and judicious of that country, is put for an unfeigned truth.

72. *He ever since doth flow beyond delightful* Sheene.

Mole's fall into *Thames* is near the utmost of the Flood, which from the *German* Ocean, is about sixty miles, scarce equalled (I think) by any other river in *Europe;* whereto you may attribute its continuing so long a course, unless to the diurnal motion of the heavens, or moon, from East to West (which hardly in any other river of note falling into so great a sea, will be found so agreeable, as to this, flowing the same way) and to the easiness of the channel being not over creeky, I cannot guess. I incline to this of the heavens, because such testimony[5] is of the ocean's perpetual motion in that kind; and whether it be for frequency of a winding, and thereby more resisting, shore, or for any other reason judicially not yet discovered, it is certain, that our coasts are most famous for the greatest differences by ebbs and floods, before all other whatsoever.

116. *Left with his* ill-got Crown *unnatural debate.*

See what the matter of Descent to the Fourth Song tells you of his title; yet even out of his own mouth as part of

* There *Alpheus* springeth again, embracing fair *Arethusa.*
[1] Herodot. Hist. ς.   [2] Idem. ζ. Polyhym.
[3] Justin. Hist. 42.   [4] Ludovic. Nonius in Fluv. Hispan.
[5] Scalig. de subtilit. Exercitat. 52.

his last will and testament, these words are reported: *I constitute no heir of the Crown of England: but to the Universal Creator, Whose I am, and in Whose Hand are all things, I commend it. For I had it not by inheritance, but with direful conflict, and much effusion of blood; I took it from that perjured Harold, and by death of his favourites, have I subdued it to my Empire.*[1] And somewhat after: *Therefore I dare not bequeath the sceptre of this kingdom to any but to God alone, lest after my death worse troubles happen in it, by my occasion. For my son* William *(always, as it became him, obedient to me) I wish that God may give him His graces, and that, if so it please the Almighty, he may reign after me.** This *William* the II. (called *Rufus*) was his second son, *Robert* his eldest having upon discontent (taken because the Dukedom of *Normandy*, then as 'it were by birthright, nearly like the Principality of *Wales* anciently, or Duchy of *Cornwall* at this day, belonging to our Kings' Heirs-apparant, was denied him) revolted unnaturally, and moved war against him, aided by *Philip* I. of *France*, which caused his merited disinheritance. Twixt this *William* and *Robert*, as also twixt him and *Henry* I. all brothers (and sons to the Conqueror) were divers oppositions for the Kingdom and Dukedom, which here the Author alludes to. Our stories in every hand inform you: and will discover also the Conqueror's adoption by the *Confessor*, *Harold's* oath to him, and such institutions of his lawful title enforced by a case[2] reported of one *English*, who, deriving his right from seisin before the Conquest, recovered by judgment of King *William* I. the Manor of *Sharborn* in *Norfolk* against one *Warren* a *Norman*, to whom the King had before granted it: which had been unjust, if he had by right of war only gotten the kingdom; for then had all

---

[1] Gul. Pictavens. in Hist. Cadomens.
* This is the bequest understood by them which say he devised his kingdom to *William* II.   [2] Antiq. sched. in Iccn. Camd.

titles[1] of subjects before been utterly extinct. But (admit this case as you please, or any cause of right beside his sword) it is plain that his will and imperious affection (moved by their rebellions which had stood for the sworn *Harold*) disposed all things as a Conqueror: Upon observation of his subjection of all lands to tenures, his change of laws, disinheriting the *English*, and such other reported (which could be but where the profitable Dominion, as Civilians call it, was universally acquired into the Prince's hand) and in reading the disgraceful account then made of the *English* name, it will be manifest.

120. *Who by a fatal dart in vast* New Forest *slain.*

His death by an infortunate loosing at a deer out of one *Walter Tirrel's* hand in *New Forest*,[2] his brother *Richard* being blasted· there with infection, and *Richard*, Duke *Robert's* son, having his neck broken there in a bough's twist catching him from his horse, have been thought as Divine revenges on *William* the First, who destroyed in *Hantshire* thirty-six parish churches to make dens for wild beasts; although it is probable enough, that it was for security of landing new forces there, if the wheel of fortune, or change of *Mars*, should have dispossessed him of the *English* Crown. Our Stories will of these things better instruct you: but, if you seek *Matthew Paris* for it, amend the absurdity of both the *London* and *Tigurin* prints in *An.* 1086, and for *Rex magnificus, et bonæ indolis adolescens*, read, *Rich. magnificus, &c.*,* for *Richard* brother to this *Red William*.

128. *Was by that cruel King* deprived of his sight.

Thus did the Conqueror's posterity unquietly possess

---

[1] Atqui ad hanc rem enucleatius dilucidandam, jure et Gentium et Anglicano, visendi sunt Hotoman. Illust. Quæst. 5.; Alberic. Gentil. de jure Belli, 3. cap. 5.; et cas. Calv. in D. Coke. lib. 7.

[2] See the Second Song.   * Matthei Paris locus sibi restitutus.

their father's inheritance. *William* had much to do with his brother *Robert* justly grudging at his usurping the Crown from right of primogeniture; but so much the less, in that *Robert* with divers other *German* and *French* Princes left all private respects for the Holy War, which after the Cross undertaken (as those times used) had most fortunate success in Recovery of *Palestine*. *Robert* had no more but the Duchy of *Normandy*, nor that without swords often drawn, before his Holy expedition: about which (having first offer of, but refusing, the Kingdom of *Jerusalem*) after he had some five years been absent, he returned into *England*, finding his younger brother (*Henry* L.) exalted into his hereditary throne. For, although it were undoubtedly agreed that *Robert* was eldest son of the Conqueror, yet the pretence which gave *Henry* the Crown (beside the means of his working favorites) was, that *he was the only issue born after his father was a King:** upon which point a great question is disputed among Civilians.[1] *Robert* was no sooner returned into *Normandy*, but presently (first animated by *Randall*, Bishop of *Durham*, a great disturber of the common peace twixt the Prince and subject by intolerable exactions and unlimited injustice under *William* II., whose Chief Justice† it seems he was, newly escaped out of prison, whither for those State-misdemeanors he was committed by *Henry*) he despatches and interchanges intelligence with most of the Baronage, claiming his primogeniture-right, and thereby the kingdom. Having thus gained to him most of the *English* Nobility, he lands with forces at *Portsmouth*, thence marching towards *Winchester:* but before any encounter the two brothers were persuaded to a

---

* *Solus omnium natus esset regiè.* Malmsb. For he was born the third year after the Conquest.   [1] Hottom. Illust. Quæst. 2.
† *Placitator, et Exactor totius regni.* Flor. Wig. et Monachorum turba.

peace; covenant was made and confirmed by oath of twelve Barons on both parts, that *Henry* should pay him yearly 2,000 pounds of silver, and that the survivor of them should inherit, the other dying without issue. This peace, upon denial of payment (which had the better colour, because, at a request of Queen *Maude*, the Duke prodigally released his 2,000 pounds the next year after the covenant) was soon broken. The King (to prevent what mischief might follow a second arrival of his brother) assisted by the greatest favours of *Normandy* and *Anjou*, besieged Duke *Robert* in one of his castles, took him, brought him home captive, and at length using that course (next secure to death) so often read of in *Choniates, Cantacuzen*, and other Oriental stories, put out his eyes, being all this time imprisoned in *Cardiff* Castle in *Glamorgan*, where he miserably breathed his last. It is by *Polydore* added, out of some authority, that King *Henry* after a few years imprisonment released him, and commanded that within 40 days and 12 hours (these hours have in them time of two floods, or a flood and an ebb) he should, abjuring *England* and *Normandy*, pass the seas as in perpetual exile; and that in the mean time, upon new treasons attempted by him, he was secondly committed, and endured his punishment and death as the common Monks relate. I find no warrantable authority that makes me believe it: yet, because it gives some kind of example of our obsolete law of Abjuration, (which it seems had its beginning from one of the Statutes published under the name of the *Confessor*) a word or two of the time prescribed here for his passage: which being examined upon *Bracton's* credit, makes the report therein faulty. For he seems confident that the 40 days in abjuration, were afterward induced upon the Statute of *Clarindon*,* which gave the accused of Felony, or Treason, although

* *Hen.* 2. ap Rog. Hoved. fol. 314.

acquitted by the *Ordel* (that is judgment by Water or Fire, but the Statute published, speaks only of Water, being the common trial of meaner persons[1]) 40 days to pass out of the Realm with his substance, which to other felons taking sanctuary and confessing to the Coroner, he affirms not grantable; although *John le Breton* is against him, giving this liberty of time, accounted after the abjuration to be spent in the sanctuary, for provision of their voyage necessaries, after which complete, no man, *on pain of life and member*, is to supply any of their wants. I know it is a point very intricate to determine, observing these opposite authors and no express resolution. Since them, the Oath of Abjuration published among our Manual Statutes nearly agrees with this of Duke *Robert*, but with neither of those old Lawyers. In it, after the Felon confesses, and abjures, and hath his Port appointed; *I will* (proceeds the Oath) *diligently endeavour to pass over at that Port, and will not delay time there above a flood and an ebb, if I may have passage in that space; if not, I will every day go into the sea up to the knees, assaying to go over, and unless I may do this within Forty continual days I will return to the Sanctuary, as a Felon of our Lord the King; So God me help, &c.* So here the forty days are to be spent about the passage and not in the sanctuary. Compare this with other authorities,[2] and you shall find all so dissonant, that reconciliation is impossible, resolution very difficult. I only offer to their consideration, which can here judge, why *Hubert de Burch* (Earl of *Kent*, and Chief Justice of *England* under *Hen.* III.) having incurred the King's high displeasure, and grievously persecuted by great enemies, taking sanctuary, was, after his being violently

---

[1] Glanvil. lib. 14. cap. 1.; cæterùm, si placet, adeas Janum nostrum li. 2. §. 67.
[2] Itin. North. 3. *Ed.* 3. Coron. 313. Lectur. ap. Br. tit. Coron. 181. Vid. Stamfordum, lib. 2. cap. 40. qui de his gravitèr, et modestè sed ἐφικτικῶς.

drawn out, restored; yet that the Sheriffs, of *Hereford** and *Essex*, were commanded to ward him there, and prevent all sustenance to be brought him, which they did, *decernentes ibi quadraginta dierum excubiis observare*:[1] And whether also the same reason (now unknown to us) bred this forty days for expectation of embarquement out of the kingdom, which gave it in another kind for retorne? as in case of 𝔇isseisin, the law hath been,[2] that the disseisor could not re-enter without action, unless he had as it were made a present and continual claim, yet if he had been out of the Kingdom in single pilgrimage (that is not in general voyages to the Holy-land) or in the King's service in *France*, or so, he had allowance of forty days, two floods, and one ebb, to come home in, and fifteen days, and four days, after his return; and if the tenant had been so beyond sea he might have been essoined *de ultra mare*, and for a year and a day, after which he had forty days, one flood, and one ebb (which is easily understood as the other for two floods) to come into *England*. This is certain that the space of forty days (as a year and a day) hath had with us divers applications, as in what before, the *Assise* of *Freshforce* in Cities and Boroughs, and the Widow's *Quarentine*, which seems to have had beginning either of a deliberative time granted to her, to think of her conveniency in taking letters of administration, as in another country[3] the reason of the like is given; or else from the forty days in the essoine of child-birth allowed by the *Norman* Customs. But you mislike the digression. It is reported that when *William* the *Conqueror* in his death-bed left *Normandy* to *Robert*, and *England* to *William* the Red, this *Henry* asked him what he would give him, *Five*

* *i.e.*, *Hertford*.—(ED.)
[1] Math. Par. pag. 507.
[2] Bract. lib. 4. tract. assis. Nov. Diss. cap. 5. et lib. 5. tract. de Esson. cap. 3. Vid. de Consuetudine in Oxonia. 21. *Ed.* 3. fol. 46. *b.*
[3] Cust. Generaulx. de *Artois*. art. 164.

thousand pounds of silver (saith he) *and be contented my son; for, in time, thou shalt have all which I possess, and be greater than either of thy brethren.*

164. *His sacrilegious hands upon the* Churches *laid.*

The great controversy about electing the Archbishop of *Canterbury* (the King as his right had him, commanding that *John* Bishop of *Norwich* should have the Prelacy, the Pope, being *Innocent* III. for his own gain, aided with some disloyal Monks of *Canterbury*, desiring, and at last consecrating *Stephen* of *Langton*, a Cardinal) was first cause of it. For King *John* would by no means endure this *Stephen*, nor permit him the dignity after his unjust election at *Rome*, but banished the Monks, and stoutly menaces the Pope. He presently makes delegation to *William* Bishop of *London*, *Eustace* of *Ely*, and *Malgere* of *Worcester*, that they should, with monitory advice, offer persuasion to the King of conformity to the *Romish* behest; if he persisted in constancy, they should denounce *England* under an interdict. The Bishops tell King *John* as much, who suddenly, moved with imperious affection and scorn of Papal usurpation, swears, *by God's tooth, if they or any other, with unadvised attempt, subject his Kingdom to an interdict, he would presently drive every prelate and priest of* England *to the Pope, and confiscate all their substance; and of all the* Romans *amongst them, he would first pull out their eyes, and cut off their noses, and then send them all packing*,[1] with other like threatening terms, which notwithstanding were not able to cause them desist; but within little time following, in public denunciation they performed their authority; and the King, in some sort, his threatenings, committing all Abbeys and Priories to laymen's custody, and compelling every priest's concubine to a grievous fine. Thus for a while continued the Realm

[1] 9. *Joann.* Reg.

without divine Sacraments or Exercise, excepted only Confession, Extreme Unction, and Baptism; the King being also excommunicated, and burials allowed only in high-ways and ditches without ecclesiastic ceremony, and (but only by indulgence procured by Archbishop *Langton* which purchased favour that in all the Monasteries, excepting of *White-Friars*, might be divine service once a week) had no change for some four or five years, when the Pope in a solemn Council of Cardinals, according to his pretended plenary power, deposed King *John*, and immediately by his Legate *Pandulph* offered to *Philip* II. of *France* the Kingdom of *England*. This with suspicion of the subjects' heart at home, and another cause then more esteemed than either of these, that is, the prophecy of one *Peter* an Hermit in *Yorkshire* foretelling to his face *that before Holy-Thursday following he should be no King*, altered his stiff and resolute, but too disturbed, affections; and persuaded him by oath of himself and sixteen more of his Barons, to make submission to the Church of *Rome*, and condescended to give for satisfaction, 8,000 pounds sterling (that name of *sterling*[1] began, as I am instructed, in time of *Hen.* II. and had its original of name from some Esterling, making that kind of money, which hath its essence in particular weight and fineness, not of the starling bird, as some, nor of *Sterling* in *Scotland* under *Ed.* I. as others absurdly, for in Records[2] much more ancient the express name *sterlingorum* I have read) to the Clergy, and subject[3] all his dominions to the Pope; and so had absolution, and, after more than four years, release of the Interdict. I was the willinger to insert it all, because you might see what injurious opposition, by Papal usurpation, he endured; and then conjecture that his violent

---

[1] Jo. Stow. in Notit. Londin. pag. 52. Vid. Camd. in Scot. Buchan. alios.   [2] Polydor. Hist. 16.
[3] Norff. 6, Rich. I, Fin. Rot. 13. et alibi in eisdem archivis vid.

dealings against the Church were not without intolerable provocation, which madded rather than amended his troubled spirits. Easily you shall not find a Prince more beneficial to the holy cause than he, if you take his former part of reign, before this ambitious *Stephen* of *Langton's* election exasperated desire of revenge. Most kind habitude then was twixt him and the Pope, and for alms toward *Jerusalem's* aid he gave the fortieth part of his revenue, and caused his Baronage to second his example. Although therefore he was no ways excusable of many of those faults, both in government and religion, which are laid on him, yet it much extenuates the ill of his action, that he was so besieged with continual and undigestable incentives of the Clergy with traitorous confidence striking at his Crown, and in such sort, as humanity must have exceeded itself, to have endured it with any mixture of patience. Nor ever shall I impute that his wicked attempt of sending Ambassadors, *Thomas Hardington*, *Ralph Fitz-Nicholas*, and *Robert* of *London*, to *Amiramully*, King of *Morocco*, for the *Mahometan* Religion, so much to his own will and nature, as to the persecuting Bulls, Interdicts, Excommunications, Deposings, and such like, published and acted by them which counterfeiting the vain name of Pastors, shearing and not feeding their sheep, made this poor King (for they brought him so poor, that he was called *Johannes sine terrâ**) even as a phrenetic, commit what posterity receives now among the worst actions (and in themselves they are so) of Princes.

107. *His* Baronage *were forc'd* defensive arms *to raise.*

No sooner had *Pandulph* transacted with the King, and *Stephen* of *Langton* was quietly possessed of his Archbishopric, but he presently, in a Council of both orders at *Paul's*,

¹ Ante alios de hiis consulendus sit Matth. Paris.
* *John Hadland.*

stirs up the hearts of the Barons against *John*, by producing the old Charter of liberties granted by *Hen.* I. comprehending an instauration of S. *Edward's* Laws, as they were amended by the Conqueror, and provoking them to challenge observation thereof as an absolute duty to subjects of free State. He was easily heard, and his thoughts seconded with rebellious designs : and after denials of this purposed request, armies were mustered to extort these liberties. But at length by treaty in *Runingmede*[1] near *Stanes*, he gave them two Charters ; the one, of Liberties general, the other of the Forest : both which were not very different from our *Graund Charter*[2] and that of the *Forest*. The Pope at his request confirmed all : but the same year, discontentment (through too much favour and respect given by the King to divers strangers, whom, since the composition with the Legate, he had too frequently, and in too high esteem, entertained) renewing among the Barons, Ambassadors were sent to advertise the Pope what injury the See of *Rome* had by this late exaction of such liberties out of a kingdom, in which it had such great interest (for King *John* had been very prodigal to it, of his best and most majestical titles) and with what commotion the Barons had rebelled against him, soon obtained a *Bull* cursing in thunder all such as stood for any longer maintenance of those granted Charters: This (as how could it be otherwise ?) bred new but almost incurable broils in the State twixt King and subject : but in whom more, than in the Pope and his Archbishop, was cause of this dissension? Both, as wicked *boutefeus* applying themselves to both parts; sometimes animating the subject by censorious exauthorizing the Prince, then assisting and moving forward his proneness to faithless abrogation, by pretence of an interceding universal authority.

16. Joh. Reg.
King *John's* Grand Charter.

175. *The general* Charter seiz'd————

The last note somewhat instructs you in what you are to remember, that is, the *Grand Charters* granted and (as matter of fact was) repealed by King *John;* his son *Henry* III.[1] of some nine years age (under protection first of *William Mareshall* Earl of *Penbroke*, after the Earl's death, *Peter de Roches* Bishop of *Winchester*) in the ninth year of his reign, in a Parliament held at *Westminster* desired of the Baronage (by mouth of *Hubert de Burch* proposing it) a Fifteen: whereto upon deliberation, they gave answer, *quòd Regis petitionibus gratantèr adquiescerent si illis diù petitas Libertates concedere voluisset.** The King agreed to the condition, and presently under the Great Seal delivered Charters of them into every County of *England*, speaking as those of King *John* (saith *Paris*) *ita quod Chartæ utrorúmque Regum in nullo inveniuntur dissimiles.*† Yet those, which we have, published want of that which is in King *John's*, wherein you have a special chapter that, if a *Jew's* debtor die, and leave his heir within age subject to payment, the usury during the nonage should cease, which explains the meaning of the Statute of *Merton* Chap. V. otherwise but ill interpreted in some of our Year Books.[2] After this follows further, that no Aid, except to redeem the King's person out of *Captivity* (example of that was in *Richard* I. whose ransom out of the hands of *Leopold* Duke of *Austria*, was near 100,000 pounds of silver, collected from the subject) make his *eldest son Knight,* or *marry his eldest daughter,* should be levied of the subject but by Parliament. Yet reason, why these are omitted in *Henry* the Third's Charter, it seems, easily may be given;

---

[1] 1225.
* That they would willingly grant his request, if he would vouchsafe them those Liberties so long desired.
† So that the Charters of both Kings are just alike.
[2] 35. *Hen.* 6. fol. 61. et 3. *Eliz.* Plowd. 1. fol. 236. atqui. vid. Bract. lib. 2. cap. 26. § 2.

seeing ten years before time of *Edward Longshank's* exemplification (which is that whereon we now rely, and only have) all *Jews* were banished the kingdom: and among the Petitions and Grievances of the Commons at time of his instauration of this Charter to them, one was thus consented to; *Nullum Tallagium vel Auxilium, per nos vel heredes nostros de cætero in regno nostro imponatur seu levetur sine voluntate et consensu communi Archiepiscoporum, Episcoporum, Abbatum et aliorum Prælatorum, Comitum, Baronum, Militum, Burgensium, et aliorum liberorum hominum:** which although compared with that of Aids by Tenure, be no law, yet I conjecture that upon this article was that Chapter of Aids omitted. But I return to *Henry:* He, within some three years, summons a Parliament to *Oxford*, and declares his full age, refusing any longer *Peter de Roches's* protection; but taking all upon his personal government, by pretence of past nonage, caused all the Charters of the Forest to be cancelled, and repealed the rest (for so I take it, although my author speak chiefly of that of the Forest) and made the subject with price of great sums, rated by his Chief Justice *Hugh de Burch*, renew their liberties, affirming that his grant of them was in his minority, and therefore so defeasible: which, with its like (in disinheriting and seising on his subjects' possessions, without judicial course, beginning with those two great potentates *Richard* Earl of *Cornwall*, his brother, and *William* le *Marshall* Earl of *Pembrooke*) bred most intestine trouble twixt him and his Barons, although sometime discontinued, yet not extinguished even till his declining days of enthroned felicity. Observe among this, that where our historians and chronologers, talk of a desire by the Baronage, to have the Constitutions of *Oxford* restored, you must understand those Charters cancelled at *Ox-*

---

* No Tallage or Aid without consent of Parliament should after be exacted. Thom. de Walsingham in 26. *Ed.* 1. Polyd. Hist. 17.

ford; where after many rebellious, but provoked, oppositions, the King at last, by oath of himself and his son *Edward,* in full Parliament[1] (having nevertheless oft-times before made show of as much) granted again their desired freedom : which in his spacious reign, was not so much impeached by himself, as through ill counsel of alien caterpillars crawling about him, being as scourges then sent over into this kingdom. But *Robert* of *Glocester* shall summarily tell you this, and give your palate variety.

The meste wo that here bel bi King Henries day
In this lond scholle biginne to tell puf Ich may,
He adde[2] thre Brethren that is Modres sons were
And the King[3] of Almaine the berthe that to heie them here,
Ac sir William de Valence and sir Eimer[4] thereto,
Elit of Wincetre and sir Guy de Lisewi also
Thoru hom and thoru the Quene[5] was so much Frenss
    folc ibrought
That of English men me told as right nought,
And the King hom let her will that each was as King
And nome poure men god, and ne paiede nothing.
To eni of this brethren puf ther pleinide eny wight
Kii sede, puf we doth ou wrong, wo ssall ou do right:
As wo seith we beth Kings, br wille we mowe do,
And many Englisse alas hulde mid hom also.
So that thoreu Godes grace the Erles at last,
And the Bishops of the lond, and Barons bespeake baste,
That the kind Englissemen of Londe hii wolde out caste,
And that long bring adoun, puf her poer laste.
Therof[6] hii nome confest, and to the King hii send,

---
[1] 42. *Hen.* 3.
[2] *Guy* of *Lusignan*, *William* of *Valence*, and *Athelmar*, his half-brothers, sons of *Isabel* King *John's* Dowager, daughter to *Aimar* Earl of *Engolisme*, married to *Hugh Browne* Earl of *March* in *Poiters*.
[3] *Richard* Earl of *Cornwall* son to King *John*.   [4] *Athelmarus*.
[5] *Elianor* daughter to *Rain* and Earl of *Provence*.   [6] They took.

To abbe[1] pite of his lond and suiche manners amende.
So ther at laste hii brought him therto
To make a Puruciance amendment to do,
And made it was at Oxenford, that lond bor to septe,
Tuelf hundred as in yer of Grace and fifty and eyghte,
Right aboute Missomer fourtene night it laste
The Erles and the Barons were well stude baste[2]
Uor to amendi that Lond as the Erle of Gloucetre,
Sir Richard, and sir Simond Erle of Leicetre
And sir Iohn le Fiz-Geffry and other Barons inowe
So that at last the R. therto hii drowe,
To remue the Frensse men to libbe[3] beyonde se
Bi nor londs her and ther and ne come noght age.[4]
And to granti god[5] lawes and the Old Charter also
That so ofte was igranted er, and so oft bndo.
Wercof was the Chartre imade and asseled bast there
Of the Ring and of other heye men that there were:
Tho nome tende tapers[6] the Bishops in hor hond
And the R. himselfe and other heye men of the lond,
The Bishops amansed[7] all that there agon were
And euer ett bndude the lawes that loked were there,
Mid berninge taperes; and such as laste,
The Ring and others seide Amen and the Tapers adoun
    caste.

If particulars of the story, with precedents and consequents, be desired, above all I send you to *Matthew Paris*, and *William Rishanger*, and end in adding that these so controverted Charters had not their settled surety until *Ed.* I. Since whom they have been more than thirty times in Parliament confirmed.

    188. *The* seat *on which her* Kings *inaugurated were.*
Which is the Chair and Stone at *Westminster*, whereon

[1] Have.   [2] Stedfast.   [3] Live.   [4] Again.   [5] Good.
[6] Kindled tapers.   [7] Cursed.

our Sovereigns are inaugurated. The *Scottish*[1] stories (on whose credit, in the first part hereof, I importune you not to rely) affirm that the Stone was first in *Gallicia* of *Spain* at *Brigantia* (whether that be *Compostella*, as *Francis Tarapha* wills, or *Coronna* as *Florian del Campo* conjectures, or *Betansos* according to *Mariana*, I cannot determine) where *Gathel*, King of *Scots* there, sat on it as his throne: Thence was it brought into *Ireland* by *Simon Brech* first King of *Scots* transplanted into that Isle, about 700 years before *Christ:* Out of *Ireland* King *Ferguze* (in him by some, is the beginning of the now continuing *Scottish* reign) about 370 years afterward, brought it into *Scotland*, King *Kenneth* some 850 of the Incarnation, placed it at the Abbey of *Scone* (in the Shrifdome of *Perth*) where the Coronation of his successors was usual, as of our Monarchs now at *Westminster*, and in the *Saxon* times at *Kingston-upon-Thames*. This *Kenneth*, some say, first caused that distich to be ingraven on it,

Ni fallat Fatum, Scoti, *quocúnque locatum*
Invenient lapidem, Regnare tenentur ibidem,

(whereupon it is called *Fatale marmor** in Hector Boetius) and inclosed it in a wooden Chair. It is now at *Westminster*, and on it are the Coronations of our Sovereigns; thither first brought (as the Author here speaks) among infinite other spoils, by *Edward Longshanks*[2] after his wars and victories against King *John Balliol*.

207. *Their women to inherit* ———

So they commonly affirm: but that denial of sovereignty to their women[3] cost the life of many thousands of their men, both under this victorious *Edward*, and his son the *Black Prince*, and other of his successors. His case stood

[1] Hector Boeth. Hist. 1. 10. et 14.; Buchanan. Rer. Scotic. 6. et 8.
* The Fatal Marble. [2] 1297. 24. *Ed*. 1. [3] *Salique* law.

briefly thus: *Philip* IV. surnamed the *Fair*, had issue three sons, *Lewes* the *Contentious*,* *Philip* the *Long*, and *Charles* the *Fair* (all these successively reigned after him, and died without issue inheritable) : he had likewise a daughter *Isabell* (I purposely omit the other, being out of the present matter) married to *Edward* II. and so was mother to *Edward* III. The issue male of *Philip* the *Fair* thus failing, *Philip* son and heir of *Charles* Earl of *Valois*, *Beaumont*, *Alenson*, &c. (which was brother to *Philip* the *Fair*) challenged the Crown of *France* as next heir male against this *Edward*, who answered to the objection of the *Salique* law, that (admitting it as their assertion was, yet) he was Heir Male although descended of a daughter : and in a public assembly of the Estates first about the Protectorship of the womb (for, Queen *Jone* Dowager of the *Fair Charles*, was left with child, but afterward delivered of a daughter, *Blanch*, afterwards Duchess of *Orleans*) was this had in solemn disputation by lawyers on both sides, and applied at length also to the direct point of inheriting the Crown. What followed upon judgment given against his right, the valiant and famous deeds of him and his *English*, recorded in *Walsingham*, *Froissart*, *Æmilius*, and the multitude of later collected stories, make manifest. But for the Law itself; every mouth speaks of it, few I think understand at all why they name it. The opinions are, that it being part of the ancient Laws made among the *Salians* (the same with *Franks*) under King *Pharamond* about 1200 years since, hath thence denomination ; and, *Goropius* (that fetches all out of *Dutch*, and more tolerably perhaps this than many other of his etymologies) deriving the *Salians'* name from 𝔖al, which in contraction he makes from¹ 𝔖adel† (inventors whereof the *Franks*, saith he, were) interprets them, as it were, *Horsemen*, a name fitly applied to the warlike and most

* *Hutin*.   ¹ Francic. lib. 2.   † As our word Saddle.

noble of any nation, as *Chivalers*[1] in *French*, and *Equites* in *Latin* allows likewise. So that, upon collection, the *Salique law* by him is as much as a *Chivalrous law*, and *Salique land*, *quæ ad Equestris Ordinis dignitatem et in capite summo et in cæteris membris conservandam pertinebat :*[2] which very well agrees with a sentence[3] given in the Parliament at *Burdeux* upon an ancient testament devising all the testator's *Salique* lands, which was, in point of judgment, interpreted *Fief*.[4] And who knows not, that *Fiefs* were originally military gifts. But then, if so, how comes *Salique* to extend to the Crown, which is merely without tenure? Therefore *Ego scio* (saith a later lawyer[5]) *legem Salicam agere de privato patrimonio tantùm.*[6] It was composed (not this alone, but with others as they say) by *Wisogast*, *Bodogast*, *Salogast*, and *Windogast*, wise Counsellers about that *Pharamund's* reign. The text of it in this part is offered us by *Claude de Seissell* Bishop of *Marsilles*, *Bodin*, and divers others of the *French*, as it were as ancient as the origin of the name, and in these words, *De terrâ Salicâ nulla portio hæreditatis mulieri veniat, sed ad virilem sexum tota terræ hæreditas perveniat,** and in substance, as referred to the person of the King's heir female; so much is remembered by that great Civilian *Baldus*,[7] and divers others, but rather as Custom than any particular law, as one[8] of that kingdom also hath expressly and newly written; *Ce n'est point une loy écritte, mais nee avec*

[1] Knights.
[2] Which belonged to the preservation of chivalrous state in the possessors.
[3] Bodin. de Repub. 6. cap. 5.; vid. Barth. Chassan. Cons. Burgund. Rubric. 3. §. 5. num. 70. as it were.
[4] Knights' fees, *or* Lands held.
[5] Paul. Merul. Cosmog. part. 2. lib. 3. cap. 17.
[6] I know that the *Salique* Law intends only private possessions.
* No part of the *Salique* land can descend to the daughter, but all to the male.   [7] Ad l. ff. de Senatorib.
[8] Hieronme Pignon. De L'Excel. des Roies. livre. 3. * This is no law written, but learned of Nature.

nous, que nous n'avons point inventée, mais l'avons puisse de la nature même, qui le nous a ainsi apris et donné cet instinct; But why the same author dares affirm that King *Edward* yielded upon this point to the *French Philip de Valois*, I wonder, seeing all story and carriage of state in those times is so manifestly opposite. *Becanus* undertakes a conjecture of the first cause which excluded *Gynæcocracy* among them, guessing it to be upon their observation of the misfortune in war, which their neighbours the *Bructerans* (a people about the now *Over Issel* in the *Netherlands*, from near whom he as many other first derive the *Franks*) endured in time of *Vespasian*, under conduct and empire of one *Velleda*,[1] a lady even of divine esteem amongst them. But howsoever the law be in truth, or interpretable (for it might ill beseem me to offer determination in matter of this kind) it is certain, that to this day, they have an use of ancient time[2] which commits to the care of some of the greatest Peers, that they, when the Queen is in child-birth, be present, and warily observe lest the ladies privily should counterfeit the inheritable sex, by supposing some other made when the true birth is female, or by any such means, wrong their ancient Custom Royal, as of the birth of this present *Lewes* the XIII. on the last of *September* in 1601 is after other such remembered.

26s. *Of these two factions styl'd, of* York *and* Lancaster.

Briefly their beginning was thus. *Edward* the III. had seven sons, *Edward* the *Black Prince*, *William* of *Hatfield*, *Lionel* Duke of *Clarence*, *John* of *Gaunt* Duke of *Lancaster*, *Edmund* of *Langley* Duke of *York*, *Thomas* of *Woodstocke*, and *William* of *Windsor*, in prerogative of birth as I name them.[3] The *Black Prince* died in life of his father, leaving *Richard*

---

[1] Vid. Tacit. Histor. 4.   [2] Rodulph. Boter. Commentar. 8.
[3] Ex Archiv. Parl. 1. *Ed.* 4. in lucem edit. 9. *Ed.* 4. fol. 9.

of *Burdeux* (afterward the II.); *William* of *Hatfield* died without issue; *Henry* Duke of *Lancaster* (son to *John* of *Gaunt* the fourth brother) deposed *Richard* the II. and to the Fifth and Sixth of his name left the kingdom descending in right line of the Family of *Lancaster*. On the other side, *Lionel* Duke of *Clarence* the third brother had only issue *Philippa*, a daughter married to *Edmund Mortimer*, Earl of *March* (who upon this title was designed Heir apparant to *Rich.* II.), *Edmund*, by her had *Roger;* to *Roger* was issue two sons, and two daughters: but all died without posterity, excepting *Anne;* through her married to *Richard* Earl of *Cambridge*, son to *Edmund* of *Langley*, was conveyed (to their issue *Richard* Duke of *York* father to King *Edward* IV.) that right which *Lionel* (whose heir she was) had before the rest of that Royal stem. So that *Lancaster* derived itself from the fourth brother; *York*, from the blood of the third and fifth united. And in time of the Sixth *Henry* was this fatal and enduring misery over *England*, about determination of these titles, first conceived in thirtieth of his reign by *Richard* Duke of *York*, whose son *Edward* IV. deposed *Henry* some nine years after; and having reigned near like space, was also, by readoption of *Henry*, deprived for a time, but restored and died of it possessed, in whose family it continued until after death of *Richard* III. *Henry* Earl of *Richmond* and heir of *Lancaster* marrying *Elizabeth* the heir of *York* made that happy union. Some have referred the utmost root[1] of the *Lancastrian* title to *Edmund*, indeed eldest son to *Henry* III. but that by reason of his unfit deformity, his younger brother *Edward* had the succession, which is absurd and false. For one whom I believe before most of our Monks, and the King's Chronologer of those times, *Matthew Paris*, tells expressly the days and years of both their births, and makes *Edward* above four years elder

[1] Ap. Polydor. Hist. 16.

than *Crook-back*.* All these had that most honoured surname *Plantagenest*[1]; which hath been extinct among us ever since *Margaret* Countess of *Salisbury* (daughter to *George Plantagenet* Duke of *Clarence*) was beheaded in the Tower. By reason of *John* of *Gaunt's* device being a Red Rose, and *Edmund* of *Langley's* a White Rose, these two factions afterward, as for cognisances of their descent and inclinations, were by the same Flowers distinguished.[2]

280. *Yet* jealous of his right *descended to his grave.*

So jealous, that towards them of the *Lancastrian* faction, nought but death (as, there, reason of State was enough) was his kindness. Towards strangers, whose slipping words were in wrested sense, seeming interpretable to his hurt, how he carried himself, the relations of Sir *John Markham*, his Chief Justice, *Thomas Burdet* an Esquire of *Warwickshire*, and some citizens, for idle speeches are testimony. How to his own blood in that miserable end of his brother *George*, Duke of *Clarence*, is showed: Whose death hath divers reported causes, as our late Chroniclers tell you. One is supposed upon a prophecy for speaking that *Edward's* successor's name should begin with G; which made him suspect this *George*[3] (a kind of superstition not exampled, as I now remember, among our Princes; but in proportion very frequent in the Oriental Empire, as passages of the names in *Alexius*, *Manuel*, and others, discover in *Nicetas Choniates*) and many more serious, yet insufficient faults (tasting of *Richard* Duke of *Glocester's* practices) are laid to his charge. Let *Polydore*, *Hall*, and the rest disclose them. But, of his death, I cannot omit, what I have newly seen. You know, it is commonly affirmed, that he was drowned in a hogs-

---

* See to the end of the Fourth Song.
[1] Name of *Plantagenest*. 33. *Hen.* 8. J. Stow. pag. 717.
[2] White and Red Roses, for *York* and *Lancaster*. Camd. Remaines, pag. 161.   [3] Of *George* Duke of *Clarence*.

head of malmsey at the Tower. One,[1] that very lately
would needs dissuade men from drinking healths to their
Princes, friends, and mistresses, as the fashion is, a Bache-
lor of Divinity and Professor of *Story* and *Greek* at *Cologne*,
in his division of Drunken Natures, makes one part of them,
*Qui in balænas mutari cuperent, dummodo mare in generosissi-
mum vinum transformaretur*,[2] and for want of another example, dares deliver, that, *such a one was* George *Earl of*
Clarence,[3] *who, when, for suspicion of treason, he was judged to
die, by his brother* Edward IV. *and had election of his form of
death given him, made choice to be drowned in malmsey*. First,
why he calls him Earl of *Clarence*, I believe not all his Professed History can justify; neither indeed was ever among
us any such Honour. Earls of *Clare*[4] long since were: but
the title of *Clarence* began when that Earldom was converted
into a Dukedom by creation of *Lionel* (who married with
the heir of the *Clares*) Duke of *Clarence*, third son to *Edward*
III. since whom never have been other than Dukes of that
Dignity. But, unto what I should impute this unexcusable
injury to the dead Prince, unless to *Icarius'* shadow dazzling
the writer's eyes, or *Bacchus* his revengeful causing him to
slip in matter of his own Profession, I know not. Our
Stories make the death little better than a tyrannous
murder, privily committed without any such election. If
he have other authority for it, I would his margin had been
so kind as to have imparted it.

[1] Francisc. Matenes. De Ritu Bibend. l. cap. 1. edit. superioribus nundinis.
[2] Which would wish themselves whales, so the sea were strong liquor.
[3] Comes Clarentiæ. Cæterùm Ævo Normanico indiscriminatim *Comes* et *Dux* usurpantur, et *Will*. Conquestor sæpiùs dictus *Comes Norm*.
[4] From *Clare* in *Suffolk*. Vid. Polydor. Hist. 19. et Camd. in Icenis.

THE SEVENTEENTH SONG. 253

306. *Upon a daughter born to* John *of* Somerset.

John *of Gaunt,* Duke of *Lancaster,* had issue by *Catharine Swinford,* John *of Beufort* Earl of *Somerset,* and Marquess *Dorset:* To him succeeded his second son, John (*Henry* the eldest dead) and was created first Duke of *Somerset* by *Henry* V. Of this *John's* loins was *Margaret,* mother to *Henry* VII. His father was *Edmund* of *Hadham* (made Earl of *Richmond,* by *Henry* VI.) son to *Owen Tyddour* (deriving himself from the *British Cadwallader*) by his wife Queen *Catherine, Dowager* to *Henry* V. and hence came that royally ennobled name of *Tyddour,* which in the late Queen of happy memory ended.

336. *Defender of the Faith*————

When amongst those turbulent commotions of *Lutherans* and *Romanists* under *Charles* V. such oppositions increased, that the Pope's three crowns even tottered at such arguments as were published against his Pardons, Mass, Monastic profession, and the rest of such doctrine; this King *Henry*[1] (that *Luther* might want no sorts of antagonists) wrote particularly against him in defence of Pardons, the Papacy, and of their Seven Sacraments: of which is yet remaining the original in the *Vatican*[2] at *Rome,* and with the King's own hand thus inscribed,

Anglorum Rex, HENRICUS, LEONI X.
*mittit hoc Opus, et fidei testem
et amicitiæ.**

Hereupon, this *Leo* sent him the title of *Defender of the Faith*†: which was as ominous to what ensued. For to-

---
[1] 13. *Hen.* 8.   [2] Francisc. Sweet. in Delic. Orbis Christ.
* *Henry,* King of *England,* sends this to Pope *Leo* X. as a testimony of his faith, and love to him.
† *Defensor Ecclesiæ,* 1. Sleidano Comment. 3.

wards the twenty-fifth year of his reign, he began so to examine their traditions, doctrine, lives, and the numerous faults of the corrupted time, that he was indeed founder of Reformation for inducement of the true ancient Faith: which by his son *Edward* VI. Queen ELIZABETH, and our present Sovereign, hath been to this day piously established and defended.

To ease your conceit of these Kings here sung, I add this Chronology of them.

1066. *William* I. conquered *England.*

1087. *William* the *Red* (*Rufus*) second son to the Conqueror.

1100. *Henry* I. surnamed *Beuclerc*, third son to the first *William.*

1135. *Stephen* Earl of *Moreton* and *Bologne*, son to *Stephen* Earl of *Blois* by *Adela* daughter to the Conqueror. In both the prints of *Math. Paris* (*An.* 1086) you must mend *Beccensis Comitis*, and read *Blesensis Comitis;* and howsoever it comes to pass, he is, in the same author, made son to *Tedbald* Earl of *Blois*, which indeed was his brother.*

1154. *Henry* II. son to *Geffery Plantagenest* Earl of *Anjou*, and *Maude* the Empress, daughter to *Henry Beuclerc.*

1189. *Richard* I. *Ceur de Lion*, son to *Henry* II.

1199. *John*, brother to *Ceur de Lion.*

* In Matth. Paris dispunctio.

1216. *Henry* III. son to King *John*.

1273. *Edward* I. *Longshanks*, son to *Henry* III.

1308. *Edward* II. of *Caernarvan*, son to *Edward* I. deposed by his wife and son.

1326. *Edward* III. son to *Edward* II.

1387. *Richard* II. of *Burdeaux* (son to *Edward* the *Black Prince*, son to *Edward* III.) deposed by *Henry* Duke of *Lancaster*.

1399. *Henry* IV. of *Bolingbroke;* son to *John* of *Gaunt* Duke of *Lancaster* fourth son to *Edward* III.

1413. *Henry* V. of *Monmouth*, son to *Henry* IV.

1422. *Henry* VI. of *Windsor*, son to *Henry* V. deposed by *Edward* Earl of *March*, son and heir to *Richard* Duke of *York*, deriving title from *Lionel* Duke of *Clarence* and *Edmund* of *Langley*, third and fifth sons of *Edward* III.

1460. ' *Edward* IV. of *Roane*, son and heir of *York*. In the tenth of his reign *Henry* VI. got again the Crown, but soon lost both it and life.

1483. *Edward* V. son to the fourth of that name, murdered with his brother *Richard* Duke of *York* by his uncle *Richard* Duke of *Glocester*.

1483. *Richard* III. brother to *Edward* IV. slain at *Bosworth* Field, by *Henry* Earl of *Richmond*. In him ended the name of *Plantagenet* in our Kings.

1485. *Henry* VII. heir to the *Lancastrian* Family, married with *Elizabeth*, heir to the House of *York*. In him the name of *Tyddour* began in the Crown.

1509. *Henry* VIII. of *Greenwich*, son to *Henry* VII.

1546. *Edward* VI. of *Hampton Court*, son to *Henry* VIII.

1553. *Mary*, sister to *Edward* VI.

1558. *Elizabeth*, daughter to *Henry* VIII.

---

370. *Great* Andredswalde *sometime*———

All that maritime tract comprehending *Sussex*, and part of *Kent* (so much as was not mountains, now called the *Downs*, which in *British*,[1] old *Gaulish*, *Low Dutch*, and our *English* signifies but *Hills*) being all woody, was called *Andredsweald*,[2] i.e., *Andred's wood*, often mentioned in our stories, and *Newenden* in *Kent* by it *Andredcester* (as most learned *Camden* upon good reason guesses) whence perhaps the Wood had his name. To this day we call those woody lands, by North the *Downs*, the *Weald:* and the channel of the River that comes out of those parts, and discontinues the Downs about *Bramber*, is yet known in *Shorham* Ferry, by the name of *Weald-dich;* and, in another *Saxon* word equivalent to it, are many of the parishes' terminations on this side the Downs, that is, *Herst*, or *Hurst*, i.e., a wood. It is called by *Ethelwerd*[3] expressly *Immanis sylva, quæ vulgò* Andredsvuda *nuncupatur*,[4] and was 120 miles long, and 30 broad.[5] The Author's conceit of these Forests being Nymphs of this great *Andredsvuda*, and their complaint for

[1] *Dunum* uti ex Clitophonte apud Plut. habet Camd. et 𝔇𝔲𝔫𝔫𝔢𝔫 Belgis dicuntur *tumuli arenarii oceano objecti.* Gorop. Gallic. 1. Alii.
[2] We yet call a Desert a wilderness from this root.
[3] Lib. 4. cap. 3.   [4] Wood, called *Andred's wood*.
[5] Henric. Huntingdon. Hist. 5. in Alfredo.

loss of woods, in *Sussex*, so decayed, is plain enough to every reader.

426. *As* Arun *which doth name the beauteous* Arundel.

So it is conjectured, and is without controversy justifiable if that be the name of the River. Some fable it from *Arundel*, the name of *Bevis'* horse: It were so as tolerable as *Bucephalon*,[1] from *Alexander's* horse, *Tymenna*[2] in *Lycia* from a goat of that name, and such like, if time would endure it: But *Bevis* was about the Conquest, and this town is, by name of *Erundele*, known in time of King *Alfred*,[3] who gave it with others to his nephew *Athelm*. Of all men, *Goropius*[4] had somewhat a violent conjecture, when he derived *Haroudell*, from a people called *Charudes* (in *Ptolemy*, towards the utmost of the now *Juitland*) part of whom he imagines (about the *Saxon* and *Danish* irruptions) planted themselves here, and by difference of dialect, left this as a branch sprung of their Country title.

432. *And* Adur *coming on to* Shoreham.

This river that here falls into the ocean might well be understood in that *Port* of *Adur*,[5] about this coast, the relics whereof, learned *Camden* takes to be *Edrington*, or *Adrington*, a little from *Shoreham*. And the Author here so calls it *Adur*.

444. *Doth* blush, *as put in mind of those there* sadly slain.

In the Plain near *Hastings*, where the *Norman William* after his victory found King *Harold* slain, he built *Battell* Abbey, which at last (as divers other Monasteries) grew to

---

[1] Plutarch in Alex. et Q. Curt. lib. 9.   [2] Steph. περὶ πολ.
[3] Testament. Alfred. ubi etiam, *Ritherumfelld*, *Diccalingum*, *Angmeringum*, *Feltham*, et aliæ in hoc agro villæ legantur Osfertho ejusdem cognato.   [4] Gothodanic. lib. 7.
[5] Portus Adurni in Notit. Provins.

a Town enough populous. Thereabout is a place which after rain always looks red, which some[1] have (by that authority, the Muse also) attributed to a very bloody sweat of the earth, as crying to heaven for revenge of so great a slaughter.

[1] Gul. Parvus Hist. 1. cap. 1.

THE EIGHTEENTH SONG.

THE ARGUMENT.

The Rother *through the* Weald *doth rove,*
Till he with Oxney *fall in love:*
Rumney would with her wealth beguile,
And win the River from the Isle.
Medway, with her attending Streams,   5
Goes forth to meet her Lord, great Tames:
And where in breadth she her disperses,
Our famous Captains she rehearses,
With many of their valiant deeds.
Then with Kent's *praise the Muse proceeds;*   10
And tells when Albion *o'er sea rode,*
How he his daughter-Isles bestow'd;
And how grim Goodwin *foams and frets:*
Where to this Song, an end she sets.

OUR *Argas* scarcely yet delivered of her son,
When as the River down through *Andredsweald*
    doth run:
Nor can the aged Hill have comfort of her child.
For, living in the woods, her *Rother* waxéd wild;
His banks with aged oaks, and bushes overgrown,   5
That from the *Sylvans*' kind, he hardly could be known:
Yea, many a time the Nymphs, which hapt this Flood to see,
Fled from him, whom they sure a Satyr thought to be;

17—2

As Satyr-like he held all pleasures in disdain,
And would not once vouchsafe to look upon a Plain ; 10
Till chancing in his course to view a goodly plot,
Which *Albion* in his youth upon a Sea-Nymph got,
For *Oxney's* love he pines : who being wildly chaste,
And never woo'd before, was coy to be imbrac'd.
But, what obdurate heart was ever so perverse, 15
Whom yet a lover's plaints, with patience, could not pierce?
For, in this conflict she being lastly overthrown,
In-isléd in his arms, he clips her for his own.
Who being gross and black, she lik'd the River well.

    Of *Rother's* happy match, when *Rumney* Marsh heard tell,
Whilst in his youthful course himself he doth apply, 21
And falleth in her sight into the sea at *Rye*,
She thinketh with herself, how she a way might find
To put the homely Isle quite out of *Rother's* mind ;
¹Appearing to the Flood, most bravely like a Queen, 25
Clad all from head to foot, in gaudy summer's green ;
Her mantle richly wrought, with sundry flowers and weeds ;
Her moistful temples bound, with wreaths of quivering reeds :
Which loosely flowing down, upon her lusty thighs,
Most strongly seem to tempt the River's amorous eyes. 30
And on her loins a frock, with many a swelling pleat,
Emboss'd with well-spread horse, large sheep, and full-fed
    neat,
Some wallowing in the grass, there lie awhile to batten ;
Some sent away to kill ; some thither brought to fatten ;
With villages amongst, oft powthred here and there ; 35
And (that the same more like to landskip* should appear)
With lakes and lesser ferds, to mitigate the heat
(In summer when the fly doth prick the gadding neat,

---

¹ A description of *Rumney* Marsh.
* The natural expressing of the surface of a country in painting.

THE EIGHTEENTH SONG.

Forc'd from the brakes, where late they brows'd the velvet
  buds)
In which they lick their hides, and chew their savoury cuds.
  Of these her amorous toys, when *Oxney* came to know,
Suspecting lest in time her rival she might grow,
Th' allurements of the Marsh, the jealous Isle do move,
That to a constant course, she thus persuades her Love :
With *Rumney*, though for dower I stand in no degree ;
In this, to be belov'd yet liker far than she :
Though I be brown, in me there doth no favour lack.
The soul is said deform'd : and she, extremely black.
And though her rich attire, so curious be and rare,
From her there yet proceeds unwholesome putrid air :
Where my complexion more suits with the higher ground,
Upon the lusty *Weald*, where strength still doth abound.
The Wood-gods I refus'd, that sued to me for grace,
Me in thy wat'ry arms, thee suff'ring to imbrace ;
Where, to great *Neptune* she may one day be a prey :
The Sea-gods in her lap lie wallowing every day.
And what, though of her strength she seem to make no doubt ?
Yet put unto the proof she'll hardly hold him out.
  With this persuasive speech which *Oxney* lately us'd,
With strange and sundry doubts, whilst *Rother* stood confus'd,
Old *Andredsweald** at length doth take her time to tell
The changes of the world, that since her youth befell,
When yet upon her soil, scarce human foot had trode ;
A place where only then, the *Sylvans* made abode.
Where, fearless of the hunt, the hart securely stood,
And everywhere walk'd free, a burgess of the wood ;
Until those *Danish* routs, whom hunger starv'd at home,
(Like wolves pursuing prey) about the world did roam.
And stemming the rude stream dividing us from *France*,
Into the spacious mouth of *Rother* fell (by chance)

* See to the Seventeenth Song.

§ That *Lymen* then was nam'd, when (with most irksome care)
The heavy *Danish* yoke, the servile *English* bare.
And when at last she found, there was no way to leave
Those, whom she had at first been forcéd to receive;
And by her great resort, she was through very need,   75
Constrainéd to provide her peopled Towns to feed.
She learn'd the churlish axe and twybill to prepare,
To steel the coulter's edge, and sharp the furrowing share:
And more industrious still, and only hating sloth,
A housewife she became, most skill'd in making cloth.[1]   80
That now the Draper comes from *London* every year,
And of the *Kentish* sorts, makes his provision there.
Whose skirts ('tis said) at first that fifty furlongs went,
Have lost their ancient bounds, now limited in *Kent*.*
Which strongly to approve, she *Medway* forth did bring,   85
From *Sussex* who ('tis known) receives her silver spring.
Who towards the lordly *Tames*, as she along doth strain,
Where *Teise*, clear *Beule*, and *Len*, bear up her limber train
As she removes in state: so for her more renown,
Her only name she leaves, t' her only christ'ned Town;†   90
And *Rochester* doth reach, in ent'ring to the bow'r
Of that most matchless *Tames*, her princely paramour.
Whose bosom doth so please her Sovereign (with her pride)
Whereas the Royal Fleet continually doth ride,
That where she told her *Tames*, she did intend to sing   95
What to the *English* Name immortal praise should bring;
To grace his goodly Queen, *Tames* presently proclaims,
That all the *Kentish* Floods, resigning him their names,
Should presently repair unto his mighty hall,
And by the posting tides, towards *London* sends to call   100
Clear *Ravensburne* (though small, rememb'red them among)
At *Detford* ent'ring. Whence as down she comes along,

[1] *Kentish* Cloth.   * The *Weald* of *Kent*.
† *Maidstone*, i.e., *Medway's* town.

She *Darent* thither warns: who calls her sister *Cray*,
Which hasten to the Court with all the speed they may.
And but that *Medway* then of *Tames* obtain'd such grace, 105
Except her country Nymphs, that none should be in place,
More Rivers from each part, had instantly been there,
Than at their marriage, first, by *Spenser** numb'red were.
   This *Medway* still had nurs'd those Navies in her road,
Our Armies that had oft to conquest borne abroad; 110
And not a man of ours, for arms hath famous been,
Whom she not going out, or coming in hath seen:
Or by some passing ship, hath news to her been brought,
What brave exploits they did; as where, and how, they fought.
Wherefore, for audience now, she to th' assembly calls, 115
The Captains to recite when seriously she falls.
   Of noble warriors now, saith she, shall be my Song;
Of those renownéd spirits, that from the Conquest sprong,
Of th' *English Norman* blood: which, matchless for their might,
Have with their flaming swords, in many a dreadful fight, 120
Illustrated this *Isle*, and bore her fame so far;
Our *Heroes*, which the first wan, in that Holy War,
Such fear from every foe, and made the East more red,
With splendour of their arms, than when from *Tithon's* bed
The blushing Dawn doth break; towards which our fame begon, 125
By *Robert* (*Curt-hose* call'd) the *Conqueror's* eldest son,
Who with great *Godfrey* and that holy Hermit† went
The Sepulchre to free, with most devout intent.
   And to that title which the *Norman William* got,
When in our Conquest here, he strove t' include the *Scot*, 130
The General of our power, that stout and warlike Earl,
Who *English* being born, was styl'd of *Aubemerle;*

* In the *Faery Queene*.   † *Peter*, the Hermit.

Those *Lacyes* then no less courageous, which had there
The leading of the day, all brave Commanders were.
 Sir *Walter Especk*, match'd with *Peverell*, which as far 135
Adventur'd for our fame : who in that Bishop's war,
Immortal honour got to *Stephen's* troubled reign :
That day ten thousand *Scots* upon the field were slain.
 The Earl of *Strigule* then our *Strong-bowe*, first that won
Wild *Ireland* with the sword (which, to the glorious sun, 140
Lifts up his nobler name) amongst the rest may stand.
 In *Cure de Lyon's* charge unto the Holy Land,
Our Earl of *Lester*, next, to rank with them we bring :
And *Turnham*, he that took th' impost'rous *Cyprian* King.
Strong *Tuchet* chose to wield the *English* standard there; 145
Poole, Gourney, Nevill, Gray, Lyle, Ferres, Mortimer :
And more, for want of pens whose deeds not brought to light,
It grieves my zealous soul, I cannot do them right.
 The noble *Penbrooke* then, who *Strong-bowe* did succeed,
Like his brave grand-sire, made th' revolting *Irish* bleed, 150
When yielding oft, they oft their due subjection broke ;
And when the *Britans* scorn'd, to bear the *English* yoke,
Lewellin Prince of *Wales* in battle overthrew,
Nine thousand valiant *Welsh* and either took or slew.
Earl *Richard*, his brave son, of *Strong-bowe's* matchless strain,
As he a *Marshall* was, did in himself retain 155
The nature of that word, being martial, like his name :
Who, as his valiant sire, the *Irish* oft did tame.
 With him we may compare *Marisco* (King of Men)
That Lord Chief Justice was of *Ireland*, whereas then 160
Those two brave *Burrowes, John* and *Richard*, had their place,
Which through the bloodied bogs, those *Irish* oft did chase ;
Whose deeds may with the best deservedly be read.
 As those two *Lacyes* then, our *English* powers that led :
Which twenty thousand, there, did in one battle quell, 165
Amongst whom (trodden down) the King of *Conaugh* fell.

THE EIGHTEENTH SONG.

Then *Richard*, that lov'd Earl of *Cornwall*, here we set:
Who, rightly of the race of great *Plantaginet*,
Our *English* armies shipp'd, to gain that hallow'd ground,
With *Long-sword* the brave son of beauteous *Rosamond:* 170
The Pagans through the breasts, like thunderbolts that shot;
And in the utmost East such admiration got,
That the shrill-sounding blast, and terrour of our fame
Hath often conquered, where, our swords yet never came:
As *Gifford*, not forgot, their stout associate there. 175
   So in the wars with *Wales*, of ours as famous here,
Guy Beuchamp, that great Earl of *Warwick*, place shall have:
From whom, the *Cambrian* Hills the *Welsh-men* could not save;
Whom he, their general plague, impetuously pursu'd,
And in the *British* gore his slaught'ring sword imbru'd. 180
   In order as they rise (next *Beuchamp*) we prefer
The Lord *John Gifford*, match'd with *Edmond Mortimer;*
Men rightly moulded up, for high advent'rous deeds.
   In this renownéd rank of warriors then succeeds
Walwin, who with such skill our armies oft did guide; 185
In many a dangerous strait, that had his knowledge tried.
And in that fierce assault, which caus'd the fatal flight,
Where the distresséd *Welsh* resign'd their ancient right,
Stout *Frampton:* by whose hand, their Prince *Lewellin* fell.
   Then followeth (as the first who have deserved as well) 190
Great *Saint-John;* from the *French*, which twice recoveréd *Guyne:*
And he, all him before that clearly did out-shine,
Warren, the puissant Earl of *Surrey*, which led forth
Our *English* armies oft into our utmost North:
And oft of his approach made *Scotland* quake to hear, 195
When *Tweed* hath sunk down flat, within her banks for fear.
   On him there shall attend, that most adventurous *Twhing*,

That at *Scambekin* fight, the *English* off did bring
Before the furious *Scot*, that else were like to fall.
   As *Basset*, last of these, yet not the least of all   200
Those most renownéd spirits that *Fowkerk* bravely fought:
Where *Long-shanks*, to our lore, *Albania* lastly brought.
   As, when our *Edward* first his title did advance,
And led his *English* hence, to win his right in *France*,
That most deserving Earl of *Darby* we prefer,   205
Henry's third valiant son, the Earl of *Lancaster*,
That only *Mars* of men ; who (as a general scourge,
Sent by just-judging Heaven, outrageous *France* to purge)
At *Cagant* plagu'd the power of *Flemings* that she rais'd,
Against the *English* force : which as a hand-sell seis'd,   210
Into her very heart he march'd in warlike wise ;
Took *Bergera, Langobeck, Mountdurant*, and *Mountguyse ;*
Leau, Poudra, and *Punach, Mount-Segre, Forsa*, won ;
Mountpesans, and *Beumount*, the *Ryall, Aiguillon,*
Rochmillon, Mauleon, Franch, and *Angolisme* surpris'd ;   215
With castles, cities, forts, nor provinces suffic'd.
Then took the Earl of *Leyle :* to conduct whom there came
Nine Viscounts, Lords, and Earls, astonish'd at his name.
To *Gascoyne* then he goes (to plague her, being prest)
And manfully himself of *Mirabell* possest ;   220
Surgeres, and *Alnoy, Benoon*, and *Mortaine* strook :
And with a fearful siege, he *Taleburg* lastly took ;
With prosperous success, in lesser time did win
Maximien, Lusingham, Mount-Sorrell, and *Bouin ;*
Sack'd *Poytiers :* which did, then, that Country's treasure hold ;
That not a man of ours would touch what was not gold.   226
   With whom our *Maney** here deservedly doth stand,
Which first Inventor was of that courageous band,
Who clos'd their left eyes up ; as, never to be freed,
Till there they had achiev'd some high adventurous deed.   230

* Sir *Walter Maney.*

THE EIGHTEENTH SONG.

He first into the prease at *Cagant* conflict flew;
And from amidst a grove of gleaves, and halberds drew
Great *Darby* beaten down; t' amaze the men of war,
When he for *England* cried, 'S. *George*, and *Lancaster!*'
And as mine author tells (in his high courage, proud)   235
Before his going forth, unto his mistress vow'd,
He would begin the war: and, to make good the same,
Then setting foot in *France*, there first with hostile flame
Forc'd *Mortain*, from her towers, the neighbouring towns to
    light;
That suddenly they caught a fever with the fright.   240
Thin Castle (near the town of *Cambray*) ours he made;
And when the *Spanish* powers came *Britanne** to invade,
Both of their aids and spoils, them utterly bereft.
This *English Lion*, there, the *Spaniards* never left,
Till from all air of *France*, he made their *Lewes* fly.   245
And Fame herself, to him, so amply did apply,
That when the most unjust *Calicians* had forethought,
Into that town (then ours) the *French-men* to have brought,
The King of *England's* self, and his renownéd son[1]
(By those perfidious *French* to see what would be done)   250
Under his guydon march'd, as private soldiers there.
    So had we still of ours, in *France* that famous were.
Warwick, of *England* then High-Constable that was,
As other of that race, here well I cannot pass;
That brave and god-like brood of *Beuchamps*, which so long
Them Earls of *Warwick* held; so hardy, great, and strong,   256
That after of that name it to an adage grew,
If any man himself advent'rous hapt to shew,
Bold Beuchamp men him term'd, if none so bold as he.[2]
With those our *Beuchamps*, may our *Bourchers* reck'ned be.

---

* *Little Britanne* in *France*.
[1] *Edward* III. and the *Black Prince*.
[2] *Bold Beuchamp*, a proverb.

Of which, that valiant Lord, most famous in those days, 261
That hazarded in *France* so many dangerous frays:
Whose blade in all the fights betwixt the *French* and us,
Like to a blazing-star was ever ominous;
A man, as if by *Mars* upon *Bellona* got. 265
    Next him, stout *Coblam* comes, that with as prosp'rous lot
The *English* men hath led; by whose auspicious hand,
We often have been known the *Frenchmen* to command.
And *Harcourt*, though by birth an alien; yet, ours won,
By *England* after held her dear adopted son: 270
Which oft upon our part was bravely prov'd to do,
Who with the hard'st attempts Fame earnestly did woo:
To *Paris*-ward, that when the *Amyens* fled by stealth
(Within her mighty walls to have inclos'd their wealth)
Before her bulwark'd gates the Burgesses he took; 275
Whilst the *Parisians*, thence that sadly stood to look,
And saw their faithful friends so wofully bested,
Not once durst issue out to help them, for their head.
    And our *John Copland;* here courageously at home
(Whilst everywhere in *France*, those far abroad do roam) 280
That at *New-castle* fight (the Battle of the Queen,
Where most the *English* hearts were to their Sovereign seen)
Took *David* King of *Scots* his prisoner in the fight.
Nor could these wars imploy our only men of might:
But as the Queen by these did mighty things achieve; 285
So those, to *Britaine* sent the Countess to relieve,
As any yet of ours, two knights as much that dar'd,
Stout *Dangorn*, and with him strong *Hartwell* honour shar'd;
The dreaded *Charles de Bloyes*, that at *Rochdarren* bet,
And on the royal seat, the Countess *Mountfort* set. 290
In each place where they came so fortunate were ours.
    Then, *Audley*, most renown'd amongst those valiant powers,
That with the Prince of *Wales* at conquer'd *Poyters* fought;
Such wonders that in arms before both armies wrought;

The first that charg'd the *French;* and, all that dreadful day,
Through still renewing worlds of danger made his way;
The man that scorn'd to take a prisoner (through his pride)
But by plain down-right death the title to decide.
And after the retreat, that famous battle done,
Wherein, rich spacious *France* was by the *English* won.
Five hundred marks in fee, that noblest Prince bestow'd
For his so brave attempts, through his high courage show'd.
Which to his four Esquires he freely gave,* who there
Vy'd valour with their Lord; and in despite of fear,
Oft fetch'd that day from death, where wounds gap'd wide
    as hell;
And cries, and parting groans, whereas the *Frenchmen* fell,
Even made the victors grieve, so horrible they were.
    Our *Dabridgcourt* the next shall be rememb'red here,
At *Poyters* who brake in upon the *Alman* Horse
Through his too forward speed: but, taken by their force,
And after, by the turn of that so doubtful fight,
Being rescu'd by his friends in *Poyters'* fearful fight,
Then like a lion rang'd about the enemy's host:
And where he might suppose the danger to be most,
Like lightning ent'red there, to his *French* foes' dismay,
To gratify his friends which rescu'd him that day. [do,
    Then *Chandos:* whose great deeds found Fame so much to
That she was lastly forc'd, him for her ease to woo;
That Minion of drad *Mars,* which almost over-shone
All those before him were, and for him none scarce known,
At *Cambray's* scaléd wall his credit first that won;
And by the high exploits in *France* by him were done,
Had all so over-aw'd, that by his very name
He could remove a siege: and cities where he came
Would at his summons yield. That man, the most belov'd,
In all the ways of war so skilful and approv'd,

* The honourable bounty of the Lord *Audley.*

The Prince* at *Poyters* chose his person to assist.
This stout *Herculean* stem, this noble martialist,
In battle twixt brave *Bloys* and noble *Mountfort*, tri'd
At *Array*, then the right of *Britaine* to decide, 330
Rag'd like a furious storm beyond the power of man,
Where valiant *Charles* was slain, and the stern *English* wan
The royal *British* rule to *Mountfort's* nobler name.
He took strong *Tarryers* in, and *Anjou* oft did tame.
Gavaches he regain'd, and us *Rochmador* got. 335
Wherever lay'd he siege that he invested not?
   As this brave warrior was, so no less dear to us,
The rival in his fame, his only *æmulus*,
Renown'd Sir *Robert Knowles*, that in his glories shar'd,
His chivalry and oft in present perils dar'd ; 340
As Nature should with Time, at once by these consent
To show, that all their store they idly had not spent.
He *Vermandoise* o'er-ran with skill and courage high:
Notoriously he plagu'd revolting *Picardy:*
That up to *Paris'* walls did all before him win, 345
And dar'd her at her gates (the King that time within)
A man that all his deeds did dedicate to fame.
   Then those stout *Percyes, John* and *Thomas*, men of name.
The valiant *Gourney*, next, deservedly we grace,
And *Howet*, that with him assumes as high a place. 350
Strong *Trivet*, all whose ends at great adventures shot :
That conquer'd us *Mount Pin*, and Castle *Carcilot*,
As famous in the *French*, as in the *Belgique* war ;
Who took the Lord *Brimewe ;* and with the great *Navarre*,
In *Papaloon*, attain'd an everlasting praise. 355
   Courageous *Curill* next, than whom those glorious days
Produc'd not any spirit that through more dangers swam.
   That princely *Thomas*, next, the Earl of *Buckingham*,
To *Britany* through *France* that our stout *English* brought,

* The *Black-Prince*.

THE EIGHTEENTH SONG.

Which under his command with such high fortune fought 360
As put the world in fear *Rome* from her cinders rose,
And of this earth again meant only to dispose.
   Thrice valiant *Hackwood* then, out-shining all the rest,
From *London* at the first a poor mean soldier prest
(That time but very young) to those great wars in *France*, 365
By his brave service there himself did so advance,
That afterward, the heat of those great battles done,
(In which he to his name immortal glory won)
Leading six thousand horse, let his brave guydon flie.
So, passing through East *France*, and ent'ring *Lombardie*, 370
By th' greatness of his fame, attain'd so high command,
That to his charge he got *the White Italian Band*.
With *Mountferato** then in all his wars he went :
Whose clear report abroad by Fame's shrill trumpet sent,
Wrought, that with rich rewards him *Milan* after won, 375
To aid her, in her wars with *Mantua* then begon ;
By *Barnaby*,† there made the *Milanezes*' guide :
His daughter, who, to him, fair *Domina*, affi'd.
For *Gregory* then the Twelfth, he dangerous battles strook,
And with a noble siege revolted *Pavia* took. 380
And there, as Fortune rose, or as she did decline,
Now with the *Pisan* serv'd, then with the *Florentine :*
The use of th' *English* bows to *Italy* that brought ;
By which he, in those wars, seem'd wonders to have wrought.
   Our *Henry Hotspur* next, for high achievements meet, 385
Who with the thund'ring noise of his swift courser's feet,
Astund the earth, that day, that he in *Holmdon's* strife
Took *Douglas*, with the Earls of *Anguish*, and of *Fyfe*.
And whilst those hardy *Scots*, upon the firm earth bled,
With his revengeful sword swich'd after them that fled. 390
   Then *Culverley*, which kept us *Calice* with such skill,

---
   * The Marquess of *Mountferato*.
   † Brother to *Galeazo*, Viscount of *Milan*.

His honor'd room shall have our Catalogue to fill:
Who, when th' rebellious *French*, their liberty to gain,
From us our ancient right unjustly did detain
(T' let *Bullen* understand our just conceivéd ire)   395
Her suburbs, and her ships, sent up to heaven in fire;
Estaples then took in that day she held her Fair,
Whose marchandise he let his soldiers freely share;
And got us back Saint *Mark's*, which loosely we had lost.

   Amongst these famous men, of us deserving most,   400
In these of great'st report, we gloriously prefer,
For that his naval fight, *John* Duke of *Excester;*
The puissant fleet of *Jeane* (which *France* to her did call)
Who mercilessly sunk, and slew her admirall.

   And one, for single fight, amongst our martial men,   405
Deserves remembrance here as worthily agen;
Our *Clifford*, that brave, young, and most courageous Squire:
Who thoroughly provok'd, and in a great desire
Unto the *English* name a high report to win,
Slew *Bockmell* hand to hand at Castle *Jocelin*,   410
Suppos'd the noblest spirit that *France* could then produce.

   Now, forward to thy task proceed industrious Muse,
To him, above them all, our power that did advance;
John Duke of *Bedford*, styl'd the fire-brand to sad *France:*
Who to remove the foe from siegéd *Harflew*, sent,   415
Affrighted them like death; and as at sea he went,
The huge *French* navy fir'd, when horrid *Neptune* roar'd,
The whilst those mighty ships out of their scuppers pour'd
Their trait'rous clutt'red gore upon his wrinkled face.
He took strong *Ivery* in: and like his kingly race,   420
There down before *Vernoyle* the *English* Standard stuck:
And having on his helm his conquering Brother's luck,
Alanzon on the field and doughty *Douglasse* laid,
Which brought the *Scottish* power unto the *Dauphin's* aid;

THE EIGHTEENTH SONG.

And with his fatal sword, gave *France* her fill of death,   425
Till wearied with her wounds, she gasping lay for breath.
   Then, as if powerful Heaven our part did there abet,
Still did one noble spirit, a nobler spirit beget.
So, *Salsbury* arose; from whom, as from a source
All valour seem'd to flow, and to maintain her force.   430
From whom not all their forts could hold our treacherous
Pontmelance he regain'd, which ours before did lose. [foes.
Against the envious *French*, at *Cravant*, then came on;
As sometime at the siege of high-rear'd *Ilion*,
The Gods descending, mix'd with mortals in the fight: 435
And in his leading, show'd such valour and such might,
As though his hand had held a more than earthly power;
Took *Stuart* in the field, and General *Vuntadour*,
The *French* and *Scottish* force, that day which bravely led;
Where few at all escap'd, and yet the wounded fled.   440
Mount Aguilon, and *Mouns*, great *Salsbury* surpris'd:
§ What time (I think in hell) that instrument[1] devis'd,
The first appear'd in *France*, as a prodigious birth
To plague the wretched world, sent from the envious earth;
Whose very roaring seem'd the mighty round to shake,   445
As though of all again it would a chaos make.
This famous General then got *Gwerland* to our use,
And *Malicorne* made ours, with *Loupland*, and *La Suise*,
Saint *Bernard's Fort*, S. *Kales*, S. *Susan*, *Mayon*, *Lyle*,
The *Hermitage*, *Mountseure*, *Baugency*, and *Yanvile*.   450
   Then he (in all her shapes that dreadful war had seen,
And that with danger oft so conversant had been,
As for her threats at last he seem'd not once to care,
And Fortune to her face adventurously durst dare)
The Earl of *Suffolke*, *Poole*, the Marshal that great day   455
At *Agincourt*, where *France* before us prostrate lay
(Our battles everywhere that *Hector*-like supplied,

---

[1] Great ordnance.

And march'd o'er murtheréd piles of *Frenchmen* as they died)
Invested *Aubemerle*, rich *Cowcy* making ours,
And at the *Bishop's Park* o'erthrew the *Dolphin's* powers. 460
Through whose long time in war, his credit so increas'd,
That he supplied the room of *Salsbury* deceas'd.

In this our warlike rank, the two stout *Astons* then,
Sir *Richard* and Sir *John*, so truly valiant men,
That ages yet to come shall hardly over-top 'em, 465
Umfrevill, *Peachy*, *Branch*, *Mountgomery*, *Felton*, *Popham*.
All men of great command, and highly that deserv'd:
    Courageous *Ramston* next, so faithfully that serv'd
At *Paris*, and S. *James de Beneon*, where we gave
The *French* those deadly foils, that ages since deprave 470
The credit of those times, with these so wondrous things,
    The memory of which, great *Warwick* forward brings.
Who (as though in his blood he conquest did inherit,
Or in the very name there were some secret spirit)
Being chosen for these wars in our great Regent's place 475
(A deadly foe to *France*, like his brave *Roman* race)
The Castilets of *Loyre*, of *Maiet*, and of *Lund*,
Mountdublian, and the strong *Pountorson* beat to ground.
    Then he, above them all, himself that sought to raise,
Upon some mountain-top, like a pyramidés; 480
Our *Talbot*, to the *French* so terrible in war,
That with his very name their babes they us'd to scar,
Took-in the strong *Lavall*, all *Main* and over-ran,
As the betrayéd *Mons* he from the Marshal wan,
And from the treacherous foe our valiant *Suffolke* freed. 485
His sharp and dreadful sword made *France* so oft to bleed,
Till fainting with her wounds, she on her wrack did fall;
Took *Joing*, where he hung her traitors on the wall;
And with as fair success wan *Beumont* upon *Oyse*,
The new Town in *Esmoy*, and *Crispin* in *Valoyes*: 490
Creile, with Saint *Maxine's-bridge*; and at *Avranches'* aid,

Before whose batter'd walls the foe was strongly laid,
March'd in, as of the siege at all he had not known ;
And happily reliev'd the hardly-gotten *Roan:*
Who at the very hint came with auspicious feet,
Whereas the trait'rous *French* he miserably beat.
And having over-spread all *Picardy* with war,
Proud *Burgaine* to the field he lastly sent to dare,
Which with his *English* friends so oft his faith had broke :
Whose countries he made mourn in clouds of smould'ring
    smoke :
Then *Gysors* he again, then did Saint *Denise*, raze.
  His parallel, with him, the valiant *Scales* we praise ;
Which oft put sword to sword, and foot to foot did set :
And that the first alone the garland might not get,
With him hath hand in hand leap'd into danger's jaws ;
And oft would forward put, where *Talbot* stood to pause :
Equality in fame, which with an equal lot,
Both at Saint *Denise* siege, and batt'red *Guysors* got.
Before *Pont-Orson's* walls, who when great *Warwick* lay
(And he with soldiers sent a foraging for prey)
Six thousand *French* o'erthrew with half their numb'red
    powers,
And absolutely made both *Main* and *Anjou* ours.
  To *Willoughby* the next, the place by turn doth fall :
Whose courage likely was to bear it from them all :
With admiration oft on whom they stood to look,
Saint *Valerie's* proud gates that off the hinges shook :
In *Burgondy* that forc'd the recreant *French* to fly,
And beat the rebels down disord'ring *Normandy :*
That *Amiens* near laid waste (whose strengths her could not
    save)
And the perfidious *French* out of the country drave.
  With these, another troop of noble spirits there sprong,
That with the foremost press'd into the warlike throng.

The first of whom we place that stout Sir *Philip Hall*,
So famous in the fight against the *Count S. Paul*,
That *Crotoy* us regain'd : and in the conflict twixt   525
The *English* and the *French*, that with the *Scot* were mixt,
On proud *Charles Cleremont* won that admirable day.

Strong *Fastolph* with this man compare we justly may,
By *Salsbury* who oft being seriously imploy'd
In many a brave attempt, the general foe annoy'd ;   530
With excellent success in *Main* and *Anjou* fought :
And many a bulwark there into our keeping brought ;
And, chosen to go forth with *Vadamont* in war,
Most resolutely took proud *Renate*, Duke of *Barre*.

The valiant *Draytons* then, Sir *Richard* and Sir *John*, 535
By any *English* spirits yet hardly over-gone ;
The fame they got in *France*, with costly wounds that bought :
In *Gascony* and *Guyne*, who oft and stoutly fought.

Then, valiant *Matthew Gough:* for whom the *English* were
Much bound to noble *Wales* in all our battles there,   540
Or sieging or besieg'd that never fail'd our force,
Oft hazarding his blood in many a desperate course.
He beat the *Bastard Bulme* with his selected band,
And at his castle-gate surpris'd him hand to hand,
And spite of all his power away him prisoner bare.   545

Our hardy *Burdet* then with him we will compare,
Besieg'd within Saint *James de Beneon*, issuing out,
Crying '*Salsbury*, S. *George*,' with such a horrid shout,
That cleft the wand'ring clouds ; and with his valiant crew
Upon the envied *French* like hungry lions flew,   550
And *Arthur* Earl of *Eure* and *Richmont* took in fight :
Then following them (in heat) the army put to flight :
The *Britan*, *French*, and *Scot*, receiv'd a general sack,
As, flying, one fell still upon another's back ;
Where our six hundred slew so many thousands more.   555
At our so good success that once a *French-man* swore

That God was wholly turn'd unto the *English* side,
And to assist the *French*, the Devil had deni'd.
  Then here our *Kerrill* claims his room amongst the rest,
Who justly if compar'd might match our very best.   560
He in our wars in *France* with our great *Talbot* oft,
With *Willoughby* and *Scales*, now down, and then aloft,
Endur'd the sundry turns of often-varying Fate:
At *Cleremont* seiz'd the Earl before his city gate,
Eight hundred faithless *French* who took or put to sword;
And, by his valour, twice to *Artoyse* us restor'd.   566
  In this our service then great *Arondell* doth ensue,
The Marshal *Bousack* who in *Beuroys* overthrew;
And, in despite of *France* and all her power, did win
The Castles *Darle*, *Nellay*, S. *Lawrence*, *Bomelin* ;   570
Took *Silly*, and *Count Lore* at *Sellerin* subdu'd,
Where with her owner's blood, her buildings he imbru'd:
Revolted *Loveers* sack'd, and manfully supprest
Those rebels, that so oft did *Normandy* molest.
  As *Poynings*, such high praise in *Gelderland* that got,   575
On the *Savoyan* side, that with our *English* shot   [fear.
Strook warlike *Aiske*, and *Straule*, when *Flanders* shook with
  As *Howard*, by whose hand we so renownéd were:
Whose great success at sea, much fam'd our *English* Fleet:
That in a naval fight the *Scottish Barton* beat;   580
And setting foot in *France*, her horribly did fright:
(As if great *Chandos*' ghost, or feared *Talbot's* spright
Had com'n to be their scourge, their fame again to earn)
Who having stoutly sack'd both *Narbin* and *Deverue*,
The Castles of *De Boyes*, of *Fringes*, took us there,   585
Of *Columburge*, of *Rewe*, of *Dorlans*, and *Daveere ;*
In *Scotland*, and again the Marches East to West,
Did with invasive war most terribly infest.
  A nobler of that name, the Earl of *Surry* then,
That famous hero fit both for the spear and pen   590

(From *Flodden's* doubtful fight, that forward *Scottish* King
In his victorious troop who home with him did bring)
Rebellious *Ireland* scourg'd, in *Britany* and wan
Us *Morles.* Happy time, that bredst so brave a man !
    To *Cobham,* next, the place deservedly doth fall :   595
In *France* who then imploy'd with our great Admirall,
In his successful road blew *Sellois* up in fire,
Took *Bottingham* and *Bruce,* with *Samkerke* and *Mansier.*
    Our *Peachy,* nor our *Carre,* nor *Thomas,* shall be hid,
That at the Field of Spurs by *Tirwyn* stoutly did.   600
Sands, Guyldford, Palmer, Lyle, Fitzwilliams, and with them,
Brave *Dacres, Musgrave, Bray, Coe, Wharton, Jerningham,*
Great Martialists, and men that were renownéd far
At sea ; some in the *French,* some in the *Scottish* war.
    Courageous *Randolph* then, that serv'd with great command,   605
Before *Newhaven* first, and then in *Ireland.*
The long-renown'd Lord *Gray,* whose spirit we oft did try ;
A man that with drad *Mars* stood in account most high.
Sir *Thomas Morgan* then, much fame to us that wan,
When in our Maiden reign the *Belgique* war began :   610
Who with our friends the *Dutch,* for *England* stoutly stood,
When *Netherland* first learn'd to lavish gold and blood.
Sir *Roger Williams* next (of both which, *Wales* might vaunt)
His martial compeer then, and brave commilitant :
Whose conflicts, with the *French* and *Spanish* manly fought,
Much honour to their names, and to the *Britans* brought.   615
    Th' Lord *Willoughby* may well be reckon'd with the rest,
Inferior not a whit to any of our best ;
A man so made for war, as though from *Pallas* sprong.
Sir *Richard Bingham* then our valiant men among,   620
Himself in *Belgia* well, and *Ireland,* who did bear ;
Our only schools of war this later time that were.

As *Stanly*,[1] whose brave act at *Zutphen's* service done,
Much glory to the day, and him his knighthood won.
  Our noblest *Norrice* next, whose fame shall never die
Whilst *Belgia* shall be known, or there's a *Britany:*
In whose brave height of spirit, Time seem'd as to restore
Those, who to th' *English* name such honour gain'd of yore.
  Great *Essex*, of our Peers the last that ere we knew ;
Th' old world's Heroës' lives who likeliest did renew ;
The soldiers' only hope, who stoutly serv'd in *France ;*
And on the Towers of *Cales* as proudly did advance
Our *English* ensigns then, and made *Iberia* quake,
When as our warlike Fleet rode on the surging Lake,
T' receive that city's spoil, which set her batter'd gate
Wide ope, t' affrighted *Spayne* to see her wretched state.
  Next, *Charles*, Lord *Mountjoy*, sent to *Ireland* to suppress
The envious rebel there ; by whose most fair success,
The trowzéd *Irish* led by their unjust *Tyrone*,
And the proud *Spanish* force, were justly overthrown.
That still *Kinsall* shall keep and faithful record bear,
What by the *English* prowess was executed there.
  Then liv'd those valiant *Veres*,[2] both men of great command
In our imployments long : whose either martial hand
Reach'd at the highest wreath, it from the top to get,
Which on the proudest head, Fame yet had ever set.
  Our *Dokwray*,[3] *Morgan*[4] next, Sir *Samuel Bagnall*, then
Stout *Lambert*,[5] such as well deserve a living pen ;
True Martialists and Knights, of noble spirit and wit.
  The valiant *Cicill*, last, for great imployment fit,
Deservedly in war the lat'st of ours that rose :
Whose honour every hour, and fame still greater grows.
  When now the *Kentish* Nymphs do interrupt her Song,
By letting *Medway* know she tarried had too long

[1] Sir *Edw. Stanley*.   [2] Sir *Francis* and Sir *Horace*.
[3] Sir *Henry*.   [4] Sir *Edmond*.   [5] Sir *Oliver*.

Upon this warlike troop, and all upon them laid, 655
Yet for their nobler *Kent* she nought or little said.
 When as the pliant Muse, straight turning her about,
And coming to the land as *Medway* goeth out,
Saluting the dear soil, O famous *Kent*, quoth she,
What country hath this Isle that can compare with thee, 660
Which hast within thyself as much as thou canst wish?
Thy conies, ven'son, fruit; thy sorts of fowl and fish:
As what with strength comports, thy hay, thy corn, thy wood:
Nor anything doth want, that anywhere is good.
Where *Thames*-ward to the shore, which shoots upon the rise,
Rich *Tenham* undertakes thy closets to suffice 665
With cherries, which we say, the Summer in doth bring,
Wherewith *Pomona* crowns the plump and lustful Spring;
From whose deep ruddy cheeks, sweet *Zephyr* kisses steals,
With their delicious touch his love-sick heart that heals. 670
Whose golden gardens seem th' *Hesperides* to mock:
Nor there the *Damzon* wants, nor dainty *Abricock*,
Nor *Pippin*, which we hold of kernel-fruits the king,
The *Apple-Orendge;* then the savoury *Russetting:*
The *Peare-maine*, which to *France* long ere to us was known,
Which careful Fruit'rers now have denizen'd our own. 675
The *Renat:* which though first it from the *Pippin* came,
Grown through his pureness nice, assumes that curious name,
Upon that *Pippin* stock, the *Pippin* being set;
As on the *Gentle*, when the *Gentle* doth beget 680
(Both by the sire and dame being anciently descended)
The issue born of them, his blood hath much amended.
The *Sweeting*, for whose sake the plow-boys oft make war:
The *Wilding*, *Costard*, then the well-known *Pomwater*,
And sundry other fruits, of good, yet several taste, 685
That have their sundry names in sundry countries plac'd:
Unto whose dear increase the gardener spends his life,
With percer, wimble, saw, his mallet, and his knife;

Oft covereth, oft doth bare the dry and moist'ned root,
As faintly they mislike, or as they kindly suit;　　　600
And their selected plants doth workman-like bestow,
That in true order they conveniently may grow.
And kills the slimy snail, the worm, and labouring ant,
Which many times annoy the graft and tender plant:
Or else maintains the plot much starvéd by the wet,　　695
Wherein his daintiest fruits in kernels he doth set:
Or scrapeth off the moss, the trees that oft annoy.
　But, with these trifling things why idly do I toy,
Who any way the time intend not to prolong?
To those *Thamisian* Isles now nimbly turns my Song,　　700
Fair *Shepey* and the *Greane* sufficiently suppli'd,
To beautify the place where *Medway* shows her pride.
But *Greane* seems most of all the *Medway* to adore,
And *Tenet*, standing forth to the *Rhutupian*[1] shore,
By mighty *Albion* plac'd till his return again　　705
From *Gaul*; where, after, he by *Hercules* was slain.
For, earth-born *Albion* then great *Neptune's* eldest son,
Ambitious of the fame by stern *Alcides* won,
Would over (needs) to *Gaul*, with him to hazard fight,
Twelve Labours which before accomplish'd by his might;　　710
His daughters then but young (on whom was all his care)
Which *Doris*, *Thetis'* Nymph, unto the Giant bare:
With whom those Isles he left; and will'd her for his sake,
That in their grandsire's Court she much of them would make:
But *Tenet*, th' eld'st of three, when *Albion* was to go,　　715
Which lov'd her father best, and loth to leave him so,
There at the Giant raught; which was perceiv'd by chance:
This loving Isle would else have follow'd him to *France*;
To make the channel wide that then he forcéd was,
§ Whereas (some say) before he us'd on foot to pass.　　720

[1] Near *Sandwich*.

Thus *Tenet* being stay'd, and surely settled there,
Who nothing less than want and idleness could bear,
Doth only give herself to tillage of the ground.
With sundry sorts of grain whilst thus she doth abound,
She falls in love with *Stour*, which coming down by *Wye*, 725
And towards the goodly Isle, his feet doth nimbly ply.
To *Canterbury* then as kindly he resorts,
His famous country thus he gloriously reports :
 O noble *Kent*, quoth he, this praise doth thee belong,
The hard'st to be controll'd, impatientest of wrong. 730
Who, when the *Norman* first with pride and horror sway'd,
Threw'st off the servile yoke upon the *English* laid ;
And with a high resolve, most bravely didst restore
That liberty so long enjoy'd by thee before.
§ Not suff'ring foreign Laws should thy free customs bind,
Then only show'd'st thyself of th' ancient *Saxon* kind. 736
Of all the *English* Shires be thou surnam'd the Free,
§ And foremost ever plac'd, when they shall reck'ned be.
And let this Town, which Chief of thy rich Country is,
Of all the *British* Sees be still *Metropolis*. 740
 Which having said, the *Stour* to *Tenet* him doth hie,
Her in his loving arms imbracing by and by,
Into the mouth of *Tames* one arm that forth doth lay,
The other thrusting out into the *Celtique* Sea.
§ Grim *Goodwin* all this while seems grievously to low'r, 745
Nor cares he of a straw for *Tennet*, nor her *Stour ;*
Still bearing in his mind a mortal hate to *France* •
Since mighty *Albion's* fall by war's incertain chance.
Who, since his wish'd revenge not all this while is had,
Twixt very grief and rage is fall'n extremely mad ; 750
That when the rolling tide doth stir him with her waves,
Straight foaming at the mouth, impatiently he raves,
And strives to swallow up the Sea-marks in his deep,
That warn the wand'ring ships out of his jaws to keep.

THE EIGHTEENTH SONG.

The Surgeons of the sea do all their skill apply,   755
If possibly, to cure his grievous malady:
As *Amphitrite's* Nymphs their very utmost prove,
By all the means they could, his madness to remove.
From *Greenwich* to these Sands, some *scurvy-grass*[1] do bring,
That inwardly applied 's a wondrous sovereign thing.   760
From *Shepey, sea-moss*[1] some, to cool his boiling blood;
Some, his ill-season'd mouth that wisely understood,
Rob *Dover's* neighbouring cleeves of *sampyre*,[1] to excite
His dull and sickly taste, and stir up appetite.

   Now, *Shepey*, when she found she could no further wade
After her mighty Sire, betakes her to his trade,   766
With sheephook in her hand, her goodly flocks to heed,
And cherisheth the kind of those choice *Kentish* breed.
Of villages she holds as husbandly a port,
As any *British* Isle that neighboureth *Neptune's* Court.   770
But *Greane*, as much as she her father that did love
(And, then the Inner Land, no further could remove)
In such continual grief for *Albion* doth abide,
That almost under-flood she weepeth every tide.

[1] Simples frequent in these places.

ILLUSTRATIONS.

BUT of *Sussex*, into its Eastern neighbour, *Kent*, this Canto leads you. It begins with *Rother*, whose running through the woods, in-isling *Oxney*, and such like, poetically here described is plain enough to any apprehending conceit; and upon *Medway's* Song of our Martial and Heroic spirits, because a large volume might be written to explain their glory in particular action, and in less comprehension without wrong to many worthies it's not performable, I have omitted all Illustration of that kind, and left you to the Muse herself.

71. *That* Limen *then was nam'd* ——————

So the Author conjectures; that *Rother's* mouth was the place called *Limen*, at which the *Danes* in time of King *Alfred* made irruption; which he must (I think) maintain by adding likelihood that *Rother* then fell into the Ocean about *Hith;* where (as the relics of the name in *Lime*, and the distance from *Canterbury* in *Antoninus*, making *Portus Lemanis*,* which is misprinted in *Surita's* edition, *Pontem Lemanis*, sixteen miles off) it seems *Limen* was; and if *Rother* were *Limen*, then also, there was it discharged out of

* *Lemannis* in Notit. Utr. Provinc.

the land. But for the Author's words read this: *Equestris pagunorum exercitus cum suis equis CCL. navibus Cantiam transvectus in ostio* Amnis Limen *qui de sylvâ magnâ* Andred *nominatâ decurrit, applicuit, à cujus ostio IV. milliariis in eandem sylvam naves suas sursum traxit, ubi quandam arcem semistructam, quam pauci inhabitabant villani, diruerunt, aliamque sibi firmiorem in loco qui dicitur* Apultrea *construxerunt,** which are the syllables of *Florence* of *Worcester;* and with him in substance fully agrees *Matthew* of *Westminster:* nor can I think but that they imagined *Rye* (where now *Rother* hath its mouth) to be this Port of *Limen*, as the Muse here; if you respect her direct terms. *Henry* of *Huntingdon* names no River at all, but lands them *ad Portum Limene cum* 250 *navibus, qui portus est in orientali parte* Cent *juxtà magnum nemus* Andredslaige.† How *Rother's* mouth can be properly said in the East (but rather in the South part) of *Kent*, I conceive not, and am of the adverse part, thinking clearly that *Hith* must be *Portus Lemanis*, which is that coast, as also learned *Camden* teaches, whose authority cited out of *Huntingdon*, being near the same time with *Florence* might be perhaps thought but as of equal credit; therefore I call another witness[1] (that lived not much past fifty years after the arrival) in these words, *In* Limneo *portu constituunt puppes*, 𝔄𝔭𝔬𝔩𝔡𝔯𝔢 (so I read, for the print is corrupted) *loco condicto orientali Cantiæ parte, destruúntque ibi prisco opere castrum propter quod rustica manus exigua quippe intrinsecus erat, Illicque hiberna castra confirmant.*‡ Out of which you note both that no River, but a Port only, is spoken of, and that the

---

* The *Danes* with 250 sail, came into the mouth of the River *Limen*, which runs out of *Andredswald:* from whence four miles into the wood they got in their ships, and built them a fort at *Apledore.* 893. † At Port *Limen* by *Andredswald* in the East of *Kent*.
[1] Ethelwerd. lib. 4. cap. 4.
‡ They leave their ships in Port-*Limen*, making their rendezvous at *Anpledoure* in the East of *Kent* (for this may better endure that name) and there destroyed one Castle and built another.

ships were left in the shore at the haven, and thence the *Danes* conveyed their companies to *Apledowre*. The words of this *Ethelwerd* I respect much more than these later Stories, and I would advise my reader to incline so with me.

412. *What time I think in hell that instrument devis'd.*

He means a Gun; wherewith that most noble and right martial *Thomas Montayne* Earl of *Salisbury* at the siege of *Orleans* in time of *Hen.* VI. was slain. The first inventor of them (I guess you dislike not the addition) was one *Berthold Swartz*[1] (others say *Constantine Anklitzen* a *Dutch* Monk and Chymist, who having in a mortar sulphurous powder for medicine, covered with a stone, a spark of fire by chance falling into it, fired it, and the flame removed the stone; which he observing, made use afterward of the like in little pipes of iron, and showed the use to the *Venetians* in their war with the *Genowayes* at *Chioggia* about 1380. Thus is the common assertion: but I see as good authority,[2] that it was used above twenty years before in the *Danish* Seas. I will not dispute the conveniency of it in the world, compare it with *Salmoneus'* imitation of thunder, *Archimedes* his engines, and such like; nor tell you that the *Chinois* had it, and Printing, so many ages before us, as *Mendoza, Maffy*, and others deliver; but not with persuading credit to all their readers.

720. *Whereas some say before he us'd on foot to pass.*

The allusion is to *Britain's* being heretofore joined to *Gaul* in this Strait twixt *Dover* and *Calais* (some thirty miles over) as some moderns have conjectured. That learned antiquary *J. Twine* is very confident in it, and derives the name from 𝔅𝔯𝔦𝔱𝔥 signifying (as he says) as much as 𝔊𝔲𝔦𝔱𝔥,

---

[1] Vid. Polyd. de Invent. rer. 2. cap. 2.; et Salmuth. ad G. Panciroll. 2. tit. 18.   [2] Achilles Gassar. ap. Munst. Cosmog. 3.

i.e., a *separation*, in *Welsh*, whence the Isle of *Wight*[1] was so called; *Guith* and *Wight* being soon made of each other. Of this opinion is the late *Verstegan*, as you may read in him; and for examination of it, our great light of antiquity *Camden* hath proposed divers considerations, in which, experience of particulars must direct. Howsoever this was in truth, it is as likely, for ought I see, as that *Cyprus* was once joined to *Syria*, *Eubœa* (now *Negropont*) to *Bœotia*, *Atalante* to *Eubœa*, *Belbicum* to *Bithynia*, *Leucosia* to *Thrace*, as is affirmed:[2] and *Sicily* (whose like our Island is) was certainly broken off from the Continent of *Italy*, as both *Virgil* expressly, *Strabo*, and *Pliny* deliver; and also the names of *Rhegium*, παρὰ τὸ 'ῥήγνυσθαι,[3] and of the self *Sicily*; which, rather than from *secare*,[4] I derive from *sicilire*,[5] which is of the same signification and nearer in analogy: *Claudian* calls the Isle

———————diducta Britannia mundo,*

and *Virgil* hath

———————toto divisos orbe Britannos;†

Where *Servius* is of opinion, that, for this purpose, the learned Poet used that phrase. And it deserves inquisition, how beasts of rapine, as foxes and such like, came first into this Island (for *England* and *Wales*, as now *Scotland* and *Ireland*, had store of wolves, until some three hundred years since) if it were not joined to a firm land, that either by like conjunction, or narrow passage of swimming might receive them from that Continent where the Ark rested, which is *Armenia*. That men desired to transport them, is

[1] Sam. Beulan. ad. Nennium.   [2] Plin. Hist. Nat. 2. cap. 88.
[3] From breaking off. Trogus. Hist. 4. et Strab. α.
[4] To cut off.   [5] Varr. de Re Rustic. 1. cap. 49.
* *Britain* pulled from the world.
† *Britons* divided from the whole world.

not likely: and a learned *Jesuit*[1] hath conjectured, that the
West Indies are therefore, or have been, joined with firm
land, because they have lions, wolves, panthers, and such
like, which in the *Barmudez, Cuba, Hispaniola, S. Domingo*,
and other remote Isles, are not found. But no place here
to dispute the question.

735. *Not suff'ring* foreign laws *should thy free customs bind*.

To explain it, I thus *English* you a fragment of an old
Monk:[2] *When the* Norman Conqueror *had the day, he came
to* Dover *Castle, that he might with the same subdue* Kent *also;
wherefore,* Stigand *Archbishop, and* Egelsin *Abbot, as the chief
of that Shire, observing that now whereas heretofore no* Villeins
(the *Latin* is *Nullus fuerat servus,* and applying it to our Law-
phrase, I translate it) *had been in* England, *they should be now
all in bondage to the* Normans, *they assembled all the County,
and showed the imminent dangers, the insolence of the* Normans,
and the hard condition of Villenage: *They, resolving all rather
to die than lose their freedom, purpose to encounter with the Duke
for their Country's liberties. Their Captains are the Archbishop
and the Abbot. Upon an appointed day they meet all at* Swanescomb, *and harbouring themselves in the woods, with boughs in
every man's hand, they encompass his way. The next day, the
Duke coming by* Swanescomb, *seemed to see with amazement,
as it were a wood approaching towards him, the* Kentish *men at
the sound of a trumpet take themselves to arms, when presently
the Archbishop and Abbot were sent to the Duke and saluted him
with these words: Behold, Sir Duke, the* Kentish *men come to
meet you, willing to receive you as their liege Lord, upon that condition, that they may for ever enjoy their ancient Liberties and
Laws used among their ancestors; otherwise, presently offering
war; being ready rather to die, than undergo a yoke of Bondage,*

---

[1] Joseph. Acost. De Natur. Novi Orbis 1. cap. 20. et 21.
[2] Th. Spotus ap. Lamb. in Explic. Verb.

and lose their ancient Laws. The Norman *in this narrow pinch, not so willingly, as wisely, granted the desire: and hostages given on both sides, the* Kentish *men direct the* Normans *to* Rochester, *and deliver them the County and the Castle of* Dover. Hither is commonly referred the retaining of ancient liberties in *Kent.* Indeed it is certain that special customs they have in their *Gavelkind* (although now many of their gentlemen's possessions[1] are altered in that part) *suffering for Felony without forfeiture* of estate, and such like, as in particular, with many other diligent traditions you have in *Lambard's* Perambulation: yet the report of *Thomas Spot* is not, methinks, of clear credit, as well by reason that no warrant of the historians about the *Conquest* affirms it (and this Monk lived under *Edward* I.) as also for his commixture of a fauxete about *Villenage,* saying it was not in *England* before that time, which is apparently false by divers testimonies. Giꝼ þeop (says King *Ine's* Laws) pýpce on Sunnan dæȝ. be hiꝼ Hlaꝼopdeꝼ hæꝛt ꝼý he ꝼꝛeo;* and, under *Edward* the *Confessor,* 𝕮𝖍𝖔𝖗𝖔𝖑𝖉 of 𝕭𝖊𝖚𝖈𝖍𝖊𝖓𝖆𝖑𝖊 grants to the Abbey of *Crowland* his Manor of *Spalding,* with all the appurtenances, *scilicet*[2] Colgrinum *præpositum meum, et totam sequelam suam, cum omnibus bonis et catallis, quæ habet in dictâ Villâ, &c. Item* Hardingum *Fabrum et totam sequelam suam;* and the young wench of *Anderer,* that *Edgar* was in love with, was a Nief. But for *Kent,* perhaps it might be true, that no villeins were in it, seeing since that time it hath been adjudged in our Law,[3] that one born there could not without cognizance of record be a Villein.

[1] Stat. 31. *Hen.* 8. cap. 3.
* If a Villein work on *Sunday* by his lord's command, he shall be free.
[2] *Colgrin* my bailiff and his issue, with all goods and chattels, &c.
[3] Itin. Cornub. 30. *Ed.* 1. *Villenage* 46. et Mich. 5. *Ed.* 2. MS. in Bibliothec. *Int. Templ.* cas. *John de Garton.*

738. *And foremost ever plac'd when they shall reckon'd be.*

For this honour of the *Kentish*, hear one[1] that wrote it about *Hen.* II. *Enudus* (as some copies are, but others, *Cinidus*; and perhaps it should so be, or rather *Cnudvs*, for King *Cnut*; or else I cannot conjecture what) *quantâ virtute Anglorum, Dacos Danósqué fregerit motúsque compescuerit Noricorum, vel ex eo perspicuum est, quod ob egregiæ virtutis meritum quam ibidem potentèr et patentèr exercuit*, Cantia Nostra, primæ Cohortis honorem et primus Congressus *Hostium usque in hodiernum diem in omnibus prœliis obtinet. Provincia quóque* Severiana, *quæ moderno usu et nomine ab incolis* Wiltesira *vocatur, eâdem jure sibi vendicat* Cohortem subsidiariam, *adjectâ sibi* Devoniâ *et* Cornubiâ.* Briefly, it had the first *English King*, in it was the *first Christianity* among the *English*, and *Canterbury* then honoured with the Metropolitic See: all which give note of honourable prerogative.

745. *Grim* Godwin *but the while seems grievously to low'r.*

That is *Godwin-sands*, which is reported to have been the patrimony[2] of that *Godwin* Earl of *Kent*, under *Edward* the *Confessor*, swallowed into the Ocean by strange tempest somewhat after the Conquest, and is now as a floating Isle or Quicksand, very dangerous to sailors, sometime as fixed, sometime moving, as the Muse describes.

[1] Joann. Sarisbur. De Nugis Curial. 6. cap. 18.
* What performance King *Cnut* did among the *Danes* and *Norwegians* by *English* valour, is apparant in that until this day, the *Kentish* men for their singular virtue then shown, have prerogative always to be in the Vant-gard; as *Wiltshire, Devonshire,* and *Cornwall* in the Rere.
[2] Hect. Boeth. Hist. Scotic. 12. et Jo. Twin. Albionic. 1.

END OF VOL. II.

www.ingramcontent.com/pod-product-compliance
Lightning Source LLC
Chambersburg PA
CBHW031332230426
43670CB00006B/325